# Fanny Lewald
# and Nineteenth-Century
# Constructions of Femininity

# North American Studies in Nineteenth-Century German Literature

Jeffrey L. Sammons
*General Editor*

Vol. 29

PETER LANG
New York • Washington, D.C./Baltimore • Bern
Frankfurt am Main • Berlin • Brussels • Vienna • Oxford

Vanessa Van Ornam

# Fanny Lewald
# and Nineteenth-Century
# Constructions of Femininity

PETER LANG
New York • Washington, D.C./Baltimore • Bern
Frankfurt am Main • Berlin • Brussels • Vienna • Oxford

**Library of Congress Cataloging-in-Publication Data**

Van Ornam, Vanessa.
Fanny Lewald and nineteenth-century
constructions of femininity / Vanessa Van Ornam.
p. cm. — (North American Studies in nineteenth-
century German literature; vol. 29)
Includes bibliographical references.
1. Lewald, Fanny, 1811–1889—Political and social views. 2. Women
in literature. 3. Femininity in literature. 4. Feminism and literature.
5. Women—Germany—History—19th century. I. Title. II. Series.
PT2423.L3 Z92    833'.7—dc21    00-034050
ISBN 0-8204-5101-0
ISSN 0891-4095


**Die Deutsche Bibliothek-CIP-Einheitsaufnahme**

Van Ornam, Vanessa:
Fanny Lewald and nineteenth-century
constructions of femininity / Vanessa Van Ornam.
–New York; Washington, D.C./Baltimore; Bern;
Frankfurt am Main; Berlin; Brussels; Vienna; Oxford: Lang.
(North American studies in nineteenth-
century German literature; Vol. 29)
ISBN 0-8204-5101-0

The paper in this book meets the guidelines for permanence and durability
of the Committee on Production Guidelines for Book Longevity
of the Council of Library Resources.

Printed in the United States of America

*For Hans-Jürgen*

# CONTENTS

# ACKNOWLEDGMENTS

I am greatly indebted to many people and to two institutions for their generous support during the work on the various phases of this book. Washington University deserves thanks for a dissertation fellowship that enabled me to write the original version of the first chapter, while financial support from Middlebury College helped to make publication of this book possible. Washington University's library, and its wonderful interlibrary loan department, and the library of Middlebury College were both helpful and friendly.

A number of people made very useful suggestions on early drafts and approaches. Lisa Hock read and commented at thoughtful length on a section of my argument. Inge Stephan read and commented, also at thoughtful length, on an earlier paper on Lewald's female protagonists. The members of my dissertation committee asked insightful questions and made recommendations, many of which I hope they will recognize in this book. I am particularly grateful to Claire Baldwin for having helped me to structure my project before I was entirely aware of what I wanted to do. Greg Baer, Cary Nathenson, Katrin Volkner, and, again, Lisa Hock offered advice on the dissertating and publication process in general and have been supportive listeners and good friends. Jeffrey Sammons has been an excellent and careful series editor, and I would like to thank him here for his early interest in this project. I am also deeply grateful to Lynne Tatlock for her constant support, her critical and painstaking readings of many drafts, her insightful suggestions and astounding knowledge, and for having introduced me to Fanny Lewald years ago in a seminar.

All mistakes, omissions, and infelicities are of course my own.

Profound thanks also go to my parents, Georgia and Robert Van Ornam, and my sister, Valerie Workman, for their unflagging interest and encouragement over the years.

My deepest gratitude is to my husband, Hans-Jürgen Homann, for having been supportive both of my work and of me for all of the years that I have been thinking about this project. This book is dedicated to him.

◆     ◆     ◆     ◆     ◆

I would also like to thank the Ulrike Helmer Verlag, Walter Erhart, and Ute Gerhard for permission to reprint sections of the following works:

Lewald, Fanny. *Meine Lebensgeschichte*. 1861-62. Ed. Ulrike Helmer. Frankfurt: Helmer, 1988–89. 3 vols.

—. *Politische Schriften für und wider die Frauen*. 1863, 1870. Ed. Ulrike Helmer. Frankfurt: Helmer, 1989.

Erhart, Walter. "'Your Uterus is the Loneliness in My Soul': Male Voices in Medical Body-Discourse (1860-1900)." Paper given at 1995 MLA Convention.

Gerhard, Ute. *Verhältnisse und Verhinderungen: Frauenarbeit, Familie und Rechte der Frauen im 19. Jahrhundert. Mit Dokumenten*. Frankfurt: Suhrkamp, 1978.

# INTRODUCTION

## "Werde Weib, Sophie!": Yes, But How?

A subplot of Fanny Lewald's *Eine Lebensfrage* (1845) treats the illicit relationship between Julian Brand, a minister of justice, and Sophie Harkourt, the French actress who is his mistress. Dressed in men's clothing and a powdered wig for a new role, Sophie proclaims in an early scene her conviction that her complete devotion to Julian, however transitory, is preferable to the half-hearted surrender of more conventionally virtuous women to the men they marry. As she puts it, "Es mag recht hübsch sein, aus den Armen der Eltern in die des Gatten überzugehen und in ihm auch den Schutz zu finden, dessen man bedarf, um tugendhaft zu bleiben. Das heißt tugendhaft vor dem Gericht der Welt, trotz der Untreue im Herzen, die oft nicht fehlt" (I: 109). Her view that passion does not require a legal promise of permanence scandalizes Julian. He attributes her daring to her costume and exclaims, "Kleide dich um und werde Weib, Sophie!" (I: 110). This dialogue suggests that gender is a matter of construction, performance, and outward conformity to social norms. How did nineteenth-century women — Lewald's protagonists and her putative readers — "become" women and what guidance might they have received from the dominant discourses of the culture? Further, how did Lewald's literary and nonfiction texts participate in the process of preserving and revising standards of femininity?

Lewald (1811–1889) was one of the nineteenth century's best-selling German women writers. A review written in 1874, for instance, maintained that "[u]nter den deutschen Schriftstellerinnen der Gegenwart...[sie] wohl unbestritten die erste Stelle ein[nimmt]" (qtd. in Rheinberg 13). By 1921, however, Martha Weber would describe her own work on Lewald as an attempt to paint a portrait of an almost forgotten author (qtd. in Rheinberg 32). Feminist Germanist circles rediscovered her work in the 1970s. Within those circles, scholarship notes Lewald's ambivalence on the subject of women in general: their "nature," their roles, their capabilities, and the feminine ideal. Critical ambivalence toward Lewald often expresses "irritation" (Di Maio 275) with her apparent willingness to perpetuate in her fiction the stereotypes of women dominant in her culture, while ignoring the real lives of her female contemporaries. According to these critics, she thus neglected an opportunity to use her fictional constructions to promote positive changes in the discourses operative in women's lives. Her nonfiction texts, on the other hand, displayed all the hallmarks of the women's movement of her day. These essays include pleas for better education for girls and expanded employment options for women. Her work in this area was highly regarded by fellow activists for women's rights. John Stuart Mill, for instance, to whom she dedicated a volume of her essays, responded to her dedication and the book she sent him with praise: "Your book is both convincing & persuasive & is singularly free from the two contrary defects one or other of which writings for the cause of women so often exhibit, of indiscreet violence & timid concession" (1703). Her writings were further described by Gertrud Bäumer in 1911 as "das Beste, was in der ganzen ersten Generation der Frauenbewegung zur Sache gesagt [worden] ist" (qtd. in Helmer, "Einleitung" 5).

Twentieth-century Lewald scholarship has thus tended to concentrate on her autobiography, her essays, and her earlier novels.[1] Their "emancipatory" content is more obvious and lends itself more readily to a reading of resistance in nineteenth-century women's writing. Strategies of dissent manifest themselves, however, in most of the many texts Lewald produced over the course of forty years. My inquiry examines the role of various discourses as agents of production of "reality" in terms of gender in Lewald's texts and focuses on her textual collusion with and resistance to this process of production. Her characters function simultaneously as advocates of change and as adherents to gendered norms. The recognizable conformity of these female figures in fact facilitates their potential subversion of actual norms and practices of Lewald's own century.

"Gender" is fashioned through creation, interpretation, and abstraction within a historical context. Generating scientific support for the doctrine of separate spheres and the polarized gender opposites presumed to inhabit them was one of the nineteenth century's great projects. The dichotomies that burgeoned to explain virtually every aspect of social organization derived their legitimacy from the discursive domains that contributed their various scientific insights, such as anthropology, pedagogy, and legal and political theory. Their conclusions can be summed up in the words of one encyclopedia published in 1894: "Dem Manne der Staat, der Frau die Familie!" (qtd. in Frevert 39).

Not every class, of course, had the "luxury" of such restrictive definitions of femininity—or masculinity. Working-class men, for instance, were not entrusted with guiding the state. Nevertheless, the encyclopedias argued that humans have achieved the highest level of civilization when women, loved and respected by their husbands, may be permitted to devote themselves to their families (Frevert 39). This determination in effect suggested that the working class was a type of primitive culture because these women were compelled to work. Gender definitions thus functioned to maintain class divisions. My own conclusions are in large part limited to bourgeois manifestations of femininity, primarily because these are the focus of Lewald's narrative efforts. Her protagonists are usually middle class, which for her was synonymous with "good." A few of her worthy heroines are of working-class origins, but their habits, their character, and their conception of family life are then always indistinguishable from the best of their middle-class peers. Further, the middle class of the late eighteenth and nineteenth century was the originator and the immediate beneficiary of the family definitions that informed the conclusions of the discourses under discussion here.

Ute Frevert has investigated the change in definitions related to gender in German encyclopedias from the eighteenth to the nineteenth century. She demonstrates how, since the late eighteenth century, "Konversationslexika" had attempted to prove the superiority of their own epochs to previous eras in the treatment of women. They further connect chaos and the fall of earlier civilizations to the deterioration of the doctrine of separate spheres. As Frevert puts it, they thus argue that cultural, social, and political stability is possible only when women and men live in harmony with their "natures" and when the division of labor reproduces the biological differences between the sexes. This message is central to the discussions about women in the nineteenth century (39–40). Encyclopedias call on history to bear witness to the nineteenth century's refinement of an inherently German capacity to honor femininity and womanly difference. The Brockhaus of 1864–1868, for instance, asserts, "Es ist bekannt, mit welcher Achtung, die fast an Verehrung grenzte, das Weib bei den Germanen behandelt wurde" (qtd. in Gerhard 393).

Lewald, however, mocks such assertions with a reference to the prison of "femininity" to which her contemporaries attempted to confine women:

> 16.Okt.[1849] Das Wort "Weiblichkeit," das die germanischen Völkerstämme vor den andern voraus haben, ist kein Zeichen der höhern Ausbildung der germanischen Frauen, sondern vielmehr ein Beweis, daß es im Wesen des Germanismus lag, die Frau von der allgemein menschlichen Bildung, von der freien, menschlichen Entwicklung zu sondern, indem es sie von der Allgemeinheit schied. So wenig die goldenen Gitterstäbe, welche die Frauen absperren, in dem Harem des Orientalen, ein Beweis sind für die Hochschätzung der Frau im Orient, so wenig ist die Verbannung in den mystischen Bereich der Weiblichkeit eine Apotheose der Frau. (*Gefühltes* 13)

Lewald's skepticism about this piece of contemporary "knowledge" disseminated by, among others, these influential reference works invites an investigation of her treatment in both fiction and nonfiction of some of the constituent parts of femininity, as the encyclopedias and the culture understood them.

Primary sources and social histories illuminate the medical, juridical, educational, and familial discourses that contributed to the construction of "femininity" in that period and to shaping the real and fictional women on which that femininity was inscribed. Aspects of these discourses are critical factors in various Lewald texts. Lewald's work in fact aptly demonstrates the process by which cultural pressures shaped constructions of femininity in the nineteenth century. I read her fiction and nonfiction in concert with social histories and contemporary documents, such as medical texts, sections of the legal code, school curricula, and handbooks for young wives, in order to investigate the function and the connection of these factors in her cultural context and her work. Any separation of the discourses on which I have chosen to focus is of necessity artificial, as the construction of gender is accomplished through a network of contingent forces. I impose that separation on my investigation, however, in order to identify aspects of each discourse in select Lewald texts. The fields of medicine, law, education, and family theory were themselves sites of struggle. I explore elements of the medical, legal, educational, and familial construction of femininity and some of the ways in which their definitions and conclusions were also in flux. The dynamic quality of the meaning being generated in these fields during the nineteenth century may have enhanced the possibility of literary influence and have invited its participation. My chapters therefore first explore the contemporary constitution of these discursive realms. In each case I include older texts that precede Lewald's historical moment, as these texts shaped the paradigms that Lewald interrogates.

These discursive realms contribute to the definition, the production, and the control of acceptable femininity in real and fictional worlds. Literature both colludes with and dissents from prevalent social and artistic conventions. Lewald's texts, too, support and subvert these conventions on the level of both character and plot. Because her plots and her characters are the site of Lewald's exploration and interrogation of contemporary representations of femininity and because the fictional texts, at least, are not well known, I examine these plots and characters in some detail. The range of characteristics and situations available to her fictional creations is admittedly not inexhaustible, but they include options that transgress the borders often drawn around women in nineteenth-century literature and life.

Gabriele Schneider notes Lewald's comment on the difficulty of finding "das rechte Maß zwischen roher daguerreotypirender Wirklichkeit und poetischer Verweichlichung." Lewald, however, also argues against portrayals that "beautify" the working class: they are dangerous in that the prosperous may then not recognize the precarious nature of working-class existence (*Zeitroman* 275). These statements suggest that she is attempting to negotiate the terrain between the "real" and the transfiguration presumably demanded by art and is aware of the practical disadvantages to real people poetically reconstructed in literature. This general principle surfaces in the construction of her female characters as well, regardless of class. Aesthetic and social conventions that demanded particular constructions of femininity, however, complicated the genesis of these characters. Lewald's own existence as a "feminine" product of her own culture must have further influenced her reading of these normative constructions.

Lewald's life was paradigmatic of both the constraints and the possibilities for escape operative in the lives of most of her female contemporaries, although she begins her three-part autobiography not with her gender but with her German-Jewish heritage: "Ich bin am 24. März des Jahres 1811 zu Königsberg in Preußen geboren, und stamme von väterlicher und mütterlicher Seite aus jüdischen Familien ab. Auch meine beiden Eltern waren geborene Königsberger" (*ML* I: 5). Her father was indifferent to "alles Dogmatische und Konfessionelle der verschiedenen Religionen," and her mother, as a result of the difficulties she and her then fiancé experienced in their attempt to get governmental permission to marry, "sah es als ein Unglück an, eine Jüdin zu sein" (*ML* I: 13). The family was so assimilated that young Fanny heard first from the neighbors that she was Jewish. She describes her childhood as happy and her parents, particularly her father, as loving. Her memoirs indicate both an attachment to her father and an undercurrent of resentment at his autocratic child-rearing methods. Her response to her mother is still more ambivalent. Because her mother had not been allowed an education and because she was initially ambitious for her daughter and proud of her accomplishments, Lewald began early to consider herself intellectually superior to her. A certain superciliousness alternates with guilt in her recounting of their various interactions: she had failed to appreciate her mother's good qualities, she laments, and was both unable and unwilling to emulate her.

Lewald received a good education for a girl of the period and distinguished herself as one of the school's best students. Her exemplary performance, however, called forth regretful comments from strangers, such as the oft-quoted "[W]ie schade, daß das kein Junge ist" (*ML* I: 88) and "Nu! Dein Kopf hätt' auch besser auf 'nem Jungen gesessen!" (*ML* I: 87). She responded with envy of boys, among them her brothers, because they were allowed to study, and had "eine Art von Geringschätzung gegen die Frauen." She concluded that "die Knaben etwas Besseres waren als die Mädchen, und daß [sie] selbst mehr und besser sein müsse, als die anderen Mädchen" (*ML* I: 88).

The school that Lewald attended closed when she was thirteen, which marked the beginning of twenty years of enforced idleness and busy work. At sixteen she met Leopold Bock, a theology student whose autocratic

tendencies rivaled her father's. Her father entered into an engagement on
her behalf with Leopold, which Lewald discovered after the fact. When
her father, without explanation, ended the relationship suddenly, Lewald
found herself emotionally unable to defy his prohibition of any subsequent
contact with Leopold. Later her father permitted her conversion to
Christianity. Although she realized shortly before her baptism that she
could not embrace Christian precepts intellectually, she convinced herself
that there must be more to Christianity than meets the eye and went
through with the ceremony. In 1831, her father changed the Jewish family
name of Markus to Lewald, which his brothers had done years earlier. To
his children's objections he responded, "Was soll Euch [an der
Universität] der jüdische Name? Was soll er Euch im Leben?…Macht
Euch also keine Gedanken darüber, ich weiß, was ich tue, und Ihr werdet
es allmählich begreifen lernen und es mir danken" (*ML* I: 243).

At twenty-one, Lewald accompanied her father on a business trip. Her
happiness at the prospect was briefly clouded by a comment she overheard:

> Ich hörte einmal, daß er mit einem Bekannten davon sprach, wie sehr lieb es
> ihm sein würde, für mich eine "passende Partie" zu finden, und wie er mich zum
> Teil deshalb mit sich genommen habe. Ich hätte vor Scham und Zorn
> aufschreien mögen in dem Augenblicke. Ich kam mir wie eine elende Ware vor,
> die man auf den Markt führte, weil sich zu Hause kein Käufer dafür gefunden
> hatte. (*ML* II: 10)

They visited various relatives, and Lewald met and fell in love with her
cousin Heinrich Simon. He apparently returned her feelings only briefly;
she then spent the next seven years in the throes of unrequited love for
him. In her uncle's home she encountered world literature, including the
novels of George Sand, and his circle of friends, who discussed the political
issues of the day. Back in Königsberg, she refused at twenty-five to marry
a lawyer she had seen twice at their home and whom her father pressured
her to accept. Her cousin August Lewald, the editor of the periodical
*Europa*, published letters she had written to him on political events in
Königsberg. He subsequently wrote to her father to suggest that Lewald
was a "dichterische Natur, und es wäre nicht zu verantworten, wenn sie
eine solche Begabung nicht benutzte und ein Feld brachliegen ließe, von
dem sie für ihre Zukunft gute Früchte ernten könnte" (*ML* II: 276).

With her father's reluctant permission and her own almost constant self-doubt, Lewald began to write. At her father's request, she published her first stories, novels, and newspaper articles anonymously. When Lewald was thirty-three, her father allowed her to move into her own apartment in Berlin, to the horror of most of her relatives and acquaintances. She associated with the literary members of Berlin society and in 1845 left for her first trip to Italy. There, as part of a group of German artists, writers, and tourists, she met Adolph Stahr, a more or less unhappily married father of five. They fell in love and spent nine years waiting for Stahr's wife to agree to a divorce. She and Stahr settled in Berlin, where several of his children lived with them for varying periods. Her success as a writer enabled them to travel frequently. In Berlin they had a well-known salon in which Lewald was pleased and proud to be the center of attention (Rheinberg 142), although the guests' admiration of the hostess was not universal: some found her rather *too* desirous of attention (Rheinberg 142–44). Their marriage was happy, and Rudolph von Gottschall, for one, saw profound creative benefits in it for Lewald:

> Eine reiche konkrete Welt- und Lebensanschauung trat an die Stelle jener einsamen abstrakten Grübeleien, mit denen sich die Dichterin bisher beschäftigt hatte, und befruchtete ihre Phantasie, die von Hause aus nicht reich und schöpferisch zu nennen war, mit einer Fülle von Bildern. Die philosophische und ästhetische Bildung Stahr's, seine Verehrung und geistige Beherrschung des Altertums mußten ihren Horizont bedeutend erweitern und sie über jene vorwiegend formellen Fragen hinaus in eine reichere Welt der Schönheit führen. (330–31)

Regula Venske evaluates Stahr's influence differently: "His tutelage has to be interpreted as a far-reaching impediment to Lewald's development of an identity of her own, and it had fatal consequences for her writing" (184). Stahr died in 1876. Lewald, deeply depressed, eventually continued to travel and to write until her own death in Dresden on 5 August 1889. She is buried with Stahr in Wiesbaden.

Lewald's popularity in the nineteenth century suggests that her contemporaries approved of her narrative vision of femininity. Irene Stocksieker Di Maio has suggested that twentieth-century critics' "vacillation between admiration for and irritation with" Lewald stems from the "tension between emancipatory and integrative impulses in her fiction and nonfiction" (275). My own reading of Lewald's texts, however, demonstrates that her response to prevailing social discourses partially, and effectively, challenged the conclusions of these discourses and that the "integrative impulses" other critics identify can be read against the grain.

Linda Alcoff's concept of "positionality" can facilitate an appreciation of Lewald's social activism within the narrative context she creates, a fictional world in dialogue with the real world of mid- to late nineteenth-century Germany. Alcoff argues for recognition of the "subject's ability to reflect on the social discourse and challenge its determinations" (417), although the subject will inevitably be to some extent shaped by these determinations (432). Positionality thus may offer an explanation for Lewald's reproduction of conventional domestic paradigms and the significant mutations of these that are also a part of her narratives.

Positionality combines two theoretical assumptions. Alcoff asserts that the category "woman" does not refer to a set of universal, ahistorical attributes. Rather, it is a "relational term identifiable only within a (constantly moving) context." She also argues for the recognition of an "identity politics" that makes the position in which women find themselves a site that "can be utilized (rather than transcended)...for the construction of meaning" (434). The changing "historical dimension" of the "habits, practices, and discourses" that contribute to the formation of subjectivity ensures the impermanence of a given construction of gender (431), as do the contributions of women themselves. Within a given relational network and within a given historical context, which involves, among other things, "the objective economic conditions, cultural and political institutions and ideologies" (433), women, as "part of the historicized, fluid movement... actively contribute to the context within which [their] position can be delineated" (434). If women in fact "use their positional perspective as a place from which values are interpreted and constructed rather than as a locus of an already determined set of values" (434), then positionality enables us read the domestic novels and female (as well as male) characters written by some nineteenth-century writers differently from those written by others. This phenomenon can account for similarities and differences among women, as well as between some men and some women.

Lewald's position as a woman writer in an age that found the professional woman anomalous and her view of the individual as a product of his/her time and its spirit (*ML* I: 24) are documented aspects of the formation of Lewald's own subjectivity. These formative influences and others suggest that while she may have regarded her own femininity as distinct from that of the female contemporaries she criticized in her letters and comments, she herself would have viewed that difference as permissible within the dominant discourse. Within the shifting parameters of that discourse—observing its conventions and adopting its nominal hierarchies—her narratives negotiate better terms for her female characters, and therefore for their historical counterparts.

Although I would like to avoid the ahistoricity Alcoff criticizes in other—even feminist—conceptions of the category of "women," Alcoff's explication of her theory reads like the subtext of the narratives I discuss. With some modification of phrasing, we might imagine this statement by Alcoff being written by Lewald a hundred years earlier:

> [B]eing a 'woman' is to take up a position within a moving historical context and to be able to choose what we make of this position and how we alter this context. From the perspective of that fairly determinate though fluid and mutable position, women can themselves articulate a set of interests and ground a feminist politics. (435)

Female patients whose illness allows them to reclaim their autonomy, women whose worthiness facilitates their victimization by the law, wives whose education makes the exercise of their domestic vocation possible, and women who are reluctant to enter into matrimony except on their own terms "articulate a set of [women's] interests" (Alcoff 435) and act to alter the historical context of which Lewald and her narratives were a part.

CHAPTER ONE

# "Wollen Sie mit einer Kranken rechten? Lassen Sie ihr den Willen!": Lewald and Nineteenth-Century Medical Discourse

In a survey of women novelists and their work, the influential literary critic Rudolf von Gottschall (1823–1909) writes disapprovingly that although the novels of Julie Burow,[1] a contemporary of Fanny Lewald and a fellow East Prussian, are distinguished by a "verstandesmäßige, naturwissenschaftliche Aufklärung," they lack a certain delicacy: "'Das Körperliche' spielt bei ihr eine allzu große Rolle, nicht im ästhetischen, sondern im medizinischen Sinne; sie bebt vor der Berührung mit ekelhaften Krankheiten nicht zurück und gefällt sich in Schilderungen, welche den Cynismus des Lazaretts nicht verleugnen können" (327–28). Although Gottschall identifies in Lewald an "Unerbittlichkeit des Verstandes" similar to Burow's, he finds more intellectual breadth, which we may read as fewer descriptions of the physical, in her work and attributes it to Lewald's origins in Kant's home, Königsberg. Unlike Burow, he argues, Lewald has left the realm of the "Familienroman." Her narrative purpose, he claims, is women's emancipation (328–29).

   Although Lewald's texts do indeed tend to elevate mind over body and to exclude consideration of "disgusting illnesses," the female body and its exigencies nevertheless play a significant role in several of her narratives. Women's bodies in fact make a contribution to her emancipatory project. Her interrogation of medicine and female illness both assents to and subverts the prevailing constructions of the female body, reshaping the "patient" from within familiar discursive representations. In her "Doktor Melchior" (1880), Lewald challenges the perception of doctors as virtually infallible "knowers" of women's bodies. In *Liebesbriefe. Aus dem Leben eines Gefangenen* (1850) she avails herself of the "sickroom" as a locus of female power. She also employs this fictional space to dispute the diagnosis of female bodies as deficient because inherently more susceptible to disease. Finally, in *Treue Liebe* (1882) she contests the view of female sterility as "selbstverschuldete" female bodily derangement. These texts work together to rewrite contemporary representations of female physiology as constituted by the masculine medical gaze. Lewald's fictional female bodies reveal their strength rather than their weakness: they make insistent demands, and their demands are met.

The body that Lewald and other writers of the period employed was a body in transition. As Thomas Laqueur's *Making Sex: Body and Gender from the Greeks to Freud* demonstrates, the female body was refashioned in medical narratives after the end of the seventeenth century. The ancients' view of women and their bodies as imperfect versions of men had yielded, although not entirely, to the concept of male and female physical complements. Literary representations of the body then utilized the various scientific and medical constructions that were circulating at the time and manipulated those representations to achieve specific narrative goals.[2] Medical manuals on women's illnesses were written both for the practicing physician and for the layperson. The numbers of each type of manual appear to have increased in the late eighteenth and nineteenth centuries, which made the medical theories of the age, as well as the ideology that informed them, more readily available to both physicians and the laity.[3] In this chapter, I cite examples from medical texts from various countries and from various points throughout the nineteenth century. Many of these books appeared in one (often revised) edition after another, referred to one another as well as to other international texts, and were translated. Further, even medical beliefs from the earlier part of the century that had been discredited by scientific discoveries in the latter half must have survived to some extent among the lay populace and among older practitioners.

I

The female body that emerged in nineteenth-century medical texts incarnated conflict, inadequacy, and existing or potential disease, primarily because this body was the terrain on which an ideological battle was waged. Nineteenth-century domestic ideology, as is by now well-known, argued for the assignment of women to the home as their nominal domain, while men governed the world outside it. The second half of the century saw increasing resistance from the women's movement to this doctrine, and the female reproductive body was then offered by the doctrine's proponents as the "scientific"—and hence incontrovertible—response (Oppenheim 186). The comparisons between male and female bodies emphasize a physiology of difference and deficiency that encompasses the blood, the nervous system, the brain, the skeletal structure, and the reproductive organs. This difference was fundamentally hazardous to women's health, both physical and mental.

Female blood, for instance, is simply not as red as that of men and therefore not as vigorous and healthy. The English lawyer and legal writer Joseph Chitty maintains in his *Practical Treatise on Medical Jurisprudence* (1836) that the blood is the "primary and principle cause of most diseases, especially fevers" (151) and that the "quantity of [red] globules in the blood, in regard to the whole mass, varies, so that the appearance of the blood has been considered as a real index of health or disease. In disease and weakness the blood is poor and colorless, whilst in health and strength it is rich and florid" (162–63). Women's blood, however, "usually contains more water and fewer red globules than that of men" (376). The widely translated Italian medical professor Paolo Mantegazza also notes that women's blood is "poorer" in red blood cells than men's (67–68), while the professor of medicine and spa physician E. Heinrich Kisch echoes the type of conclusions Chitty draws from this impoverishment. Kisch's discussion of chlorosis, a kind of anemia to which women are "predisposed," refers to the conclusions of many other researchers. They base their work generally on the assumption that the disease is linked to uterine development, the onset of menstruation, and toxins produced by the ovaries (*Life* 89–91).[4] Women, compared to the male standard, are thus intrinsically weak and diseased.[5] They can also be expected to faint more frequently, because, although usually due to an inadequate supply of blood reaching the brain, fainting can also be attributed to "the state of the blood itself" (Chitty 167). Obligingly, nineteenth-century fiction tipped its hat to medical research with a plethora of swooning heroines.

Although Chitty considers the blood the most significant factor in health and disease and notes with satisfaction that many others now support this view (151), he acknowledges a competing doctrine: the idea that "most diseases, whether mental or affecting the body, are attributable to the influence of the nervous system" (271). Nineteenth-century medical investigations into its effects further suggest that the female nervous system predisposes women to emotional disorders and leaves them almost unfit even for domestic roles. Chitty articulates the prevailing view that body and mind are "intimately connected" (312) and that "all acts that affect the mind and passions may be baneful in their consequences upon the nervous system. Surprise, fright, terror, anger, and indignation, are not infrequently productive of apoplexy, paralysis, epilepsy, convulsions, syncope, and almost innumerable other maladies, bodily as well as mental" (287). Fear, he claims, can even engender cholera (315).

The examples Chitty provides, however, indicate whose bodies succumb most readily to the nervous system and its passions. He cites "[n]umerous instances...on record" of an attempted burglary having "induced so powerful an effect upon the nerves of the most sensible and healthy females, as to occasion continued sleeplessness and anxious nights for months, and even decline, if not speedily removed." He also argues that parents should ensure that nursemaids never frighten the children in their care, "lest their minds should be permanently affected," and insists that pregnant women exposed to "terror" of some sort may miscarry or die (317). Women and children, even when otherwise healthy, are equated in their vulnerability to fear and its allegedly physical effects, whereas the few nervous men whose cases he describes are condemned prisoners or are already debilitated and dying, often of wounds sustained in war. Walter Erhart discusses the nineteenth century's assumption of difference in the etiology of male and female "nervousness," neurasthenia and hysteria, respectively. He claims that "[a]lthough, from 1850 on, medical theory can hardly distinguish the clinical symptoms, hysteria is always coded female, neurasthenia is coded male." "[H]ysteria comes from within the female body, neurasthenia is caused by the outside—the stress of the modern world that weakens the male body" and makes it female. "[T]rembling hands," "sensitive nerves," "lack of will and control over his body," and "loss of inner strength" are the markers of this feminization (2).

Janet Oppenheim cites the medical professor Thomas Laycock's assertion in the 1860s that "[w]oman, as compared with man, is of the nervous temperament.... Her nervous system is therefore more easily acted upon by all impressions, and more liable to all diseases of excitement." Oppenheim demonstrates that for most medical men the "principal cause of [women's] nervous ailments" was the reproductive functions that defined them as female (187), yet reproduction and motherhood constituted the overriding purpose of their lives. She also points to an irreconcilable contradiction in the imaging of the female nervous system itself: although evolutionary theory argued that women had "stalled at a less lofty stage of cerebral development" than men (183) and therefore "lacked the most intricately developed nervous structures, the so-called highest nervous centers that the will was thought to occupy" (184), the same proponents of this theory paradoxically insisted on the "delicacy and complexity of women's nerves," which explained women's greater "sensibility and excitability." Rather than confronting the incongruity of these opposing representations, the "medical profession... reiterate[d] that a woman's nervous instability was closely related to her reproductive system" (193). And, according to Mantegazza, "die Geburtsarbeit [erschüttert] das Nervensystem so gewaltig..., daß es den Grenzen des Wahnsinns nahe kommt" (367–68). Every woman is a potential madwoman; because women play an unfortunately crucial role in the continuation of the species, they must be preserved from additional strain that might overwhelm them entirely.

In the work of medical authorities, female blood and the female nervous system joined forces with the female brain and the female skeleton to "prove" women's predetermination for motherhood and their unsuitability for intellectual labor. According to Oppenheim, beginning in the late 1860s, the findings of craniology provided the definitive argument for women's alleged intellectual inferiority. Craniologists measured the female skull, determined that it was smaller than that of the male, and concluded that size mattered. Medical researchers with access to actual brains then weighed them, and a "consensus emerged that, on the average, the female brain weighed about five ounces less than the male. In those missing ounces lay all the vigor that women lacked, especially the power of rigorous self-control under the will's sovereign direction." These researchers rejected the thesis that difference in brain size might simply reflect general size differences (Oppenheim 185–86).

Londa Schiebinger describes the general European attempt, beginning in the second half of the eighteenth century, to locate sex differences in the skeleton, the body's structural frame, which would "penetrate every muscle, vein, and organ attached to and molded by the skeleton" (53). Because this search for difference was, as noted above, precipitated by demands for social equality for women, the anatomists focused on "politically significant" structures: women's smaller skulls and larger pelvises (Schiebinger 42–44). The drawings they produced, which were intended to "capture the details...of a universal and ideal type," were "laden with cultural values" (Schiebinger 60–61). In these illustrations the female pelvis is much wider than the male's, and the ribs and the shoulders are much narrower. The skull is either smaller in proportion to the body — obvious evidence for the proposition that women are less intelligent than men — or proportionally larger and accompanied by drawings of or references to children. Because children's heads are indeed larger in proportion to their bodies, they served as proof for the assertion that women — and their intellectual powers — are child-like (Schiebinger 58–66). Delineation of the "ideal" extended to the relative proportions of husband and wife: women of small stature married to men of "normal height" are far more fertile than women of medium height married to such men (Kisch, *Sterilität* 57–58). This assertion privileged marriages in which the wife really did appear child-like in relation to her husband.

In his response to the question of whether women's anatomy makes them inferior or superior to men, Mantegazza appears to acknowledge the cultural uses to which anatomy has been put — "die Anthropologen [haben] dieselbe verschieden beantwortet, je nachdem sie in der Anatomie Gründe suchten, um das Weib herabzusetzen oder ihm zu schmeicheln" (62) — and then expounds on his support of the view that "in dem Skelett des Weibes...selbst der kleinste Knochen den Eindruck des weiblichen Charakters [trägt]" (186). He examines the bones of the skull for such proof and finds it. After admitting that many anatomists see no difference between males and females in this respect, he trots out himself and a colleague as proof of his claim that, in fact, one can — with a three to five percent rate of failure — distinguish the skulls from one another (43–50).

His measurements/evidence are often his own, and when he cites other researchers, it is apparent that there is disagreement among them. However, listing all the differences anyone has asserted enables him to present a lengthy catalog of comparative traits. The net effect suggests the incompetence of the medical men who had professed their inability to find gender in the human skull.

All of them, however, professed to find it in the pelvis. The grotesquely wide pelvises the anatomists characterized as the female anatomical ideal point again to the primary focus of the investigations into difference: the reproductive organs. The organization of medical textbooks can emphasize that focus indirectly. Chitty, for instance, whose nominal concern is human physiology, refers to the disparities between male and female bodies only in his section on female reproductive organs, although he finds some of those alleged differences in the composition of blood, bone structure, and the nervous system and might have treated them in the chapters on those subjects. His book is in fact about male physiology. Female bodies become meaningful only in the context of reproduction.[6]

Nineteenth-century medical researchers argued that woman's reproductive organs and capacity are the locus of her identity and the source of the mental and physiological weakness that is a defining feature of that identity. Ornella Moscucci summarizes their pronouncements as follows: "Not only did woman's biological functions blur into disease; they were also the source of a host of psychological disorders, from strange moods and feelings, to hysteria and insanity" (102). A review of the English urologist William Acton's *The Functions and Disorders of the Reproductive Organs*, a hefty volume that concerns itself exclusively with male reproductive organs, asserts that "sexual feelings" govern the "whole life of the female, from the time at which she dandles her first doll to the time when she teaches her grandchild 'pattycake, pattycake'" (Acton: facing title page). Like his contemporaries, Mantegazza finds that virtually all of the physiological differences he identifies between men and women derive from their disparate reproductive roles (37). This conclusion brings to mind Laqueur's revision of Freud's assertion: anatomy is destiny, but only because destiny has been located in anatomy.[7] As Mantegazza puts it, "Das Weib ist Mutter; um diesen Kern, um dieses biologische Skelett gruppieren sich alle seine Kräfte, fast alle seine Tugenden, fast alle seine Schwächen" (188).

Medical authors were primarily absorbed in detailing these "Schwächen." Their work demonstrates that women's physiology is inadequate to the body's presumptive task: the maintenance of mental and physical health. Thus, the "events" of women's reproductive lives — puberty, the onset and recurrence of menstruation, intercourse, childbirth, and menopause — constitute windows of opportunity for malfunction and disease. Each such period "demanded heavy payments of nerve force" (Oppenheim 188). Moscucci quotes the gynecologist Robert Barnes, who wrote in 1882 that gynecology bears "the most instructive testimony to the law which declares that there is no proper boundary between physiology and pathology; that pathology is but a chapter in the history of physiology" (102). Researchers detailed the increased risks of disease of the reproductive organs themselves at each stage of a woman's life, as well as the ailments caused or aggravated by these stages. Menstruation itself was no longer a "healthy release of plethoric body fluid, as it had sometimes been viewed in past centuries, but a condition that definitively marked women's morbidity." It was the "chief reason for the physical fragility and nervous irritability that placed women at such a disadvantage in comparison to men" (Oppenheim 190). Pregnancy and childbirth are particularly dangerous: pregnancy can result in enlargement of the thyroid, hernias, wandering internal organs, tooth decay, tumors, bone damage, psychosis, retinitis, deafness, and skin diseases; childbirth carries even greater risks (Kisch, *Life* 221–23), not least of which is the borderline insanity induced by labor pains (Mantegazza 368). Early menopause, however, according to medical texts, is not a liberation for women from the perils of their reproductive lives. Rather, it is "sexual death" (Kisch, *Life* 2), which entails the loss of social esteem. As Kisch puts it, "a woman in whom the sexual life is short quickly loses value and significance, both in domestic and in social circles" (*Life* 33), although the postmenopausal woman will probably live longer than men of the same age because she is "more cared for" (Moscucci 103).

But how much pleasure would she or anyone else derive from her longevity? Mantegazza argues that a woman is "wahrhaft Weib" only during her thirty to thirty-five years of fertility (87). In her late forties she undergoes a horrifying "Schiffbruch der Form," which signals the death of all sexual desirability (88). Kisch concurs with this assessment, citing approvingly Mantegazza's claim that "the beauties peculiar to women are one and all sexual" (*Life* 23). As with all the stages of women's reproductive lives, menopause also entails health risks: Mantegazza maintains that these years are the "critical" ones "wegen der Gefahren, welche [das Weib] bedrohen, wegen der vielen Leiden, welche seine Gesundheit trüben" (84–85). According to these narratives, a woman's opportunity to reproduce constitutes the sole point of her bodily existence, and that opportunity should be enhanced and prolonged.

Discussions of a maternal imperative are rare in late twentieth-century medical texts,[8] but the medical, social, and literary discourses of the nineteenth century generally cooperated in the assertion of the maternal instinct and urge. Texts from these discourses also sought and found affirmation in each other's narratives. Chitty, for instance, argues that all mothers want to "provide a comfortable reception for their young." Preparations such as the acquisition of baby clothes thus suggest that a woman does not intend to kill her child or conceal its birth and are therefore relevant evidence in trials for infanticide. He finds support for his statement in the actions of a female character in one of Sir Walter Scott's Waverley novels (411). Oppenheim identifies a depiction of the "infantile quality of the adult woman" that was shared by science, society, and literature. In fact, "science was as much influenced by popular prejudices and literary stereotypes in this respect as novelists and poets were impressed by the findings of science" (206). Physicians commented privately and publicly on the tendency of female patients to manipulate their loved ones with their imagined illnesses, and Oppenheim suggests that perhaps "literary sources encouraged medical men in this frame of mind, for the invocation of nervous debility to gain some personal advantage provided a recurrent motif in nineteenth-century fiction" (208–09). The nineteenth-century body in flux was apparently subject to manipulation and exploitation from all sides, including literature.

## II

"Scientific" access to women's bodies was mediated through physicians and other medical researchers, whose medical identity and authority became a part of the knowledge they disseminated in the form of textbooks, consultations, case studies, illustrations, and determinations in general of gendered anatomical, skeletal, and physiological possibility.[9] Edward Shorter maintains that the "essence" of the modern doctor—the medical paragon that held sway between 1880 and 1950—was the "ability correctly to diagnose disease: not to cure it, but to recognize what it was the patient had." This ability was the outcome of a nineteenth-century "revolution in medical thought" that employed the new germ theory to determine the etiology of specific diseases and correlated tissue changes observed in autopsies with symptoms recorded during the patient's life. In other words, even the general practitioner had become a researcher who held the microscopic keys to the patient's body and therefore had access to the absolute truth about the patient's ailment. As such he had far more credibility than his traditional predecessor (*Doctors* 75–78).

In answering a question he poses himself ("Are women as intelligent as 'we' are?"), Mantegazza makes his own status as a "Naturforscher" part of the support for his response ("No"): "Ich bin nicht Advokat, sondern Naturforscher, daher ist mir die Kunst, die Gedanken zu verwirren, der Logik einen Possen zu spielen, das Weiße schwarz und das Schwarze weiß erscheinen zu lassen, ganz unbekannt" (377). Medical researchers, in other words, are by definition objective, logical, and possessed of the ability to see things as they absolutely are. As Laqueur has demonstrated, however, what a given medical investigator might "see" was determined in large part by what he expected to see. Nevertheless, the now more general credibility of physicians conferred obvious benefits on those in the medical field who propounded viewpoints that could still be framed as biological issues for the nineteenth-century reader.

Kisch suggests to the physician-readers of his *Die Sterilität des Weibes* (1886) that they use the doctor's superior qualities consciously in their interactions with patients: the "volle Autorität des Arztes" must be deployed, for instance, in cases of husbands reluctant to submit to an examination of their semen when their wives fail to conceive (147–48). Embarrassed wives can be induced to respond to questions about the marital relationship when they see that "der Arzt mit sittlichem Ernste und mit würdiger Ruhe an seine schwierige Aufgabe herantritt" (146). Additionally, a doctor's perspicacity can ascertain whether a woman truly is experiencing painful intercourse and how her "subjective" statements can be confirmed:

> Ein Zustand, welcher nur auf subjectiven Angaben der Frau beruht, ist selbstredend schwer zu constatiren und noch schwerer zu controliren. Hat man einmal auf diesen Punkt seine Aufmerksamkeit gerichtet und stellt man

diesbezügliche Fragen, so wird eine gewisse Anzahl von Frauen ganz ungerechtfertigt Dyspareunie heucheln, um Interesse zu erregen, als lieblos auf dem ehelichen Altare Liebesopfer bringend. Indess sind häufig die Angaben vollkommen glaubwürdig, besonders wenn sie durch die Aussagen des Gatten als richtig bestätigt werden. (101)

Here physicians consult husbands as colleagues and impartial witnesses.

Kisch's monograph also emphasizes the physician's ability to diagnose. Although he admits in his preface that the finer physiological mechanisms of reproduction as well as the pathology that prevents it are not completely understood (iii), the substance of Kisch's entire text on female sterility asserts that doctors *know* and that what they know are the bodies of their female patients.[10] The gynecologist was paradigmatic of the omniscient physician: the "gynecological practice allowed the doctor to probe more deeply into the secrets of the living human body—a body that is always female—than any other medical practice at that time" (Tatlock 306).[11] Perhaps because of this assumption of access and of what might be called the diagnostic imperative, doctors "knew" what they at the time could not possibly have known.

The issue of the causes of infertility is particularly instructive: according to Laqueur, the "outlines of our modern understanding of the hormonal control of ovulation were unknown" until the 1930s (9). Although the most common cause of female infertility is "failure to ovulate, due to hormonal failure" (Heidenstam et al. 274) and although "a significant number" of infertility cases still cannot be explained (Cox 254), gynecologists in the late nineteenth century rarely confessed in their publications to bewilderment as to the origin of a patient's sterility. A list of the causes of infertility for 250 of Kisch's own spa patients identifies many women with more than one disorder. He does not mention any cases for which he could find no explanation. He also cites the similar findings of a number of other physicians. Those of the "well-known gynecologist Mayer in Berlin" are typical: his statistics, published in 1836, revealed that out of 272 cases of infertility, there were six in which no pathology was evident. The unassuming Mondot stands alone with his admission of 217 patients (out of 750) for whose infertility he could find no cause (*Sterilität* 133–42).

Nineteenth-century gynecology, as Lynne Tatlock notes, "offered a particularly crass example of asymmetrical relations between the sexes": "the doctor, the one who speculated, was always male; the patient, the object of speculation, was always female. To practice gynecology the male doctor presumed to read the female body" (306). Judging from the citations in Kisch's text, gynecologists—with the exception of the hapless Mondot—read that body with an almost exuberant confidence.[12] The nineteenth-century gynecologist's confidence in the examining room might have been in part a function of gendered social hierarchies outside it. The new confidence of the medical profession in general in the latter part of the century derived from and translated into an upward social mobility unthinkable for earlier generations of doctors. Shorter discusses the traditional disparity in social status between doctors and patients, which had worked to undermine not only the self-esteem of the doctor but the patient's opinion of the advice he dispensed (*Doctors* 102–03). This dynamic illuminates the comment of a character in one of the Lewald novels discussed below: Konrad, the physician in Lewald's *Liebesbriefe*, voices his desire to work and learn more rather than remain the "unbekannte Dorfarzt...der den Hut in der Hand, demüthig und verlegen dasteht vor dem reichen Kranken" (113).

Shorter argues that the "halo of science" helped to transform physicians in their own minds and in the minds of their patients into superior beings (*Doctors* 130). The fact that "knowing" reaped both tangible and intangible benefits presumably exerted pressure on the medical profession for continued certitude—hence the diagnostic triumphs of Kisch and his colleagues. Paul Heyse articulates the public's perceptions and expectations in a letter to Theodor Storm in 1887 about a physician character in Storm's work in progress, *Ein Bekenntnis*:

> Ich weiß nicht, ob ein Arzt, der die Novelle lies't, nicht stark den Kopf schütteln wird.... Ein Arzt...der über den Sitz eines solchen Leidens—doch wohl Unterleibskrebs—nach sorgfältiger Untersuchung nicht ins Reine kommt, der zufällig herumtastend erst Gewissheit erlangt, wird seinen Collegen mit Recht verdächtig werden. (qtd. in Tatlock 308)

Even Heyse diagnoses with confidence when projecting himself into his physician-reader, whose knowledge he assumes to be vast and common to his profession.

A comparison of Tatlock's discussion of Storm's novella and of Lewald's "Dr. Melchior" reveals useful parallels and divergences between the two literary texts, which highlight Lewald's revision of the physician ideal. Storm's male protagonist had given his wife the poison she requested while suffering from what he, a gynecologist, believed was an incurable cancer of the uterus. After her death he discovers a new and promising operation, the hysterectomy, in the medical journals he had left unread during her illness. Tatlock argues that the "sin" that he confesses to the novella's narrator is "not so much his assisting in his wife's death but rather his failure always to keep current on the advances in medicine" (305). She thus maintains that Storm's protagonist ultimately confirms the contemporary view of physicians as subscribing to a "creed of knowledge" (301), a creed that is gendered male and dominant. The protagonist eventually decides to "serve humanity in Africa." Storm sets this decision in 1859, but his novella was written in 1887. Because the 1880s were the most active years of Germany's colonial period, the protagonist's "medical practice is consistently and inextricably intertwined with dominion" (310).

Although Lewald sets her own narrative in 1850, her "Doktor Melchior" (1880) was written in the same decade as Storm's. Her text, however, questions the new infallibility and superiority of medical knowledge and practitioners. A female "patient," Juliane, falls victim to what Melchior, her doctor, blinded by the very masculinity that was allegedly the guarantor of impartial scientific acuity, could not and would not see. Lewald's text in fact argues that characteristics traditionally coded feminine improve the practice of medicine.

The female narrator hears Melchior's tale from the doctor himself. When she meets him, he is over seventy and is tall, upright, strong, determined, and refined. She wonders why such a clever doctor, whose patients travel great distances to seek his advice and who is an intelligent and educated man who could win renown in society, would choose to spend his life in a country practice. He is the head of the "Julianenstift," a small hospital located on the neighborhood estate where he also lives. His profession is part of male family tradition: both his father and grandfather were respected physicians in their community, and he had never doubted that he would become a doctor. The aristocratic owners of the estate where he now lives had left after the death of the daughter, Princess Juliane. The doctor actually lives in the princess's old rooms, which are filled with both the artifacts of scientific masculinity—many books, laboratory equipment, and a pipe stand—and those of delicate femininity—porcelain decorated with rococo figures, a sewing table, paints and brushes, and a small, carefully selected book collection (249–50).

Melchior claims that one can be satisfied if one can look back on one's life with the conviction that one has acted "nach bestem Wissen und Gewissen" and that such certainty is particularly crucial to a doctor's peace of mind (256). His narrative, however, suggests that he wavers in that conviction with respect to his own romantic history and that, by adhering to a masculine code of ethics, failing to recognize his own worth as a middle-class success story, and attempting a particular cure without regard for the needs of the patient, he caused the death of the woman he loved.

That woman is Juliane. Shortly after receiving his medical credentials Melchior meets her brother, Lothar, and heals a wound the latter has received in a duel. The grateful patient invites him to the family estate, where Melchior meets Lothar's ambitious mother, who dotes on her son, and his neglected sister, Juliane, a "zartes, körperlich etwas zurückgebliebenes, bleiches Kind" of ten or eleven (264). While walking with Lothar and Melchior one day, listening to them discuss their plans for a journey, she says that she needs Melchior with her because she is sick. Now Melchior recognizes her illness, which is a "typhöse[s] Fieber" (270–71) and does in fact keep him with her for the four months of her "lange, schwere Krankheit" (275).

Miriam Bailin's study of the function of the "sickroom" in Victorian fiction, which I will discuss in more detail below, identifies illness as both solution to and evidence of social and narrative dilemmas. Her conclusions illuminate Lewald's fictional sickroom as well. Juliane's illness indeed accomplishes a number of narrative tasks, making manifest the mother's lack of love for her daughter and establishing Juliane as a character who can and will protect herself. She, for instance, avenges herself for a lifetime of neglect by banning her mother from her sickroom (276). Primarily, however, Juliane's illness establishes a more or less permanent doctor-patient relationship between herself and Melchior, who determines that she has "gerade jetzt ebenso wohl geistig wie körperlich eine vorsichtige Behandlung nöthig" (279). Lewald sets up the apparent authority of the medical man with Melchior's cures for Juliane's body and soul, with the dependence of even her haughty mother on his advice on how best to influence Juliane's behavior, and with the patient's own insistence on interpreting herself as the product of his care. Once recovered, Juliane regards herself as actually belonging to the doctor because he saved her life (283). When Melchior realizes at last that he loves Juliane, he refers to her as, among other things, "das liebe Kind, das ich einst dem Tode in langer Sorge abgerungen" (323), and in the decisive scene in which he tells her ("for her own good") to marry another man, he hears the loud, slow ticking of the clock, "wie in der entscheidenden Stunde an schwerem Krankenbett" (371).

Just as Juliane is repeatedly defined as Melchior's patient, the narrative continues to define Melchior by his profession: he travels home to join his father's medical practice, and years later Lothar's mother asks him to return to care for her son, who has been wounded in battle and has also fallen victim to "Lazarethfieber." While Melchior attends his friend, his father dies. Once Lothar recovers, he provides Melchior with a medical practice and a hospital. Melchior discovers that the intervening years have moderated Juliane's tempestuous behavior. He realizes that he loves her and struggles with the idea of leaving, but because he believes his love unreturned—he misreads the significance of her "openness" in his presence ("Ich sagte mir: so frei, so offen, wie sie mit Dir umgeht, giebt man sich keinem Manne für den man mehr als Freundschaft, mehr als ein achtungsvolles Vertrauen empfindet" [325])—and because Lothar asks him to protect his sister and mother in his absence, he stays. He also promises Lothar that he will aid him later in persuading Juliane to marry her uncle, a much older man. Melchior suffers in silence for several years, convinced that even if he had not promised Lothar to support the uncle's suit, class differences could never permit him to hope for Juliane himself. On the ten-year anniversary of their first meeting, however, he realizes that Juliane does love him—and he rebuffs her overtures. Mental anguish follows: is it more unmanly and dishonorable to break his word to Lothar or to reject the woman he loves? Could he provide for her? And could he endure being both unable to provide for his wife *and* someone whose word cannot be trusted? His concern for his own masculine honor and for the code of ethics that bind him to Lothar will be fatal to Juliane and, tellingly, to his own chances of happiness.

The uncle arrives and proposes on schedule. Juliane puts her fate in Melchior's hands as the one who "knows" her best: "Sie werden besser als ich ermessen, was ich kann, was ich nicht kann und was ich thun soll. Ich weiß, Sie sind nicht eigennützig, Sie lieben mich und uns Alle. Sie sollen mir rathen, sollen entscheiden, wo ich's nicht vermag" (367–68). He is, however, "eigennützig"—he cannot endure the shame of failing to keep a

promise to Lothar, of perhaps failing to provide for his wife, and of being
laughed at as a "vermessener Bourgeois" (328)—and he ignores the
evidence of her character that Juliane herself had provided earlier. In his
presence she had told her brother that she would "niemals eines Mannes
Eigenthum [werden] als aus freier Wahl." She quotes Gertrud in Schiller's
*Wilhelm Tell*: "Die letzte Wahl steht auch dem Schwächsten offen, / Ein
Sprung von dieser Brücke macht mich frei" (321). Gertrud here
encourages her husband to rebel against the "Landvogt," assuring him that
she is ready to risk death to gain independence from an unjust ruler. With
this reference, Juliane asserts a similar desire for an independent choice.
Melchior had assumed that a woman would be incapable of such candor
in front of a man she loved, but he was unable to decipher its obvious
warning to him. Now telling himself that he must think only of her
happiness, Melchior advises her to marry her uncle. With this piece of
advice, he proves himself as blind to her ailment now as he had been to the
beginning stages of the fever she had had as a child. She consents but then
comes to his rooms—on an alleged last tour of her castle home—while he
is away visiting a patient. She steals a bottle of "Opiumtinktur" from his
pharmaceutical supply and drinks it alone by the pond. Her suicide note
to her mother states that although she had tried, she had concluded that
she could not be happy simply pleasing others.

Melchior had not only failed to ask his patient the right questions, he
had embarked upon a course of treatment without asking her any
questions at all. He simply assumed he knew best. In this he reflects the
behavioral model for the medical profession apparent in textbook after
textbook.[13] He had also disregarded the signs that would have led to other
conclusions. Lewald's narrative makes clear to the reader that Juliane
cared nothing for the trappings of her aristocratic life and would have been
happy to spend her life with this worthy member of the middle class.
Melchior's selfishness clouds his judgment, and his mistake leads to the
death of the patient who had entrusted herself to his care since childhood
and who had reiterated her understanding of their relationship when she
requested that he decide her fate. She, of course, reclaims her right to self-
determination by choosing the "alternative open to even the weakest," but
Lewald's text uses Juliane's suicide to underscore Melchior's involvement
in her death. Rather than "leaping from a bridge" or drowning herself in
the convenient pond, she took medical poison—*his* medical poison.

Melchior does not formulate his "guilt" in terms of the contents of his pharmacy, but the narrative does. The authorities interrogate his nurse, for instance, as to how she had overlooked Juliane's interest in the medicine cupboard (392), and the servants suspect Melchior of foul play because the bottle from the cupboard was found near Juliane and her mother now refuses to see him (389). Here one might draw a parallel to *Madame Bovary* (1857). Just as Flaubert indicts the new bourgeois model of the apothecary Homais by making it *his* arsenic that kills Emma Bovary, Lewald indicts Melchior with Juliane's own suicide method.

Overcome by guilt and sorrow, Melchior joins Lothar at the front and later returns to the estate to live out his days as a country doctor. The last words of his narrative are "Möge Ihr Schicksal Sie *vor Schuld bewahren* und das Glück getheilter Liebe Ihrem Leben leuchten! [my emphasis]" (400). He may have done a great deal of good for the patients he did not abandon for a lucrative metropolitan practice and by keeping himself informed of medical advances—an aspect of his characterization that particularly evokes the era of scientific discoveries in which Lewald wrote her story— but his life of penance has brought him no real redemption for his misdiagnosis of Juliane.

Schiebinger maintains that over the course of the previous two centuries, "scientists excluded a specific set of moral and intellectual qualities defined as feminine"—"feeling and instinct"—that "were thought to dull [women's] abilities to practice science." "[T]rue scientists" were men of "reason and truth" (72). True nurses, on the other hand, were defined by their characters rather than by their medical knowledge and practical abilities. Florence Nightingale's list of characteristics for those suited to the "calling" of nursing included "honesty, truthfulness, quietness, cheerfulness, cleanliness, calm, and chastity" (Bailin 35).[14] The importance of a nurse to the comfort of a patient elevates the nurse herself, and yet she paradoxically achieves that elevation through self-abnegation. As Bailin puts it, "the selfless compassion of the nursing ideal can be based on a crippling attenuation of self as well as serving as a means to self-fulfillment" (38). Although her study includes nurses and patients of both genders, Bailin notes that "these roles and the nature of the conflicts they adjudicate are inescapably related to the social roles and modes of self-presentation that are primarily associated with women" (24). In fact, "nursing has long been associated with the maternal role—with affection, intimacy, compassion, and tendance" (25).

At the risk of overstating the case, I maintain that after Juliane's death, Melchior begins to display the more feminine "feeling and instinct," as well as "selfless compassion," and to distance himself somewhat from rigidly defined masculine "reason." Gendered artifacts and attributes mingle in the rooms in which he lives, in his refusal to reap much in the way of rewards for his medical skill beyond the pleasure of selflessness, and in an early statement to the narrator: "was ist im Grunde mit allem unserem Wissen, mit unserem sogenannten Wissen von den Dingen gethan? Je mehr man davon weiß, um so geheimnißvoller und größer werden die Wunder, in denen wir werden, leben und vergehen" (254). Bailin's assertion that "the nurse and the patient are two sides of the same self," a relationship that is often "evidenced by the exchange…of nurse-patient roles between one pair of characters" in a given text (26), also points to Lewald's protagonist as ambiguously gendered: Melchior, the doctor, becomes on one occasion the (feminized) patient. He had nursed Lothar during the latter's recovery from "masculine" wounds sustained in a duel and in battle, but after Juliane's death he turns to Lothar as the one person who will be able to comfort him, "den Schiffbrüchigen, Zerschlagenen": "Ich war jetzt der Kranke, er der Arzt" (396). Melchior, however, has not succumbed to external injuries but to internal anguish and uncertainty, the province of female hysterics.

In Lewald's fictional world, however, the conjoining of male and female traits and the ability to be a patient make Melchior a better doctor. Lewald takes the contemporary construction—propagated by the medical profession and the public alike—of the "scientific" physician as her starting point, but she feminizes that construction in the character of Melchior, thereby destabilizing the categories of "masculine" and "feminine" themselves. Melchior fulfills the requirements of masculine science—professional skill, cognizance of medical progress, and the display of equipment used in scientific experimentation—but now cloaks these in the gentleness, the instincts, and the self-abnegation of the female nurse. What this doctor "knows"—and what has informed all of his actions since Juliane's death—is that he once succumbed to a destructive code of masculinity and that his susceptibility to it killed the patient for whom he was responsible.

## III

Although the despairing Juliane took her own life, the conclusions of contemporary medical sources suggest that unhappy lovers might just as well wait to be carried off by "natural causes." Somewhat in opposition to his own assertions about the importance of the blood, Chitty argues that "although some diseases may originate in the vascular system, yet more frequently are they attributable to some deviation from the due performance of the Nervous Function, and are greatly influenced by the passions, mental faculties, and still more by a troubled conscience" (243). Further, "mental excitement is capable of disturbing all the bodily functions, and of exasperating every symptom of fever" (312). In fact, "fear" may create fever patients: the physical symptoms and appearance of fear are so similar to the effects of "excessive cold, to the symptoms of typhus, and the first stage of intermittent fevers, that no one can doubt of the pernicious influence of this passion in predisposing the body to the like diseases, and in aggravating their symptoms" (316–17). We may recall which gender, according to Chitty's own examples, is most susceptible to fear and its "pernicious influence."

Fear was not alone in its effects. The "passions" vie with one another in the accounts of Chitty and the American physician John C. Gunn for the status of the most murderous emotion. Gunn devotes the opening 109 pages of his extremely popular book on "domestic medicine," the first edition of which was published in 1830, to warnings against the deadly effects of various "passions," while Chitty maintains that "as there is no passion so turbulent, so there is none so immediately dangerous as excessive anger" (319) and that "[e]xcessive sorrow has been the frequent cause of rupture of the heart and sudden death...or of confirmed or permanent melancholy, loss of memory, imbecility of mind, or nervous fevers" (318).[15] The Austrian medical professor and practitioner Ignaz Rudolf Bischoff supports these conclusions in his treatise on fever, published in 1830. The predisposing causes of most of the fevers he discusses include "Leidenschaften" (151, 176, 183, 189, 208, 233, 239, 252), which he summarizes as "Gemüthsbewegungen sowohl aufregender als niederschlagender Art, als Zorn, Schrecken, Freude, Furcht, Verdruss, Kummer, Traurigkeit, gekränkter Stolz, unglückliche Liebe" (98). Even Alfred Hudson, who attributed fever to the presence of a "fever poison,"

wrote in 1867 in his acclaimed *Lectures on the Study of Fever* that "[c]auses
which act as predisponents, through the agency of the nervous system, are
chiefly the depressing emotions of fear, grief, shame, anxiety, and the
deadening influence of prolonged cold" (52). Bischoff acknowledges that
people of all ages, both sexes, all body types, all occupations, and all
lifestyles can succumb to fever, but maintains that the "[v]orzügliche
Anlage ist in einer gewissen Reizbarkeit begründet, daher sanguinische,
kindliche und jugendliche Menschen, wie auch das weibliche Geschlecht,
sehr zu Fiebern geneigt sind" (97). It seems that nineteenth-century
medical science was at pains to urge moderation of the passions for the
ostensible sake of one's health and that both men and women were the
objects of this advice and these warnings of dire consequences.[16] However,
it perhaps behooved women to exercise particular restraint lest they, with
their greater susceptibility, fall ill with a life-threatening fever.

One such fever was the so-called "Nervenfieber," the definition of
which seems to have been a matter of some debate. The Grimms' *Deutsches
Wörterbuch* defines it as a "fieberhafte krankheit, bei der das gehirn und
nervensystem schwer ergriffen ist, typhus" and/or a condition indicating
a "nervöse erregtheit." James Currie, popularizer of the "cold water
affusion" treatment for fever, brings many definitions under one umbrella:
his "low contagious fever" is "the Typhus of Dr. Cullen; the contagious
fever of Dr. Lind; the Febris inirritiva of Dr. Darwin. In popular language
it is sometimes called the nervous fever, and where particular symptoms
appear, the putrid fever" (27). John Armstrong takes issue with such
conflation of terms and with Cullen's suggestion that any common fever
could become "typhus" (421). The Missouri doctor and inventor of "anti-
fever pills" John Sappington is another of the conflaters. He refers to
"mild typhus, or nervous fever" (149), although "nervous" in his sense
refers to symptoms rather than cause. Bischoff's description, on the other
hand, suggests that a "Nervenfieber" expresses itself both in symptoms
that show the "Leiden des Nervensystems"—such as confusion, dizziness,
sleeplessness, delirium, indifference, an alteration of the senses and of the
pulse, constant thirst, and so on (203–04)—and in the origins of the fever,
which can include various "Leidenschaften" (208).

An illness brought on by passions is an obvious boon to a novelist,
particularly one participating in the century's work of moderating
passion.[17] Illness in general offers an opportunity for both an author and

her protagonist to influence a course of events in a manner that would not otherwise be credible or acceptable. A "Nervenfieber" in particular underscores women's emotional delicacy and refinement and makes the narrative demand for particular consideration of women's emotional needs, a demand that is quite consistent with nineteenth-century German feminism.

Bailin argues that the "sickroom scenes" that are a staple of Victorian fiction "serve, in themselves and in their relations to larger narrative structures, as an adaptive strategy to encode and mediate competing personal, social, and aesthetic imperatives" (1). She asserts the following functions of the sickroom: it is, for instance, a refuge that makes manifest the conditions from which it serves as sanctuary (6, 18); it is a site that demands the suspension of prior conflicts and considerations, in tacit acknowledgment of the weightier issues of life and death embodied by the patient (18–19, 23–24); it is a narrative solution for the otherwise insoluble and an alternative to the narrative recognition of phenomena less acceptable or manageable than illness (15); and it is a means of combatting the limitations on women's lives. The sickroom, for instance, can give a female caregiver the authority of the nurse and compel for the female patient the consideration perhaps otherwise denied (26–38). It is also a place where gender hierarchies can be both re-imagined and confirmed (39–47).

Bailin's conclusions on the social and narrative functions of the fictional sickroom illuminate Lewald's use of the female protagonist's nervous fever in *Liebesbriefe. Aus dem Leben eines Gefangenen* (1850). Beset by her parents' demands that she break her engagement and by her fiancé's urging that she abandon both Catholicism and her own definition of love, the protagonist sinks into a life-threatening illness that resolves her familial and romantic conflicts and extricates the author from her narrative dilemma: can one demonstrate that women in love are women in thrall to their lovers' expectations and still make those women conform to the expectations of readers looking for romance? The difficulty of reconciling romance with self-assertion lingers as the lesson of this character's illness.

*Liebesbriefe. Aus dem Leben eines Gefangenen* is an epistolary novel that concerns itself more with the life of the eponymous prisoner's betrothed, Mathilde. The narrative in fact suggests that love itself is a type of imprisonment and Mathilde a captive as well. In a letter to her fiancé,

Edmund, she recalls the early days of their relationship:

> Ich hatte meinen Herrn gefunden. Auf Deiner Stirne thronte mein künftiges
> Schicksal. Ich zitterte bei dem Gedanken, meine Freiheit verloren zu haben,
> Dir unterthan zu sein, und doch zog es mich, vor Dir in das Knie zu sinken und
> Dir zu sagen, wie willig ich mir die Fesseln anlegen ließe, die Du für mich
> bereit hieltest. (17)

Her alleged "willingness," however, functions here and elsewhere as
compensation for her portrait of her fiancé as jailer and their relationship
as disadvantageous to her. Edmund, a Polish nobleman, is in prison in
Berlin, awaiting trial for his role in a Polish nationalist uprising. Mathilde
is with her parents in Switzerland, living in the home of Swiss farmers,
who, like all the other farmers in the area, rent rooms to tourists in the
summer. Konrad, the son of the Swiss hosts, has returned from medical
school in Bern, which has alienated him from his humble roots. He falls in
love with Mathilde. She, meanwhile, discovers to her consternation that
her beloved Edmund has been in love before—with a woman who had
sacrificed her own freedom in order to liberate him from an earlier
imprisonment—and that he believes it possible to love more than one
person at a time. She responds acerbically, asking him how she can forgive
herself for loving him so much when he does not seem to value her love.
Nevertheless, her next letter is awash in humility and the insistence that
he does not understand how "das ganze Dasein einer Frau…in einer
großen Liebe [aufgeht]." "Eure Männerherzen sind weiter, umfassender,
Euer Geist ist stärker. Ich lebe nur noch in Dir, liebe mich denn, damit ich
leben kann" (139–41). Despite her characteristic retreat into self-
abnegation, however, her statement insists that she must have his love on
her own terms because she—and all women—are denied other venues for
satisfaction.

Edmund has coerced Mathilde into an atheism/pantheism at odds with
the Catholicism that had once been her source of comfort. He lauds
himself for having rescued her from the "dunkeln Wolken des christlichen
Dualismus" with which she had been "umnachtet" (65), but she reiterates
in her letters to him the ensuing sense of loss and her envy of those who
are still able to pray. She has since substituted him and their love for the
God in whom she had previously believed. Edmund responds by telling
her that she must give up this "religion" as well, saying that their
separation has made her ill and has resulted in an "unnatürliche

Spannung" of her nerves. He, after all, must be able to work for his country without fearing that his death will deprive her of her new "God." Mathilde concludes that Edmund no longer loves her. With characteristic bathos, she writes him a long letter about how happy she had been in the refuge of Christianity before he had overturned the altars at which she had knelt and, "mit dem hellen Blitz [seines] Verstandes," had destroyed her world of faith: "Aus dem Asyl hast Du mich mit starken Armen entführt" (185–86). She tells him further that she will die if she cannot have him "ganz und ungetheilt" as a substitute for what she has lost (190). Meanwhile, her parents reproach her for her rejection of another suitor and her commitment to Edmund. She collapses after sobbing out her physical and emotional pain to Konrad: "[M]ir ist, als ob ich sterben werde. Das Blut stockt in meinen Adern, das Herz liegt mir wie todt in der Brust. Meine Eltern haben mir gesagt, ich beraube ihr Alter des Glückes...und Edmund glücklich zu machen, fühle ich mich zu schwach, denn er liebt mich nicht mehr!" (195–96). Later that night Konrad is called to her bed, where she is delirious with fever. He sends for a medical professor and tells his sister that Mathilde is dying (198–99).

With this narrative development, Lewald makes good on her protagonist's promise to die rather than give up her need to adore something or someone. The illness also constitutes Mathilde's act of penance for having voiced resistance to Edmund's rules of (their) engagement. As such, this episode of "Nervenfieber" is both the narrative's conciliatory gesture and its unrescinded indictment of Edmund and the "shackles" he had held ready for Mathilde. The text foregrounds that indictment in Edmund's receipt of the news of Mathilde's illness simultaneously with her anguished letter, in her mother's insistence that Edmund is to blame for Mathilde's fever, and in Edmund's repeated—and unanswered—appeals to the mother, to Konrad, and to Mathilde herself that they absolve him of that guilt.

Konrad attends Mathilde in her illness and finally takes the drastic step of cutting off her hair and submitting her to a "Sturzbad," which saves her life.[18] Her illness and recovery effect a number of changes. An aspect of Bailin's thesis surfaces in Konrad's desire for Mathilde's fever to last because of the benefit it brings him—the opportunity to sit at her bedside, holding her head in his arms—and in the prerogative he enjoys by virtue of his position as her doctor: he can forbid Mathilde to write lengthy letters to Edmund. The recipient of these newly short letters eventually feels some guilt for his role in the mental state that led to her collapse, despite his initial resistance to the charge. Mathilde's illness also reveals itself as the "cure" for a submission that had been harmful to her health, as it permits and enables her to resist a world view that is inimical to her own. In the same letter in which she writes that she is once again "[ihres] Körpers Meister," Mathilde tells Edmund that she has returned to the church. Responding to his question of whether he was the cause of her illness, she writes,

> Wollte ich Dich, mein theurer Edmund, beruhigen…ich würde Dir sagen: weil ich so aufgeregt war, mißverstand ich Deinen Brief und litt davon. Aber es ist nicht so. Ich bekenne Dir vielmehr, ich habe seit Monaten gelitten durch Deine Briefe, weil ich zu dem Bewußtsein gelangt war, daß ich mich in einem, meiner Seele unnatürlichen Zustande bewegte auf dem Gebiete Deiner Weltanschauung.
>
> Die Krankheit hat diese Spannung gebrochen. Sie war die Krisis, welche Gott herbeiführte, mich auf's Neue glücklich zu machen, und mir durch den wiedergewonnenen Glauben an ihn, die verlorne Ruhe zu gewähren. (246–47)

Edmund responds with gracious condescension: although he can never share her convictions, she is "künftig gesichert" from any attempt on his part to force her to accept what she is not able to grasp (264–65). Nevertheless, the narrative makes clear that Edmund has no choice but to accept defeat. Mathilde's illness, the insights she attributes to it, and the proof it constitutes of the extent to which she had been weakened by the attempt to adopt his views have erased any chance that she will ever embrace his atheism/pantheism. In fact, in order to avoid any "Gemüthserschütterung," she no longer reads his old letters (277–78). Despite the inevitable flood of humility (for example, "das Beste in mir [ist] Dein Werk, Dein Eigenthum" [276]) that follows Mathilde's assertion of her right to determine her own spirituality, she has attained the promise of the dream she had had in her fever-induced delirium: "Nicht getragen von Dir, sondern mit eigenen, mächtigen Flügeln, mich selbst erhaltend neben Dir, knieten wir Beide im Aether, das Lichtmeer anzubeten, Jeder auf seine Weise" (250). While she may seem to glory in the romantic conventions that demand grateful feminine humility, she reclaims the right to her own wings.[19]

Lewald appears to accept the nineteenth-century assertion of women's susceptibility to both internal and external disturbances. Unlike the medical explicators of this theory, however, for whom the theory was salutary proof of inherent female inferiority, Lewald employs it to support her own argument that women's effacement in romantic and familial constellations can be life-threatening for them. She resorts to the plot device of illness and thereby makes manifest the difficulty of negotiating the competing demands of the self and the behavioral norms operative for the woman in love. At the same time, however, she wields her protagonist's fever and her ailing body as a powerfully assertive instrument.

Lewald's own life "plot" demonstrates awareness of the power to be gained in the sickroom, in her case as a nurse. Brigitta van Rheinberg argues that Lewald's husband, the physically frail Adolph Stahr, was someone for whom she could "wie eine Mutter sorgen" (144). Rheinberg relates an anecdote recounted by the painter Ludwig Pietsch: during the painting of a portrait of Stahr, "wich Fanny Lewald keinen Augenblick von seiner Staffelei und kritisierte ständig an dem Bild herum, bis sie 'ihr Urteil in die…Worte zusammenfaßte: "Nein, lieber P., Stahr ist viel kränker, viel kränker!"'" (266, note 28). The brushstrokes that would make her sickly husband still more of an invalid were to serve Lewald's own purposes, as was her protagonist's interpretation of her fever as a "crisis"—that is, as the turning-point that heralds recovery. Mind and body have cooperated in this character's recovery from the "illness" of her conformity to her lover's demands.

### IV

According to nineteenth-century medical texts in general, mind and body are in fact inextricably intertwined. This view is not without currency in the late twentieth century, but Lewald's contemporaries often read the dualism as supportive of traditional gender norms. According to these texts, the female mind and body work in tandem to express the limits and achieve the goals of female physiology. Acton asserted in 1865 that "every step in physiological science seems to reveal to us something more of that mysterious connection between the perishing frame and the imperishable part which at once rules, and is so largely influenced by its earthly companion." This connection is particularly true of the "generative organs," because they and the "feelings, instincts, and tendencies of which they are the exponents, are perhaps the most powerful social and moral agents in the world" (xiv). A woman's body can thus be implicated in and also bear witness against her morals and behavior, and the way in which she *performs* her morality reveals much about her maternal suitability.

Body, behavior, and maternity in fact become conflated in the case of the female subject of medical narratives. Mantegazza's *Die Physiologie des Weibes* contains relatively little information on women's physical bodies, but has chapter after chapter on the behavior of women and girls, existing and potential mothers, in various cultures. The organization of Beck's text on medical jurisprudence suggests, as Chitty's work does more subtly, that female crime is inseparable from female reproduction. The crimes in which women figure exclusively or most prominently in Beck's examples are rape, concealment of pregnancy, infanticide, abortion, and the substitution of children for inheritance purposes. These criminal issues take up most of the first volume of two on medicolegal questions, which indicates the primacy of this type of case for the author and his readership. His text includes hundreds of pages of female defendants and plaintiffs whose bodies testified against them, rendering their denials or claims of recent birth void and their charges of rape groundless, or whose bodies, when interpreted by the medical practitioner, supported their assertions. Chitty's treatise on physiology for lawyers, courts, and legislators retains a murderous mother to lurk in the margins of his text and hauls her periodically into view. His section on human skeletal structure, for instance, notes that the dimensions of fetal bones would reveal whether the child had "quickened" at the point that "criminal means were used to cause miscarriage" (57), while his chapter on the lungs asserts that the lungs of an infant who has breathed are twice the size of one who has not, which is one of the tests used to establish "whether or not a child has been born alive" (102).[20] Sterility—the failure to realize the biological imperative— can lead to crime as well: Mantegazza asserts that childless married women kill more often than women with children (367).

Infertility can also point an accusing finger at the woman deprived of "Mutterglück," because it is a symptom of "mannigfacher Sexualer-krankungen wie allgemeiner Störungen im Organismus" (Kisch, *Sterilität* iii). In his study of female infertility, *Die Sterilität des Weibes: Ihre Ursachen und ihre Behandlung*, Kisch lists many self-induced "disturbances" that suggest that a woman's inability to conceive was the starting point for an exploration of her character. They include alcoholism (161), inappropriate behavior (such as dancing, jumping, ice skating, and horseback riding) (151), and masturbation (62, 92, 107), which can lead to malformed genitals and reproductive organs incapable of conceiving. Should the infertile wife fail to confess to her vice, the hypertrophy, the discoloration, the pain, and the displaced uterus and ovaries will rouse the astute physician's suspicion that "die abnorme Geschlechtsbefriedigung" has caused her sterility. In support of his assertion, Kisch cites several English and German medical authors who blame masturbation for sterility, nymphomania, and underdeveloped sexual organs (107).[21] Too much lust in general can contribute to infertility, because "übermässige geschlechtliche Erregung, wie diese vorzugsweise bei Meretrices vorkommt," can hinder the incubation of the egg (123). If an infertile woman was not a proven prostitute, she might be suspected at the very least of unseemly arousal.

A degree of lust was perhaps necessary to conception, however. Kisch maintains that "die sexuelle Erregung des Weibes bei der Cohabitation eine nicht zu unterschätzende Rolle spielt, wenn dies auch noch nicht genau definirt werden kann" and that a woman's "actives Verhalten" during intercourse is "nicht irrelevant" to conception (99). He cites other medical writers who concur, as well as the "seit alten Zeiten im Volke herrschende Meinung" that "zur Befruchtung eine Wollusterregung des Weibes nothwendig sei" (100). In fact, Kisch asserts, although there are cases in which women have conceived as the result of rape or while asleep or intoxicated, these are exceptions, the credibility of which is often in doubt (104–05).

Kisch offers a patient's "experience" as evidence that supports his views on the contribution of female desire to conception. The patient, "eine gebildete Dame, Mutter mehrerer Kinder," had announced to him that she not only knew immediately when intercourse had resulted in conception, but that she had it in her power to determine her own fertility. If she remained passive during coitus, she could prevent conception, and if she allowed herself to be moved by passion to active participation, pregnancy would follow (100).[22]

Although Kisch's patient took responsibility for her own fertility, women were not necessarily responsible for their own frigidity. Some blame for lack of female desire and ensuing sterility could be attributed to husbands, Kisch continues, since a wife's revulsion toward her husband could result in painful intercourse and the subsequent inability to conceive (103). Kisch also concludes that "eine sexuelle Disharmonie" alone can hinder conception and supports his conclusion with the assertion that infertile couples who have divorced often have children with new partners. One of his sources refers to the problem of such couples as a "Mangel an übereinstimmender Liebe" (103–04). An emotionally satisfying marital relationship apparently plays an important role in maximizing fertility; "love" becomes coterminous with "desire" in the case of virtuous married women. There are also additional dimensions of the marital relationship that are relevant to the quest for fertility. In his *The Sexual Life of Woman in Its Physiological, Pathological and Hygienic Aspects*, Kisch asserts that women "who are healthy, who lead a regular life, are well fed, free from the pressure of anxieties, with their sexual functions sufficiently exercised" can extend their sexual—that is, reproductive—lives longest (33). The subtext of this assertion is the responsibility of husbands to ensure the "regularity" of their wives' existences, to free them from anxiety, and to sleep with them on a regular basis. Thanks to the linkage of mind and body, what disturbed the former would affect the function of the latter. Because women's physiology designed them solely for reproduction, a husband's failure to provide his wife with the optimal conditions for conception thwarted her very existence. Thus, once an infertile woman's own character had been interrogated and acquitted, her childlessness was a potential indictment of her husband.

Lewald took up the issue of women's reproductive lives in *Treue Liebe* (1883), raising the question of what women want and how their physiology helps them to get it. Her answer incorporates the issues of female desire, the nineteenth-century version of which, as we have seen, was often combined with "love" even in medical narratives, and the effect of a wish fulfilled—in this case, for the kind of "regular life" Kisch describes. Lewald's text transforms the alleged weakness of the reproductive female body into a self-preserving recalcitrance: the heroine's body cannot and will not conceive until its physical and emotional needs have been met.

Urika, the ailing female protagonist of *Treue Liebe*, has been married for ten years to George Grayville, during which time they have traveled constantly. Grayville has, after what the text implies were a number of affairs, recently become enamoured of an illegitimate Italian countess. At the hotel where her husband has deposited her, Urika meets Chlodwig, a sturdy and stable German who is the antithesis of her dissipated and inconstant English husband. Chlodwig is drawn to this "leidende" woman with the "müde Lächeln" (27–28), who, thanks to his company and the "Ruhe" she now enjoys, begins to recover (69). Urika has never been happy with the wandering life she leads with Grayville, but, as her former guardian, Jenkins, explains to Chlodwig, she is adaptable, compliant, and a good wife for a traveler: "'denn sie spielt nicht das hilfsbedürftige Frauenzimmer. Sie findet sich überall zurecht, und es ist Verlaß auf sie — mehr als auf ihn!' setzte er mit Lächeln leiser hinzu" (41). Jenkins accepts Grayville's dalliances and assumes that Urika's life and her unfaithful husband have not been injurious to her.

Urika, however, wants a child but has been unable to conceive. Kisch's directives on the "regular life," the health, and the lack of anxiety conducive to female reproduction (*Life* 33) suggest the source of her infertility, as does Chlodwig's conclusion that Urika no longer loves her husband (83). Lewald's narrative in fact paints Grayville as eminently unlovable. When he at last returns to the hotel for Urika, he brings the Italian countess with him and insists on the countess accompanying them on their next journey. She takes every opportunity to deride Urika; Urika's health deteriorates further. When Urika asks him to send the countess away, Grayville excuses his own behavior with the reproach of Urika's childlessness: "Vielleicht — hätten wir Kinder, so würden diese mir die Abwechslung und den Zeitvertreib gewähren, deren man in dem Alleinsein, in der kinderlosen Ehe entbehrt" (173).

One by one, however, Lewald clears her female protagonist of all potential charges that might implicate her in her own infertility. She has been compelled to travel when she longs for a permanent home, subjected to the emotional turmoil occasioned by her husband's adulterous attachments, and made increasingly ill by her journeys and, lately, by her spiteful rival. Her husband's actions suggest that if Urika's love for him has died — and with it the desire presumed by some medical men to be necessary to conception — it is entirely his own fault. Those actions serve an additional narrative purpose in that Lewald's female protagonist further proves her worth by refusing to extricate herself from her untenable situation. Despite Grayville's behavior and despite the dawning awareness of her own love for Chlodwig, she refuses to leave her husband. She is

convinced that she must free him from the seductive countess (178) and
be true to her vows (91). This conviction establishes her virtue and her
willingness to sacrifice herself for her husband, characteristics that
presumably elevated her in the esteem of nineteenth-century readers
steeped in expectations of wifely duty.[23] Finally, however, further travel
and the continuing presence of the countess weaken Urika to the point of
life-threatening collapse. At this point she seeks a divorce.

Urika's heightened illness is significant: it serves to convince Jenkins,
Grayville, and Urika herself that a separation is unavoidable. Lewald
makes explicit Jenkins's position as a proponent of traditional marriage
arrangements, which include acceptance of a double standard, and draws
a parallel between his position and that of the law itself: desperate for help,
Urika concludes that she cannot turn to Jenkins because of his
conservative views on women's roles and "[w]as in England die Trennung
einer Ehe auf sich habe, war ihr auch bekannt" (179). What the law
refuses to permit, however, can be won by the ailing female body. The
next morning brings a dramatic turn for the worse in Urika's health, a
change that Jenkins notices. Still feeling that she may not want a divorce,
Jenkins "ermahnte sie aber dringend, endlich einmal den Rath eines in der
Behandlung von Nervenleiden bewährten Londoner Arztes einzuholen"
(212), because she was "zum Tode erschöpft" (213–14). (Note Jenkins's
matter-of-fact assumption that Urika's physical illness is indeed caused by
a "nervous ailment." She is, among other things, pale, thin, weak, chills
easily, and has a cough.) Jenkins's support of Urika's right to recover is
crucial because it is he who negotiates her release from Grayville; she is
too ill to attempt it herself (216). Jenkins tells Grayville that he has
advised Urika that it is a "Pflicht der Selbsterhaltung" "in
Zurückgezogenheit und Ruhe einmal ausschließlich sich und ihrer
Herstellung zu leben" (218–19) and that he will accompany her to
whatever place "der zu befragende Arzt für sie als den geeignetsten
bezeichnen würde" (219). Urika's former guardian weighs in with both his
own and the borrowed authority of a physician yet to be named, and
Grayville understands the challenge to his previously undisputed right to
dispose of his wife as he sees fit. Jenkins emphasizes the apparently
paramount issue of Urika's now critical illness: although Grayville is of
course "Herr über [seine] Frau, und sie...sich zu fügen [hat]," he asks him
whether it is appropriate "einer Leidenden Ihr Herrenrecht mit Härte

fühlbar zu machen? Wollen Sie mit einer Kranken rechten? Lassen Sie ihr den Willen! Sie haben ja den Ihren bisher nach allen Seiten durchgesetzt; und am Ende bewegen Sie sich freier ohne Ihre—ohne eine kranke Frau" (220–21). He employs Urika's position as a "sick woman" to gain Grayville's permission for his wife's departure, permission that she requires for her own peace of mind and to protect herself legally. Her illness thus takes precedence over a husband's "right" to dominate his wife. Illness constitutes *her* rights, rights she does not have by law.

Because one cannot "mit einer Kranken rechten," Urika's physical weakness gains her the power to determine her own place of residence and recovery and ultimately to divorce. When she finally petitions for a divorce, Jenkins tells Chlodwig that he will do his best to bring about a quick resolution of her case, "da die überreizten Nerven unserer Freundin eher nicht zur Ruhe kommen können" (251). Lewald's choice of Jenkins, whom she has written as conservative, as Urika's savior underscores the seriousness of her illness and the irreparable state of the marriage. Readers who share Jenkins's traditional viewpoint must presumably bow to their representative's conclusion that Urika's "Selbsterhaltung" demands a separation—and that a wife's "Selbsterhaltung" is a legitimate goal. Despite waiting for her husband's permission to leave (a hesitation that again underscores her character's laudable sense of nineteenth-century wifely duty), Urika does manifest an instinct for self-preservation that is independent from Jenkins's admonishments. Reunited with Chlodwig, she tells him that her conscience had demanded that she stay with her husband as long as there was any hope for their marriage, and that she had stayed until she felt herself "zum Tode ermattet" (261).

The subservience to her husband's whims that brought about Urika's illness, as well as the illness itself, belongs to this character's femininity. While the British novels Bailin examines depict both male and female invalids, Lewald's narratives tend to portray only female sufferers positively. Men who experience something other than acute illness and who do not recover in a timely fashion become objects of narrative scorn.[24] Illness in *Treue Liebe* is in general coded female, although only "true" illness gains the narrative's acceptance. When the countess pretends that even she has succumbed to the fatigue of their traveling life, Grayville finds her "mit dem Ausdruck der Ermüdung, den sie geschickt erheuchelte, reizender denn jemals…*da es sie weiblicher erscheinen machte* [my emphasis]" (233). But although this "feminine" fatigue/illness appeals to Grayville, the text makes its distaste for the dissembling countess clear. Urika's fatigue is another matter: Chlodwig, Lewald's narrative suggests, is drawn to Urika in part because of her sickly appearance and takes great satisfaction in her recovery. The extent and significance of that recovery point to the fact that female illness in this text becomes a literary solution to the social problem of female powerlessness: it makes women attractive, helps them to obtain male assistance, and allows them to transcend legally and socially sanctioned gender hierarchies.

Illness, however, marks only a turning point, because Lewald wants her characters to realize tangible profits from their virtue. Good health rewards this character for negotiating her life's legal and social pitfalls successfully, and her reproductive body confirms the improvement in her situation. Illness in the fictional world of *Treue Liebe* is not the harbinger of a long sojourn in the sickroom. Rather, it serves to precipitate change for a female character for whom the presumptive alternatives are unacceptable. These alternatives—to acknowledge her love for another man and/or to desert a husband under the spell of a femme fatale—violate the norms of a category valorized by both the character and the text: the dutiful wife. Still a dutiful wife, now to Chlodwig, and living on a German family farm, Urika recovers her health and bears a child. Secure within the four walls for which she had once longed (36), she finds herself in the rural German environment that the text has been at pains to portray as physically and socially healthiest for both women and men. Earlier in the narrative, for instance, Chlodwig had maintained to Grayville that "das Wanderleben...nicht produktiv [ist]" and that without a "festzusammen-gehaltene" family, the state is unthinkable (108). The metaphor of the family as the state in miniature was ubiquitous in the nineteenth century, and married life on Chlodwig's own estate proves his assertions correct. None too coincidentally, he himself leaves home only for sessions of the "Volksvertretung" to which he has been elected (263). The factors that secure Urika's reproductive health appear conducive to the health of representative government as well. And just as Urika's previous infertility was emblematic of the debilitating nature of her wandering life, the unproblematic birth of a son with Chlodwig indicates the salubriousness of her quiet life on his family estate. The discovery in the neighborhood of a "reiche, warme Bittersalzquelle, wie keines der gleichartigen Bäder sie besser hat," whose waters, chemists have confirmed, are among the "heilkräftigsten" (140), emphasizes the healing qualities of Urika's new home. In fact, the estate owners of the area want to open a spa (141).

A stay at a spa was alleged in the nineteenth century to be one of the most efficacious means of curing infertility. Kisch, for one, alleges this quite vigorously, although his status as a physician at Marienbad may have been partly responsible for his enthusiasm. His text on female sterility includes many examples of apparently hopeless cases who conceived after a trip to a spa and makes suggestions as to which type of infertility might benefit from which type of waters. One also finds evidence of a more widespread attribution of such powers to the various spas in a comment by Luise Mühlbach, a writer who was an acquaintance of Lewald's. Writing in 1873 about an earlier visit of Empress Eugénie of France to the spa at Ems, a place about which "[k]inderlose Frauen…einander von den außerordentlichen, dort erzielten Erfolgen ins Ohr [flüsterten]," Mühlbach poses the question of whether the empress was interested in exploring the "Wirksamkeit der Quellen." She answers her own query with "Nein,…das Kaiserreich hatte einen Erben" (247).[25]

Just as Lewald clears her protagonist charge by charge of any guilt in her own infertility, her conclusion multiplies the aspects of Urika's new life that are conducive to conceiving the child she wanted, the child who is heir to the way of life of which Lewald's text is an unrepentant partisan. She has a permanent home and a stable life with a man she loves and respects, whose mere presence promotes her health and whose national and familial roots are exemplified by the healing powers of the neighborhood's superior mineral baths.

Despite the uncomfortable similarity of Lewald's plot to the narratives of domestic ideology, the fact remains that Urika and the body that makes her medically and socially meaningful get what the heroine wants. Weak, ill, and infertile with the husband she no longer loves, the husband who would not provide her with the stability for which she longed, she leaves him in a gesture of self-affirmation and finds health, "treue Liebe," and— not coincidentally—fertility in the arms of another man. Lewald builds on contemporary medical texts that suggest the necessity of female love/desire to conception and prescribe a "regular life…free from the pressure of anxieties" for the extension of women's sexual lives to insist that if women are to fulfill the role assigned to them, they must be able to love their husbands, who must be capable of arousing their passion and willing to offer them the contentment they desire. In effect, she employs the very proscriptions of these medical writers to advance the female self-determination that their case studies attempt to close off.

## V

Lewald's construction of the nineteenth-century female body as an insistent advocate for women is at odds with the prevailing view of women's bodies as evidence that female social subordination was "natural" and therefore unalterable. This ideology affirmed women's "inferiority" in countless engravings, illustrations, and cross-sections, labeled their reproductive organs with a large red arrow—"YOU ARE HERE"—and stamped these cultural products with the seal of science. Although Lewald generally assents to the "facts" of women's physiology as they were delineated at the time, she consistently declines to interpret female physical weakness as indicative of an ailing morality or potential derangement. Rather, she employs it to improve the terms of the domestic arrangements in which her female characters—as did her historical contemporaries— almost invariably find themselves: as dependent daughters, wives, and mothers.

As we shall see in Chapter Two, this dependence was buttressed by the legal code. Family law mandated the subordination of women by excluding them from the legal arena in which the financial arrangements of their lives and their access both to divorce and to marriage were determined. Here, too, Lewald uses her female protagonists to examine the effect of prevailing definitions of "femininity" on women's lives.

# CHAPTER TWO

## "Die Frauen sind die Repräsentanten der Liebe wie die Männer des Rechts": Lewald's Revisions of the Female "Rechtsperson"

On 25 May 1854 Fanny Lewald and Adolf Stahr signed a prenuptial agreement that stipulated Lewald's complete and continuing control over her property and earnings (Schneider, *Zeitroman* 369). This agreement was based on the *Allgemeines Landrecht für die Preußischen Staaten* (1794)[1] and its provisions for the regulation of marital property arrangements that deviated from the legal norm. The norm was a "Gütergemeinschaft" that was administered entirely by the husband and, predictably, often worked to the disadvantage of wives who had not had Lewald's foresight prior to their own marriages.

In various narratives, Lewald addresses the gap between women's needs—resulting primarily from their experience of marriage—and the legal possibilities and protection available to them. The fictional experiences of her protagonists are determined by nineteenth-century legal codes and judgments and act as a critical commentary on those laws and decisions. Legislation and the courts that applied it created female legal subjects whose rights, and the lack thereof, reflected their subordinate position in the social order. The degree of subordination and concomitant legal dispossession varied with the historical (and, presumably, personal) situation. Ute Gerhard terms the *ALR* relatively sympathetic to women, for instance, but claims that the revisions to it over the course of the nineteenth century reflected increasing hostility toward women and a growing desire for male control of female family members (156–79). Legislative response to nineteenth-century male anxiety had constructed a female subject who could make few legal claims that would limit male power over her. Like Charlotte Perkins Gilman's intangible woman trapped behind the ostensibly innocuous pattern of yellow wallpaper, there is a "strange, provoking, formless sort of figure, that seems to skulk about behind that silly and conspicuous front design" (Gilman 18). She is the unequal "partner" to the marriage contract, the woman with no actual rights even to the property she has allegedly retained, and the common whore who cannot claim support for herself and her illegitimate child.

Lewald illustrates the disastrous effects of these laws on the fictional lives and bodies of her female protagonists. Her narratives not only document historical "reality," but attempt to change it through their affecting portraits of women suffering under laws that are in principle not irrevocable. Her fiction offers a view of the female "Rechtsperson"[2] that opposes that of the code. Moral, hard-working, and reluctant to step outside gendered role parameters, her female protagonists are victimized by laws that fail to recognize their worthiness, a worthiness that makes them particularly susceptible to legal and social exploitation. Three Lewald texts, written in the decades in which women's legal possibilities were being increasingly circumscribed, address specific obstacles for women in the realm of family law and argue for changes in the laws in question. *Eine Lebensfrage* (1845) argues for greater access to divorce; "Das große Loos" (1856), published two years after the signing of Lewald's own prenuptial agreement, criticizes marital property arrangements that deprive women of all control over their own assets; and "Kein Haus. Eine Dorfgeschichte" (1856) illustrates the consequences of marriage restrictions and of the law's growing tendency to censure unwed mothers.

Family law was the arena in which women's representation under nineteenth-century law was most overt and of greatest disadvantage to them. Gerhard argues that the advent of family law created a kind of "Sonderrecht"[3] for (married) women that ran counter to the universal claim to human rights and the generalizing principles of civil law and hindered the recognition of women as "Rechtspersonen." She also calls the history of family law a "Tummelplatz politischer, religiöser und sittlicher Ideen" (154), and thus identifies it as a promising starting point for an investigation of a culture's attempt to construct and reconstruct its representatives.

The legal code with which Lewald would have been most familiar was the *ALR* and its various revisions. The *ALR* reveals its roots in Enlightenment philosophy early on: "Die Rechte beyder Geschlechter sind einander gleich, so weit nicht durch besondre Gesetze, oder rechtsgültige Willenserklärungen, Ausnahmen bestimmt worden" (I 1 §24). Various provisions of the code nevertheless reveal that even a belief in, for instance, the educability of all humans, a primary Enlightenment precept, did not result in the construction of a female subject equal to men in the eyes of the law. This disparity should perhaps not surprise us. As the American legal scholar Catharine MacKinnon argues in her discussion of the "liberal state" (157–70), a legal system established solely by men necessarily reflects only the prerogatives of that gender and the social inequality that preceded legislation, and women may need special protection from the legal code itself. Lewald's texts indicate her own belief in gender difference. This belief was fully consonant with contemporary German feminism and meant that she would neither demand nor desire equality in every legal particular. Nevertheless, her narratives call for legislation that does not mandate subordination or disadvantage on the basis of perceived gender difference.

Susan Sage Heinzelman and Zipporah Batshaw Wiseman argue in their book on the "intersection of Anglo-American common law, literature, and feminism" (vii) that women increasingly turned to "literary representation to campaign against their exclusion from legal representation, an exclusion that became more determined and rigid after the late eighteenth century." They suggest that the novel "afforded these writers a forum in which transgressive—'illegal'—female stories could be represented and, unlike in the male-dominated courtroom, be authorized— that is, shown as credible and realistic" (250–51). The texts discussed in this chapter indeed give an insistent voice to women excluded and disadvantaged by the law, bestowing on these characters and their historical counterparts the presence that the law's own narratives had denied them.

I

The story of the *ALR*'s origins reflects the influence of the Enlightenment, which manifested itself in the desire for a kind of equality under the law, as well as the conflicting debt the code owed to Roman law and its concept of "patria potestas," the power of the father over his wife and children. In 1907, in an exhaustive survey of the legal position of women throughout the ages, Marianne Weber argued that wives and mothers in Roman culture enjoyed high esteem in "römische Sitte und Moralanschauung," but that their *"rechtliche* Unterordnung hier in der altrepublikanischen Zeit geradezu ihren Tiefpunkt innerhalb des Kreises der Kulturvölker erreichte" (158). This ambiguous position offers an interesting parallel to women's sociolegal situation in nineteenth-century Europe and perhaps contributes to an explanation of women's legal disadvantage in countries whose legal codes were based on Roman law.[4] The gendered social inequality evident in Roman law predated the law itself, however, and the inequality was written into Prussia's new code in large part because it was never specifically written out. The *ALR* nominally aspired to gender equality, but fell short of that Enlightenment goal because of the legal and social traditions it confronted. As we will see, the *ALR*'s framers also wished to create a document that would reflect the culture it was to legislate. They and the lawmakers who made revisions to the code were more successful in this attempt. The effect of their incorporation of cultural anxieties, in particular, into the laws they made became the focus of the critique practiced by Lewald's texts.

Nigel Foster examines the evolution of the German legal system, tracing its development from the "customary law" of the Germanic tribes to the highly codified system currently in place. He argues that the "most outstanding feature of this history is the almost complete adoption of roman law in the late-middle ages in preference to the indigenous Germanic and largely customary laws" (6). His summary of the reasons for the eventual precedence of Roman law suggests that it was primarily the result of the lack of a unified German state. There was no viable legal alternative, despite the increasing need for one in a world of expanding commercial relationships. The system that had been the basis for canon law therefore took over (16–17).

Nineteenth-century German legal codes were also influenced by the

School of Natural Law, whose "basic precept was a study of what law was perceived to be or what it should be, and not, in contrast to the views of the School of Historical Law, law as the historically determined product of civilisation."

> Those influenced by this natural school of thought considered how law had been applied in the past and sought to abstract general principles of what law should be, in an attempt to develop reasoned universal or rational laws. This reasoning seemed logically to give rise to the ordering or systematisation of the abstracted principles. In other words, the general rules discovered could be seen to make up an orderly and comprehensible system. Although there was no necessity to choose roman law, those principles appeared to natural law scholars as good examples of how natural law principles should be, and thus much of their study concentrated on roman law. (Foster 18)

Both the Bavarian and the Prussian legal codes of the eighteenth century were the products of this legal philosophy and were therefore "largely based on developed and systemised roman law principles." The *ALR* was, however, "criticised as being too detailed and hence too complex. No interpretation of these very complete statements of legal life was allowed, which meant that there was no room for manoeuvre to suit changing circumstances or times" (Foster 19). The *ALR* nevertheless superseded all previous laws within Prussian territory until it was replaced by the *Bürgerliches Gesetzbuch* (*BGB*) in 1900 (Foster 19).

Hans Hattenhauer's introduction to a twentieth-century edition of the *ALR* of 1794 details the original code's inception, the obstacles to its adoption, and the historical developments that quickly made it obsolete, despite the fact that at least parts of it remained in force until 1900. Two primary influences on the development of the Prussian legal code emerge in Hattenhauer's narrative: Roman law, which Foster emphasizes, and Enlightenment ideals, particularly as represented in Montesquieu's "De l'esprit des lois." Montesquieu's essay was published in 1748 and was widely read (twenty-two editions were published within two years). The "kluge und zugleich einfache Art" in which Montesquieu summarized Enlightenment thought and formulated it as a call to the lawmakers of his age, Hattenhauer argues, made his publication the eighteenth century's most important treatise on constitutional law. Moreover, the most important consideration for Montesquieu and his world was the belief that all nations have laws corresponding to their individual circumstances:

"ihrer Geschichte und Sprache, ihrer Wirtschaft und Kultur, ihren Sitten und ihrer Religion, ihrer geographischen Lage und ihrem Klima, etc." (1).

Friedrich II, who in 1746 had authorized the current "Chef der Justiz," Samuel Cocceji, to draft a Prussian legal code, echoed Montesquieu's demands in a treatise of his own in 1749. Here he called for a code that would cover all eventualities, so that a state run according to the laws outlined therein would resemble an "Uhrwerk...in dem alle Triebfedern nur einen Zweck haben," and in which one would find profound knowledge of the human heart and the national character (Hattenhauer 1–2). Cocceji's draft did not become law, and it was not until 1779 that the Prussian king's irritation with the legal profession's obscurantism and the bias and deliberate delays in the administration of justice cleared the way for three reformers (Hattenhauer 2–4), all of whom had been deeply influenced by Enlightenment ideals. Hattenhauer describes their generation as the one in which the Enlightenment was carried from the universities into the courts, but these ideals represented a threat to the "Ständestaat," whose beneficiaries opposed their work and who, after the death of Friedrich II, succeeded in forcing through a compromise document (7, 14). Obsolescence set in rather quickly, however. Competing royal edicts continued, political developments brought new reforms, and in the middle of the nineteenth century other legislation replaced parts of the *ALR* prior to its total replacement in 1900 by the *BGB*. It had its defenders throughout the last century (Hattenhauer 27–29), however, and has inspired Hattenhauer's and to some extent Gerhard's admiration as well.

Hattenhauer states, "Wer ein Gesetzbuch lesen will, muß nach den Leitbildern seiner Verfasser, nach deren Wertekatalog und dem daraus entstandenen Sozialmodell fragen" and points to the Enlightenment "Leitbild" of the *ALR*'s framers: "Erziehung des Individuums zur Freiheit und dadurch zum Glück" (20). But was the "Individuum" in question gendered?

Hattenhauer praises, for instance, the *ALR*'s framers' view of human freedom as fundamental. In this context he explains that a free man ("Freier") who voluntarily enters into serfdom can be pronounced the guilty party "im Sinne des Eherechts" (21), but one must turn to the actual paragraphs in question (II 7 §97–101) for an explanation of the pertinence of marriage law. There one discovers that the free man in such a case is a husband, whose wife cannot, as a rule, be forced to follow him into servitude. She may apply for divorce, and her husband will be declared at fault, unless the judge determines that the husband's decision "zum gemeinschaftlichen Besten beyder Eheleute gereiche." In such a case the wife may still insist on a divorce, but her husband cannot be held accountable. If she follows her husband, she must inform the seigneurial lord within eight days that she is free; otherwise she too will become "unterthänig." These provisions assume a remarkable legal astuteness on the part of a woman so poor that her husband has just delivered himself into serfdom. They also suggest that her freedom is not a matter of course. Whereas her husband may act to relinquish his, she may act only to preserve hers, and she must act quickly. The picture that emerges within four paragraphs of the code is of a female legal subject subordinate to the will and the decisions of three men—husband, judge, and lord—and who therefore no longer meets the criteria of humanity as defined by Hattenhauer on the basis of the evidence provided by this document: "Die Freiheit [ist] in der Natur des Menschen begründet" (21).

In addition, the Prussian legal reformers were convinced that "[j]eder Mensch...die Pflicht [habe], sich und seinen Stand zu vervollkommnen" (Hattenhauer 21) and that parents should be required to educate their "children" "zu künftigen brauchbaren Mitgliedern des Staats, in einer nützlichen Wissenschaft, Kunst, oder Gewerbe" (II 2 §108). In the next nine paragraphs, however, nongendered "children" have disappeared; the education of "Söhne" is the sole point of concern. "Kinder" (a category now rendered suspect) return in a paragraph (II 2 §119) that forbids parents to force their children into marriage. Literature suggests that parents pressured children of both sexes into marriages of convenience, although female children figure more often in fictional dilemmas of this sort. The paragraph (I 1 §24) on the presumptive legal equality of men and women—unless stated otherwise—now seems disingenuous. Women's rights clearly are not equal to men's, as they do not have equal access to the determining characteristics of the enlightened humanity the code attempts to promote.

Further, the category "Mann/Männer" does not appear in the *ALR*'s index, while "Frauenspersonen" refers the reader to a number of different laws that name women specifically (including one that mandates compensation for reduced marriageability, should the defendant have somehow disfigured a woman). Although the code claims equality for women and men, except when otherwise indicated, the language of its statutes indicates that men are the legal "Menschen" it attempts to regulate, while women represent the sometimes bizarre exception to the norm and its rules. The effects of the contemporary legal manifestations of this inequality form the background to Lewald's narrative complaint that laws pertaining to women—or ignoring them—are inadequate to address their particular needs. In other words, the "besondre[n] Gesetze" to which the *ALR* refers serve only to disadvantage women, while laws that assert gender blindness ignore social realities that make their enforcement constitute a hardship for women in particular.

Gerhard points to a number of reasons for women's exclusion from and disadvantagement under nineteenth-century law. Her book, *Verhältnisse und Verhinderungen: Frauenarbeit, Familie und Rechte der Frauen im 19. Jahrhundert*, demonstrates that law is the result of the collision of economic, political, and social forces and suggests that nineteenth-century laws pertaining to women reflect male anxiety about loss of political and domestic power. She argues, for instance, that after the failure of the bourgeois revolution of 1848, bourgeois men "versuchte[n], [ihre] politische Bedeutungslosigkeit durch die 'Herrschaft im Hause,' die sich Verinnerlichung nannte, zu kompensieren" and that all women, not only wives, suffered from the "patriarchalischen Machtzuwachs und der erneuten Benachteiligung" (172). Although domestic ideology asserted the superiority of women's moral position in the home, legislation supported a hierarchy that left men on top in every tangible respect. According to Gerhard, women's legal situation in the nineteenth century further illustrates the contradictory nature of civil law: although both men and women were freed from serfdom at the beginning of the century, reactionary family law ensured a feudal sort of dependence for wives on their husbands. They could not even sell their own labor without the permission of their husbands and an eye to the familial duties that took precedence (14–15). The influential nineteenth-century sociologist Wilhelm Heinrich Riehl suggests that women's exclusion from the law stems from gendered "Naturunterschiede" that are mirrored in the relationship of society to the state: "Die Sitte, die bewegende Kraft der Gesellschaft wird gehegt und bewahrt vom Weibe, das Weib steht im Naturleben der Sitte; der Mann erst schafft aus dem Rechtsbewußtsein das Gesetz, die bewegende Kraft des Staates" (qtd. in Gerhard 150).

Five years before the publication of Riehl's *Naturgeschichte des Volkes* (1855), a woman pseudonymously identified as "Friederike" reported in the *Frauen-Zeitung* on what the exclusion of women from the law could mean within a marriage:

> Die Gesetze für die Ehe sind von Männern entworfen, und die bibelfesten Gesetzgeber vergaßen dabei nicht das anziehende Gebot des alten Moses: "und der Mann soll dein Herr sein!"
>
> Es könnten vielleicht viele Leser der Meinung sein, ich übertreibe die Schutzlosigkeit der Frauen, ich will zur Bestätigung der Wahrheit meines Ausspruchs daher einige Beispiele solcher Ehen anführen, die ganz in meiner Nähe vorkamen. Ein Justiz-Beamter behandelte seine, nur in der Liebe zu ihm Glück findende junge, hübsche Frau mit der ausgezeichnetsten Brutalität, diese, endlich der vielen Mißhandlungen müde, drohte, ihm sein Betragen beim Gericht anzugeben; worauf dieser Herr das Landrecht holte, ihre langen Haare um die andere Hand wand, sie zu Boden warf, mit Füßen trat und ihr dabei die darauf Bezug habenden Paragraphe vorlas, mit der Versicherung, daß er wisse was ihm erlaubt sei. (qtd. in Gerhard 239)

The right to which this anonymous husband referred was the "Züchtigungsrecht" that he enjoyed as long as his wife was not pregnant, although the paragraph in question (II 20 §736) rather obscurely gave him this right only as one of "diejenigen, denen sonst das Recht der mäßigen Züchtigung zukommt." But who are "diejenigen"? One of the original framers of the *ALR* had published a book of excerpts and explanations of the new code in 1793 in an attempt to have its initial suspension lifted (Hattenhauer 17); the framer's description of this paragraph gives us more information: they are "Väter, Ehemänner und Obrigkeiten" (qtd. in Gerhard 239).

The fact that it was unnecessary to list in the code itself those who held that right points to the kind of pre-existing social inequality to which MacKinnon refers and indicates that the legal code's support of that inequality was a foregone conclusion. One might compare this law's implicit construction of wives as subordinate with the similar construction of "Gesinde" and "Untertanen," who were also subject to "mäßige Züchtigungen." Masters were, incidentally, exhorted to avoid types of punishment that would violate "Schamhaftigkeit," particularly that of *female* servants (II 7 §227). Women are thus explicitly constructed by the law as "schamhaft," a quality that should be honored and preserved in them. Gerhard notes that even in the first half of the nineteenth century, the right to flog servants was justified by the assertion that the common man had little in common with "einem Menschen" and would have to be further educated and civilized before potential corporal punishment could be eliminated (21). In their similar legal susceptibility to this type of punishment, women too are identified as being not quite "Menschen."

MacKinnon's discussion of the liberal state and its inherent biases suggests that a legal code generally favorable to women, or at least gender blind, was an impossibility in the *ALR*'s cultural context. Given the judicial decisions and the legal theorists she cites, MacKinnon's "liberal state" is America. Its founders and the framers of its constitution were of course steeped in the same Enlightenment philosophy that produced the *ALR*. Her investigation of the limitations of legislation produced by such a state enables us to pinpoint the limitations of the *ALR* as well. MacKinnon notes that the measure of the liberal state is how well it does *not* interfere in citizen's lives, but argues that the freedom it thereby preserves is male freedom. Social inequality preceded the system that was set up to reflect and maintain the status quo. Given that inequality, women may need intervention to protect them from men's exercise of the prerogatives the system gives them (163–67). She asserts that the "liberal state coercively and authoritatively constitutes the social order in the interest of men as a gender—through its legitimating norms, forms, relation to society, and substantive policies" (162). It insists on its "neutral" approach on issues of constitutionality, but the "foundation for its neutrality is the pervasive assumption that conditions that pertain among men on the basis of gender apply to women as well—that is, the assumption that sex inequality does not really exist in society." Meanwhile, "[t]hose who have freedoms like equality, liberty, privacy, and speech socially keep them legally, free of governmental intrusion. No one who does not already have them socially is granted them legally" (163).

MacKinnon's argumentation can serve to reveal the basic gender inequality of the *ALR* as well: while the *ALR* recognizes some "difference," particularly in its delineation of the specific rights and duties of husbands and wives, it asserts an equality for men and women under the law that in fact does not and could not exist. This pre-existing fundamental inequality enabled the *ALR*'s "Revisor"[5] to argue in 1830 that support for unwed mothers and their children should be continued because it was not conducive to promoting "gute Sitten" (presumably on men's part) to lay all the blame for a mistake on the "von Natur aus schwächeren Teil," while also permitting legislators in 1854 to insist that any woman making a claim for such support was quite likely an "Allerwelts-Hure" (Gerhard 176). According to MacKinnon, "special protections," which American courts based on the "unique frailty, dependency, and breeding capacity" that "placed [women] 'at a disadvantage in the struggle for subsistence'" may or may not have helped women, since they reiterated women's inferiority in the attempt to "protect" them (165). These judicial decisions "saw women legally the way men see women socially: as breeders, marginal workers, excludable" (167). Early nineteenth-century German textbooks for jurists presage these decisions: they speak of the "'Zurücksetzung' oder 'Begünstigung des weiblichen Geschlechts in Erwägung seiner Hülflosigkeit und Schwäche'" (qtd. in Gerhard 186). On the other hand, MacKinnon argues that because women are not represented by the constitution in the first place, refusing to "give them a voice" on the grounds that the court's role is not one of activist intervention is in fact a type of intervention that benefits men (166). It also ignores the fact that the creation of law in judicial decisions pertaining to women's particular situation "could be adequate to women's distinctive social exploitation" (167). Similarly, Gerhard notes that after the 1840s the same sort of allegedly "'fortschrittliche' Redeweise" represented by such refusal appears in German legal textbooks: "Die Geschlechter stehen sich im Allgemeinen einander gleich, so daß die rechtliche Verschiedenheit als Ausnahme von der Regel besonders begründet sein muß" (qtd. in Gerhard 186). While this statement is apparently the same kind of assertion found in the *ALR*'s early paragraph, this textbook was published in an era that had witnessed judicial decisions increasingly hostile to the few rights granted to women by the *ALR*. In this context, the statement seems at the very least willfully disingenuous.

Returning to MacKinnon's argument, the court's "neutrality" assumes that "access to the conventional political realm might be available in the absence of legal rights" (167). Gerhard's citation of Johann Georg Schlosser, an early critic of the *ALR* and Goethe's brother-in-law, suggests that this assumption was prevalent in 1789 as well: Schlosser argues that wives should turn over all rights to their property to their husbands, and, should a husband be too severe in his exercise of those rights, the wife may avail herself of the power of "Liebkosungen und der nächtlichen Umarmungen" (qtd. in Gerhard 87). This suggestion allocates wives only an invisible, presumptive position under the law, a position they achieve by virtue of sexual talent, and indicates that for this influential critic the true nature of the marital relationship regulated by the law is one of a prostitute represented in court by a benevolent patron. Five years later the *ALR* closed even this questionable route to legal personhood: it prohibits either spouse from denying her or his partner "nächtliche Umarmungen," unless the unwilling spouse is ill or is a "säugende Ehefrau" (II 1 §178–180).[6] Again a clause suggests that even laws that claim gender neutrality are, on closer inspection, directed more at one gender than the other.

Although Gerhard points to examples of women's inequality under the *ALR*, she asserts that it was in fact "frauenfreundlicher" than the nineteenth-century commentaries and judicial decisions based on it and the *BGB* that followed it (156–57). In 1874, after German unification in 1871 brought the "desire for a reform in the law on the basis of legal nationalism and national sovereignty," work began on a new civil code. The first draft of this code "reflected the prevailing ideology of individualism" (Foster 22). If Gerhard's suggestion that the *BGB* represented a significant weakening of the legal position of women is accurate, then women were being sacrificed to the definition of the individual as male. Like the *ALR*, however, the *BGB*'s provisions were also criticized for not "reflect[ing] the social and economic concerns of the day or subsequent changes." Foster calls them "abstract and, at times, rigid codes containing little social conscience," which have been considerably modified to meet changing cultural expectations (23). If such modification was possible in the nineteenth century as well—which, based on the response in the 1840s to the imminent reform of laws pertaining to divorce, appears to have been the case—then Lewald's texts operated within a gray zone of persuasive possibility. In other words, she might reasonably expect to effect change with her novels by addressing the gap between women's legal limitations and the consequences of those limitations on their lived lives.

## II

Gerhard asserts that the *ALR*'s liberal marriage laws were a particular focus of opposition for some of the early critics of the new code (156). The *ALR*'s view of marriage as a contract was new and was directed against the canonical conception of marriage as both sacrament and contract and against the church's claims to jurisdiction in marital matters, since such claims were irreconcilable with the state's view of itself. Marriage, which was the most important relationship in life and the one on which "bürgerliche Ordnung" and the mental well-being of the people were founded, could not be under the control of independent powers, since this would challenge the state's authority (Gerhard 157). The contract was the form on which the enlightened state, in accordance with the Natural Law theory of the social contract, based its jurisdiction in this realm. The state guaranteed the concept of marriage as a purely legal arrangement, a voluntary contract that necessarily excluded force and coercion (Gerhard 158). Such a view would seem to lead inevitably to the possibility of dissolution of said voluntary contracts.

According to Gerhard, the paragraph that caused the most indignation was "Der Hauptzweck der Ehe ist die Erzeugung und Erziehung der Kinder" (II 1 §1) (158). Critics overlooked as much as possible the fact that marriages could also be entered into for mutual support, which in effect makes the first paragraph irrelevant and suggests that the basic principle of the *ALR*'s view of marriage is the "Gleichwertigkeit, wenn nicht Gleichberechtigung der ehelichen Vertragspartner" (Gerhard 158–59). In an edition of his *ALR* commentary published in 1871, Christian Friedrich Koch referred to the code's first paragraph as a "Schamhaftigkeit verletzende" definition, taken directly from Kant and Adelung and explicable only in the context of an age that regarded marriage as a "polizeiliche Anstalt zur Fortpflanzung der Menschen." However, he continues,

> Die Ehe, ein natürlich-politisch-sittliches Rechtsinstitut, begründet eine dauernde und ausschließliche innige Gemeinschaft aller Lebensverhältnisse zweier bestimmter Personen verschiedenen Geschlechts. Sie hat außer sich keinen Zweck, sie selbst ist ihr Zweck und hat das, was der §1 als den Hauptzweck angiebt, nur zur natürlichen Folge, wie denn auch die wechselseitige Unterstützung daraus folgt. (1, note 1)

His firm assertion of a contemporary conception of marriage opposed to the *ALR*'s supports Gerhard's allegation of a nineteenth-century transformation of the definition of marriage. The law's conception of marriage as an institution, which became generally accepted during the period of the divorce reform movement in the *Vormärz*, became, according to Gerhard, a pillar of reactionary family law hostile to women (167). The history of this reform movement reveals the close political connections between the authoritarian interests of the state and the so-called "Sittlichkeit des Familienlebens," which, not coincidentally, is equated with the "Sittlichkeit" of women (Gerhard 168).

The liberal provisions of the *ALR* with respect to divorce had always been a source of irritation to clerics and conservatives in and around Prussia, who saw them as lax and frivolous, proof that the age was hedonistic and immoral, and who also argued that judicial practice was "noch laxer und weichherziger" than the law itself (Gerhard 169). Gabriele Schneider points to the relatively high divorce rates in Prussia compared to those of other German states: between 1838 and 1840, there were 57 divorces per 100,000 inhabitants in Berlin (*Zeitroman* 155; 161, note 6). Only when Friedrich Wilhelm IV came to power, though, did the conservative and clerical circles have a chance to put an end to these liberal provisions. In 1842 the king made Friedrich Carl von Savigny, who was an influential legal professor and "Geheimer Oberrevisionsrat" at the court of appeals for the Rhein province, his minister for legislation. The king gave marriage law reform a top priority, with the goal of removing provisions that contradicted Christian teachings (Gerhard 169). E.L. von Gerlach, a strict church jurist,[7] drafted the divorce reform, which included the elimination of eleven grounds for divorce (especially the possibility of no-fault divorce in the case of childless marriages and divorce in the case of "unüberwindliche Abneigung" on the part of one spouse) and insisted on punishment of the "guilty" party with a prison sentence, even when not requested by the "innocent" spouse. Women would receive punishments twice as severe as those given to men (Gerhard 169–70). A woman's crime, as the partner who embodied the ideals of "Sittlichkeit," was presumably greater.

In the fall of 1842, the draft of the proposed legislation was leaked and published in a newspaper that Karl Marx edited. The nearly universal indignation it roused brought Prussia to the brink of a state crisis. The king capitulated (Gerhard 170–71). Instead, legislation that transferred jurisdiction in matters of divorce to the higher regional courts (Oberlandesgericht) was enacted, which in itself made divorce more expensive and thus less readily obtainable (Blasius 64–65). Gerlach's mentor, Savigny, wrote a justification of himself in 1844 in which he developed the idea of the "nature" of marriage as institution, which was taken up by jurisprudence and became the marriage model for the *BGB* (Gerhard 171). Although he argued that the "höhere sittliche Stellung des weiblichen Geschlechtes," not to mention the blessings of family life and society's moral legacy to subsequent generations, were endangered by the possibility of divorce in cases of mutual consent, the general public expressed its opposition to the same reforms Savigny supported in similar terms: compulsion applied to marriage desecrates and corrupts ("entweiht und entsittlicht") the family (Gerhard 172). In other words, each side accepted the same values and attempted to claim them for its cause.

Fanny Lewald added her voice to those protesting the proposed divorce reforms; she too argued that they would profane marriage as an ideal. In her autobiography, *Meine Lebensgeschichte*, she identifies the inspiration for her third novel, *Eine Lebensfrage*, which was published in 1845. Several years earlier, she explains, she had found the following statement in an article on the proposed Prussian divorce law: "Es gibt Fälle, in welchen die Trennung einer Ehe eine hohe sittliche Tat sein kann!" Because she found the idea so disconcerting, she had attempted to imagine such a situation (III: 111). The male protagonist of *Eine Lebensfrage* eventually repeats this opinion almost verbatim: "Glauben Sie denn nicht…, daß in tausend Fällen die Trennung einer Ehe eine hohe, sittliche That sein könne, daß sie zur heiligsten Pflicht werde." His male interlocutor affirms this view, adding that every divorce honors the idea of marriage (I: 138–39). Lewald's autobiography describes the novel as addressing the "sittliche Berechtigung der Ehescheidung, wenn die Ehe aufgehört hat, eine Ehe im höheren Sinne des Wortes, das heißt: die durch gegenseitige Liebe und Wertschätzung nach allen Seiten förderliche Verbindung der Eheleute zu sein" (III: 214). With this description she identifies her conception of marriage as one that avails itself of both the *ALR*'s suggestion that a marriage should be conducive to mutual support and the alleged spirit of the new legislation, which claims to honor marriage as a moral institution that has worth in and of itself. Cleverly, Lewald appropriates the concepts of the reformers in order to argue against their legislation.[8]

But does a novelist have the authority to launch an argument against contemporary legislation? In *Eine Lebensfrage*, Lewald's characters answer the question with an emphatic yes. They argue that writers should treat contemporary issues (II: 27–28) and that a novel, "der nicht in genauer Beziehung zu der Zeit steht, in der er geschrieben ward...selten ein gelungenes Werk sein [wird]" (I: 198). Historical themes are for those whose nations and people have achieved perfection, which does not apply to Germany (I: 201), and writers should not succumb to readers' desire merely to be entertained (I: 200). Lewald thus assigns herself the task of edifying her readers within the narrative framework of a contemporary situation that demonstrates the imperfection of the age: the social inequality that can lead to bad marriages and the legislation that makes it difficult, if not impossible, to extricate oneself from such a marriage. Her text also illuminates the way in which Prussian divorce reform would work against its own alleged goals. Lewald introduces the subject of a potential reconsideration of the proposed reforms with one character's declaration that he would not consider burdening himself with a wife now that the "Staatsrath ernstlich daran denkt, die goldenen Ketten der Ehe in ganz solide Fesseln zu verwandeln" (II: 93). She follows that with another character's reference to the large number of divorce cases currently before the court, due to anxiety about the proposed new law (II: 124). In other words, marriages legally conceived as prisons result in the avoidance of marriage, presumably not the goal of a state that wanted to promote the "Sittlichkeit des Familienlebens."

Although the main character of *Eine Lebensfrage* is male, women's unique experience of both existing and proposed divorce law is also at issue in Lewald's text. The female corollary to the male protagonist, Alfred von Reichenbach, is Madame Marie Berent, whose unhappy marriage and troubled prospects for divorce become a subplot in the novel: she sues for divorce in response to the rumor that it will soon become even more difficult to obtain. The legal situations that Lewald constructs for both Alfred and Madame Berent work together to make the author's point about the potential "morality" of divorce, particularly for women.

From Alfred's point of view, he and his wife Caroline are unhappily married as a result of their profound incompatibility. Renate Möhrmann demonstrates that Alfred suffers from the "Zwang der Konvenienzehe" in that he had felt obliged to marry the fiancée from whom he had drifted apart. Raised for nothing but marriage, she would have been doomed to eternal waiting had he left her (140).[9] The characters of husband and wife are established in the opening scene and serve to put the reader on notice that these are two natures that will never reconcile themselves to one another: he is wealthy, poetic, a little melancholy; she is an "üppige Blondine" who is loud, inconsiderate, uninterested in literature, and a shrewish and even ineffective manager of the domestic environment. Even their ten-year-old son understands Alfred better than does the self-absorbed Caroline. Lewald's narrative attributes this incompatibility to her lack of education and the "unlovable" character she developed in the absence of better role models. Educational norms and legal possibilities collide in this text's indication of just where the typical education of girls might be expected to lead them: straight into divorce court, because good looks and "Liebkosungen" (I: 34) are not enough. Their son Felix suffers from the marriage as well, which Alfred makes a part of his decision to leave his wife. Caroline is a manifestly bad mother: she does not encourage Felix's noble young character, she does not put his needs and concerns before her own, she wants him to lie to his father, she exposes him to her unseemly behavior, and she wants to raise him as a Catholic. As Schneider points out, Lewald criticized the Catholic Church harshly in several novels, although less because of "religiöse Inhalte" than "despotische, feudale Strukturen" (*Zeitroman* 149).

Beating the reader over the head with such excessive marital incompatibility and such spousal and maternal inadequacy presumably contributed to the nineteenth-century reader's acceptance of this eminently desirable divorce. The reader, as eyewitness to the characters' absolute polarization, takes on the role of a Prussian judge. According to Koch, in cases in which only one partner expresses aversion to the other, the judge may,

> nachdem er 'Acta' gelesen hat, sich der inneren Ueberzeugung unmöglich erwehren...: daß aus der Fortsetzung dieser Ehe nie etwas herauskommen werde; daß die Abneigung des Klägers nicht etwa bloß simulirt, sondern sehr ernstlich und tief eingewurzelt sei; und daß man nicht den geringsten wahrscheinlichen Grund habe, je wieder eine Aussöhnung desselben mit dem Beklagten zu hoffen.

Once convinced, the judge can use the latitude granted him by a decree of Friedrich II, which expressed the view that since unhappy marriages are unlikely to produce much in the way of population growth, they should not necessarily be continued at all costs.[10] Koch rescinds some of the judicial freedom he has just acknowledged, however: he adds that if one of the parties is interested in continuing the marriage, then the situation is perhaps not hopeless, and that rewarding a spouse for the stubborn insistence on divorce may inspire other malcontents (186, note 53).

In other words, however compelling Alfred's aversion may be, he needs other ammunition, which Caroline's maternal failings provide. The disadvantages to Felix of remaining with both his parents are critical to Alfred's legal position, because the *ALR* in general prohibited divorce in cases where children were involved, even when both parties agreed. Judicial latitude had been granted, however, by the commentary of one of the *ALR*'s original framers to the effect that "es auf die Moralität der Kinder unmöglich einen vortheilhaften Eindruck machen könne, wenn sie unter den Händen zweier so sehr gegen einander aufgebrachten Eltern erzogen würden" (qtd. in Blasius 31). A secret codicil in his uncle's will further hinders Alfred's pursuit of a divorce: the dissolution of the marriage would cost him much of the property he wants to preserve for Felix.

Other complications arise when Alfred realizes he loves Therese, a woman with whom he had felt an intellectual affinity during the period of his engagement to the hapless, uneducated Caroline and whom he had reencountered after separating from his wife. The text makes clear that Caroline and Therese are complete opposites, even contrasting their behavior toward Felix. Therese's brother Julian, an old friend who happens to be a minister of justice, gives him legal advice. Alfred eventually decides to pursue his divorce, thereby throwing off the shackles of both the church—since an evil priest is orchestrating Caroline's opposition to the divorce—and conventional morality.

Although Lewald argues that incompatibility is in itself grounds for divorce, primarily by suggesting that Alfred's marriage leads him to despair and makes him the prey of unscrupulous clerics, Madame Berent's case emerges as the more tragic situation. However, it is critical to the women for whom she stands that even Alfred's unilaterally asserted incompatibility be established as permissible grounds for divorce, because the Madame Berents of the world, due to the conjunction and cooperation of various social and legal forces, may have no other legal recourse. The secret codicil affecting Alfred's estate ownership, which constitutes a significant part of his identity as both patriarchal employer and prosperous father, finds its parallel in the social exposure and subsequent loss of reputation to which a woman attempting to dissolve her marriage in court will be subject.

Theophil, a young lawyer-in-training who is living with Julian and Therese, tells Madame Berent's story. Close examination of that story illuminates a number of the intertwined social and legal constraints to which nineteenth-century women were subject and with which Lewald chooses to burden her female protagonist. According to Theophil, Madame Berent is one of many of those living in unhappy marriages who now seek a divorce as a result of "die Besorgnis vor dem neuen, die Ehescheidungen erschwerenden Gesetze" (II: 124). Her husband is known to be a "wüster Gesell" and a gambler, while her intelligent expression and neat and tidy poverty had caught Theophil's eye at her hearing. In her petition to the court she had explained that she had two daughters and that the three of them had supported themselves for years through their needlework, because her husband had no income. Whenever he happened to have money, he spent it elsewhere. She had never been happy with her husband; her parents had forced her into the marriage.[11] Nevertheless, she believed that she had fulfilled her duty and patiently endured the brutality of her husband (II: 124–25). Because that brutality was increasing, her health was broken, and her daughters were also suffering from his tyranny, she felt she had to ask for a divorce before it became impossible to obtain. She had, Theophil continues, obviously written her petition herself and had appeared in court in person because she could not afford to hire an attorney. He assures his listeners that he had dealt as gently as possible with her during the hearing. Her husband, who had first been an officer, then a civil servant who had been dismissed for "Dienstvergehen," a transgression on which the text does not further elaborate, was contesting the divorce, "weil es ihm bequem zu sein scheint, Wohnung, Speise und Kleidung für sich erwerben zu lassen, während er in Spielhäusern und Weinschenken die Zeit verschwendet, oft betrunken heimkehrt, bisweilen wüste Gesellen mit sich nach Hause bringt und Frau und Töchter auf das äußerste quält" (II: 125–26). However, because the husband had never verbally abused his wife in the presence of others, had never beaten her, was not being charged with adultery, and would not consent to the divorce, her chances of being granted it were bleak. The husband had appeared in court, and his wife had suffered visibly during his account of their marital relationship. He accused her of never having loved him, of having loved someone else before their marriage, and, because of that previous relationship, of having been so cold that she had

driven him out of the house. Theophil indicates that the man seemed to be
lying, and, as the husband had continued in this vein, finally accusing his
wife of infidelity with this same first love, she had cried, "Großer Gott!
auch das noch und vor all den Männern! und sank in einem Anfall von
Starrkrampf zusammen, der so arg wurde, daß man sie hinaustragen
mußte." After expressing his indifference to her condition, the husband
had departed (II: 127–28). While Madame Berent was still unconscious,
her first love, now a lawyer, happened by. He roused her to consciousness
merely by speaking her name and, after she had been sent home in a
carriage, told Theophil and Julian the story of their unfortunate
relationship, which had ended with her parents' insistence that she marry
Berent, then wealthy, although already dissolute. He had seen her today
for the first time since her marriage; she had become a "bleiche,
gramdurchwühlte Frau...erliegend unter der Last häuslichen Jammers,
geschmäht von einem Manne, der ihr das Leben zur Hölle gemacht hat."
His first thought, as is the reader's, had been "Wie stellen wir es an, die
Unglückliche frei zu machen!" His solution is to offer Berent money,
through Julian, to agree to the divorce (II: 130–31), and this offer is
eventually accepted. This transaction points to marriage as traffic in
women:[12] her parents profit from the first sale and her husband profits
from the second. In no case does the object realize any profit for herself.
The text suggests that her first love's desire to help her stems from
nostalgia rather than renewed or continuing love and that her chance for
happiness with him has passed.

Nevertheless, although the narrative does not attribute his generosity
to romantic love, Madame Berent's "Jugendliebe" hires a lawyer for her
in order to spare her another personal appearance before the court (II:
132). Her obviously homemade petition, the legal self-representation to
which her financial situation compels her, Theophil's attempt to question
her gently, as though such consideration were unusual, and her collapse
in response to her husband's predictable rebuttal indicate that the female
witness is not a courtroom norm and is ill-prepared for her task. In her
analysis of trial testimony in novels by Charlotte Elizabeth Tonna,
Elizabeth Gaskell, and George Eliot, Christine L. Krueger points to the
ways in which these writers construct their female characters as silenced
by the act of bearing witness, because the "legal discourse [is] structurally
incapable of admitting female difference" (345). Although Krueger

interrogates nineteenth-century British legal and literary texts, her conclusions on the female experience of the courtroom apply to German texts of the same period. In the novels she examines, "a female witness experiences the trauma of being made a public spectacle and, if she is not immediately shamed into silence, she suffers the maddening frustration caused by her authorial illegality" (338). Krueger also discusses the historical case of an English woman, Caroline Norton, whose husband attempted in 1856 to avoid responsibility for her debts by reviving an alleged infidelity of which her supposed lover, and therefore she herself, had been acquitted seventeen years earlier (340–41). Krueger quotes Norton on this second trial, in which she was called as a witness and attacked and humiliated as a defendant by her husband:

> I felt giddy; the faces of the people grew indistinct; my sentences became a confused alternation of angry loudness and husky attempts to speak. I saw nothing—but the husband of whose mercenary nature Lord Melbourne himself had warned me I judged too leniently; nothing but *the Gnome*,—proceeding *again* to dig away, for the sake of money, what remnant of peace, happiness, and reputation, might have rested on the future years of my life. Turning up as he dug—dead sorrows, and buried shames, and miserable recollections—and careless who was hurt by them, as long as he evaded payment of a disputed annuity and stamped his own signature as worthless!

As Krueger puts it, "Here patriarchal and legal power were quite literally synonymous, rendering Norton helpless to defend herself" (341).

In the case of Lewald's Madame Berent, similar in both the husband's motivations for manipulating the law and the wife's experience of that law, the court appearance of the injured wife shames her into an insensibility that not only precludes her speaking, but is a necessary element of her character. Her silence is predetermined by the modest, middle-class womanhood she represents, which cannot allow her either to engage in a verbal battle with her husband or to endure assaults on her reputation with equanimity "vor all den Männern." Theophil's statement that he dealt as gently with her as possible, followed by his apparent inability to restrain or redirect her husband's testimony, indicates that court procedure ignores the social constraints under which female witnesses operate and gives free rein to those whom law *and* culture permit a voice. The law privileges the male voice: because there were no witnesses to the husband's abuse of his wife, his denial invalidates her testimony to that abuse. It is literally his word against hers, and the court bestows no authority on her assertions. The text further underscores Madame Berent's silence when it assigns her "Jugendliebe" the task of exonerating her while she is on her way home in the carriage the sympathetic lawyers have provided. Because the court and the law do not acknowledge the "female difference" that must render Madame Berent unconscious rather than allow her to reply to her accuser, Lewald's text argues that the law should give women the opportunity to sue for divorce on the grounds of "einseitige Abneigung." Such a possibility would write into the record the mute testimony of the women, real and fictional, for whom speaking under such circumstances is synonymous with a violation of the socially mandated self, and would effectively silence her husband instead.

Lewald's construction of Madame Berent and her history portrays her as confronted by an array of sociolegal forces that will, without intervention, overwhelm her. Her case allows the author to inveigh against these forces and also points to the urgency of women's need for legal access that takes into account the way they are socially situated. Although Lewald compellingly argues Alfred's divorce suit, the nominal case presented to the reader as judge, Madame Berent's suit is the one that moves even Lewald's representatives of the legal system to action and to acknowledgment that their action must take place largely outside the law.

It is more difficult to establish the extent of Alfred's need for a divorce, since male characters, particularly successful, benevolent writers and estate and factory owners, must ignore social and literary conventions in order to act, or rather to endure, as victims. Theophil's appearances in the text, for instance, are devoted largely to his headaches and to the impatience of other characters with his apparent lack of desire to emerge from the melancholy induced by a failed love affair. He is introduced with a comment from the narrator on his "fast weibliche Züge" (I: 147), and gains the text's respect only when he falls in love with an adolescent girl who adores him. When Alfred finally decides to insist on a divorce, he obtains both it and Therese. The law will give him custody of his son (II 2 §93) and will allow him to raise his son in his own religion (II 2 §76).[13] Removing Felix from Catholic influence requires Alfred's own conversion to Protestantism, but the text has in any case been at pains to point out that Alfred's noble character is in fundamental disagreement with the nefarious tenets of Catholicism. Because Alfred is neither socially nor legally a persuasive victim, Ruhberg, the evil priest, becomes a necessary feature of the plot. Alfred's desire for a divorce becomes a battle between two men, one of whom is using the other's wife as a pawn in order to defraud him of his patriarchal role as estate owner and autonomous father. Alfred must resist this attempt by divorcing Caroline in order not to contradict the other elements of his own construction.

Although the author seeks and wins reader sympathy for Alfred's case, she obtains it with fewer strokes of the pen for Madame Berent. The reader can and does fill in the gaps of Madame Berent's shorter story with the awareness of the fictional and social conventions that constitute the sort of pre-existing social inequality, reflected in legislation, to which MacKinnon refers. The long-suffering wife and daughters living in hard-working poverty are a staple of life and art that must contrast favorably to the equally ubiquitous image of the drunken and abusive husband. The text implicitly compares Madame Berent's situation and Alfred's: she is trapped in the house whose rent she pays, while he can travel between his estate and Caroline and the city and Therese; she suffers her husband's verbal violence and the drunken behavior of his dissolute friends, while he squirms under Caroline's lack of education; and she loses her first love, in addition to her youth and beauty, while he regains Therese. Her husband's potential for reprehensible behavior is also much greater than Caroline's, since the same gendered norms and occupations that consign Madame Berent to a life of marital "duty" limit Alfred's wife, too. Women's opportunities for "Dienstvergehen," for instance, behavior that seems to verge on treason to the fatherland and may taint the whole family with its unspecified crime, are limited. Because the legal code and its potential divorce reforms, including double punishment for female offenders, ignore the greater susceptibility of women to exploitation, humiliation, and domestic tyranny, Lewald's text insists that the marriage contract must be dissoluble by either partner with a claim to aversion. Alfred has the legal, social, and financial resources to obtain his divorce under even adverse conditions; Madame Berent does not. Lewald's narrative argues for laws that facilitate the process for him, because those same laws will open up the possibility for women like Madame Berent to obtain a divorce at all.

Theophil's account of Madame Berent's case also serves to introduce a discussion of why the state deems itself entitled to defend marriages. Lewald uses her narrative to express her opinion that the legal code's involvement in "private" matters is inappropriate, a view she states in at least one of her nonfiction texts as well.[14] Her choice of a spokeswoman on this issue is significant. Eva, a young friend of Therese and Julian, functions elsewhere in the text to remind Alfred of the fundamental appeal of the gravity and intelligence she lacks. When she hears Madame Berent's story, however, she asks how the state can justify its interest in Madame Berent's divorce when it had not concerned itself with the forced nature of her marriage. She continues:

> Die Frauen sollte man beschützen, sie sollte man fragen, wenn man neue Gesetze über die Ehe entwirft…und nicht Gesetze geben, die einer Unglücklichen befehlen, das harte Joch zu tragen, wenn es ihr zu schwer wird. Es ist schlimm genug, daß Eltern und Verhältnisse ein Mädchen zwingen können, sich gegen ihren Wunsch zu verheirathen; der Staat braucht nicht die Ungerechtigkeit hinzuzufügen, daß er verlangt, man solle verheirathet bleiben mit einem Manne, den man nicht liebt, nicht achtet, den die Frau hassen muß, wenn er sie gegen ihren Willen zu fesseln begehrt. (II: 134–35)

She herself was married at fifteen by her mother to a friend of her father, but her story had ended happily: her indulgent husband had been kind enough to die three years later. Her stated lack of interest in education presumably explains her ignorance of the law that forbids parents to force their children into marriages. She does not need to know about that law, because it is irrelevant: parents can and do force their daughters, legally "unmündig" until they are married, despite their age, into marriages of convenience. Because Eva is so uninformed and because she has experienced a marriage of convenience, her response to the news about divorce reform is one unmediated by any legal sophistry. Julian further legitimizes her viewpoint by acknowledging that this response has been nearly universal and that he himself believes that punishing those who wish to divorce lies outside the state's jurisdiction (II: 135–37).

Julian in fact reads the "state as family, husband as ruler" argument against the grain: just as the state does not tolerate criminals, it must free individual families from family members who endanger its well-being (II: 139). He does not gender the family member in question, but, given the context of the Berent family's story, Julian's argument criminalizes a bad husband rather than crowning him an absolute monarch whose rule must be upheld for the good of the state that he and his family allegedly embody in miniature. Lewald's revision of the family/state analogy makes the good spouse, in this case the wife, the state whose health and prerogatives must be protected by law, if not by custom. If the "contract" signed by both marital partners injures one of those partners, the state can and should permit its dissolution.

### III

Gerhard notes that the conception of marriage as a contract also forms the basis of the regulation of marital property laws. Although the *ALR* assumes that as a rule women's property will devolve on their husbands after marriage, another clause gives women full rights of ownership to property that they have retained either by law or by contractual agreement (II 1 §205). This paragraph and others suggesting that women could contract with their husbands to keep their own wages were quite controversial, even in the legislative phase, signifying as they did the reduction of "ständischer, hausherrlicher Gewalt" (162–63). Schlosser's opposition to the *ALR* before it was instituted was based partly on his fear that it would make "das preußische Land bald zu einem wahren Paradies der Weiber" (qtd. in Gerhard 215, note 42). The response to the controversy was a compromise (Gerhard 163), which is evident in the following representative paragraph: "Was die Frau in stehender Ehe erwirbt, erwirbt sie, *der Regel nach*, dem Manne [my emphasis]." Laws that gave women some control over their own money in fact reflected social reality: 30% of the women in the "handarbeitenden Classen" worked. Laws that denied wives access to their own earnings threatened to make them their husbands' slaves, which was, as one of those working on the code asserted, contrary to the marital relationships of the age (the late eighteenth century) (Gerhard 163).

One legislator's construction of the female victim of such statutes outlines the terms under which lawmakers could be swayed; his word choices are indicative of those terms. He describes the "berühmte" woman painter, "X," who earns ten times more than her "fauler" husband and who, with "Fleiß und Mühe" over the course of thirty years, accumulates some capital. She "hofft sich damit in ihrem Alter, wenn sie nicht mehr arbeiten kann, zu ernähren," but when her husband dies, his "lachende," greedy heirs take it all and push her into "Dürftigkeit und Armut." The legislator calls on justice to consider the situation of the "Unwissenden, [die] Armen und Nothleidenden," since not even that which has been acquired with one's own talent and skill, with one's own work—"das unstreitigste Eigenthum des Menschen"—is safe from such heirs. The debates over these issues resulted in the insertion of the phrase "der Regel nach," which meant that an individual wife was entitled to use whatever "Durchsetzungsvermögen" she possessed to make more favorable arrangements with her husband (Gerhard 164–65).

As noted in the case of Madame Berent, however, female "Durchsetzungsvermögen," in opposition to social norms represented by the "rule" that appears more prominently in the law than its exception, can be presumed in short supply. In order truly to promote women's access to property, the law would have had to insist on each "partner" retaining all rights to his or her property. Once again the legal code reveals that women are something other than "Rechtspersonen," since it takes as its starting point the idea that a woman cannot keep any of her property unless she contractually reserves it as her own, much as the wife of a voluntary "Untertan" must assert her own freedom to the "Gutsherr" in order to avoid assuming her husband's servitude.

Lewald addresses the issue of women's disadvantage in marital property law in "Das große Loos." The story's female protagonist, Christel, is the victim of the *ALR*'s paragraph II 1 §205, which states: "Durch die Vollziehung der Ehe geht das Vermögen der Frau in die Verwaltung des Mannes über; in so fern diese Verwaltung der Frau durch Gesetze oder Verträge nicht ausdrücklich vorbehalten worden." Protecting herself financially from her husband would require considerable "Durchsetzungsvermögen." However, the construction of this fictional character, Lewald's surrogate for the millions of historical women Christel represents, precludes the development and the exercise of that ability.

When women did attempt to gain access to their property after mid-century, the court tended to assume that they had not actually reserved that property. The commentaries supported this trend with various legal tricks and sophistry (Gerhard 166). Koch indicates that, in contrast to "allgemeinen Beweis- und Prozeßregeln," husbands do not have to prove that their wives' property was actually transferred to them. Rather, wives must prove that they specifically retained it (80–81, note 1a). Although it appears that the courts were simply upholding what the law actually stated, the limitations and expansions of various definitions were more insidious. A "Schuldschein, welchen der Mann seiner Ehefrau über ein

Darlehn, mit Zinsversprechen und Kündigungs-Stipulation ausgestellt hat," for instance, is not adequate indication of a wife's retention of property (Koch 82, note 4b). Additionally, wives are limited in their rights to dispose of "their" property: no one should agree to auction or buy a woman's jewelry without the knowledge and, in some cases, permission of her husband (II 1 §223), since he is his wife's "Vormund" in cases involving her "relative Handlungsunfähigkeit" and can act for her as though she were a minor (Koch 86, note 15). Further, Koch notes, "eingebrachtes Eigenthum" also includes lottery winnings, even when the wife gambles only with the money she has contractually retained. Here he adds that the framers of the *ALR* had included a provision on "Glücksfälle" (II 1 §212) "um die Spielsucht der Frauen einzuschränken" (83–84, note 9).[15] The actual laws indicate that the *ALR* viewed women and their potentially disruptive behavior suspiciously, despite permitting the possibility of contractual arrangements that were more favorable than the norm. Judicial decisions and commentaries that carried that suspicion even further are unsurprising, given the jaundiced views of the original document.

The law reflects and attempts to allay the anxieties and desires of the sociohistorical context, which are evident in contemporary commentators' insistence on the eminent reasonableness of a husband's control of his wife's property. Schlosser expresses his opposition to the possibility of a wife legally retaining rights to some of her property in the following argument: "Wenn die Frau ihrem Mann den Leib, ihre Ehre, ihre Kinder, ihre ganze Glückseligkeit, ihr Leben und alle ihre Kräfte anvertrauen muß, so ist es…an sich eine Kleinigkeit, daß sie ihm auch ihr Vermögen anvertraue" (qtd. in Gerhard 87). In his etiquette manual for the middle class, *Über den Umgang mit Menschen* (1788), Adolf von Knigge offers behavioral tips for husbands whose wives bring money into the marriage:

> Hätte meine Frau mir großes Vermögen zugebracht, so würde ich mich doppelt bestreben, ihr zu beweisen, daß ich geringe Bedürfnisse hätte…. Ich würde ihr beweisen, daß ich dies Wenige mit meinem Fleiße mir erwerben könnte; Ich würde ihr Kostgeld geben; Ich würde nur der Verwalter ihres Vermögens seyn; Ich würde Aufwand im Hause machen, weil das sich für reiche Leute schickt; aber ich würde ihr zeigen, das dieser Aufwand meine Eitelkeit nicht schmeichelte…, daß ich keiner Aufwartung bedarf, daß ich gesunde Beine habe, die mich ebenso weit, wenn gleich nicht so schnell fortbringen, als ihre vergoldeten Wägen; und *dann würde ich, wie es dem Hausherrn zukömmt, über die*

*Anwendung ihres Vermögens unumschränkte Gewalt verlangen!* (qtd. in Gerhard 126;
Gerhard's emphasis)

Seventy-six years later, commentators argued still for the "naturalness" of
the property merger: "Sobald man erwog, wie schwer es oft ward, die
verschiedenen Bestandtheile der Güter wieder genetisch auszuscheiden
und der Idee, daß die Ehe eine volle und innige Lebensgemeinschaft sei,
mit Eifer nachging, so gelangte man bald und leicht an jenes Ziel"
(Bluntschli 615). Although Johann Kaspar Bluntschli also considered
other possibilities, the natural administrator of this "Gütergemeinschaft"
would seem to be the husband. After all, Bluntschli argued, "[d]as
organische Verhältniß in der Familie bestimmt zunächst, wer im einzelnen
Falle die Vormundschaft zu üben habe: der Ehemann über die Frau, der
Vater über die Kinder, der nächste mündige Schwertmag über die
unmündigen Waisen und die ledigen Weiber" (563).

Lewald's "Das große Loos," however, questions the legal code's
assumption that the husband is the "bessere Finanzverwalter in der Ehe"
(Schneider, *Zeitroman* 104).[16] Lewald's female victim of the laws regulating
marital property might have been modeled on the situation of the famous
painter "X," as framed by that sympathetic legislator: here too a worthy
woman who wanted only to provide for herself in her old age is defrauded,
in this case by the shiftless husband himself, with the aid and consent of
the law. Christel is a village seamstress with a gentle manner and an
unusual story: her mother was a poor woman who had bought a lottery
ticket and become relatively wealthy. She and her daughter live alone until
the mother dies after extracting a promise from the lady of the manor to
protect Christel and her money. The "gnädige Frau" assures Christel's
mother, "Daß [sie] nicht um das [Ihrige] käme, dafür sorge das Gericht
schon von selbst" (31). The lady of the manor and the schoolteacher then
arrange to have him made her guardian. The schoolteacher's son,
Ferdinand, is Christel's future husband and is away at school in the city
when Christel becomes his father's ward. There he spends his free time at
the theater and eventually goes astray, becoming a dissolute "Komödiant."

The law violates Christel in ways that either elude or surprise her, but
Lewald prepares the reader both for the violation and for Christel's
inability to defend herself against it. Christel's mother's experience of the
law and Christel's own character and dependence presage disaster for
herself and for other, similarly constituted women in her situation. When

her mother wins the lottery, the Jewish peddler from whom she had bought the ticket advises her not to tell anyone. Her peasant neighbors, however, notice with increasing envy that she now drinks coffee on a regular basis and are quick to denounce her when a few silver spoons are stolen from the castle. She wants to be taken before the "gnädige Frau," but the constable, "der immer kurzen Prozeß machte," a phrase that suggests that he is judge and executioner in the short work he makes of her arrest, takes her off to jail in the city. To her horror, he forces her to walk next to his horse like a vagabond (22–23). The villagers assume that if her story is true, the peddler will confirm it and she will be back the same evening. However, Christel relates, "Du lieber Gott! die wußten nicht, daß es vor den Gerichten mit dem bloßen Sagen nicht so abgetan ist" (24). After three weeks Christel's mother is freed, but the experience has broken her and she withdraws, indicating that she on some level shares the opinion of the villagers who ask how she can let herself be seen, "da sie doch einmal kriminal gesessen hätte" (26). The law's intervention destroys her reputation and happiness; the lady of the manor would, presumably, have listened to and believed her. The proven innocence of this female character victimized by her environment, by social codes, and by the law and its representatives is irrelevant now. Christel, whose "sanftes Aeußere [und] stilles Wesen für sie ein[nahmen]" (3) and whom the text portrays as even worthier than her hard-working mother, also finds that no amount of feminine worthiness will protect her from the law. In fact, that gendered virtue makes her a particularly susceptible victim to the laws that fail to protect her from a guardian with a conflict of interest and give her husband complete control over her property.

Christel is content living with the schoolmaster and his wife: "Das Gericht zahlte für mich; ich konnte es gar nicht besser treffen" (32–33). Women, other than the mother or grandmother of the ward in question, cannot be named to guardianship (II 18 §143). The lady of the manor is never at issue as a potential legal guardian, despite the fact that Christel's mother has commended her daughter to her care and despite the indication that she would have prevented Christel's marriage to Ferdinand had it been in her power to do so. This woman concurs in the choice of the schoolteacher as guardian, but the text suggests that she is either unaware or initially approving of what everyone in the village seems to know: as Wilhelm, the son of a prosperous farmer, informs Christel, "Der

Schulmeister hat Dich ja bloß aufgezogen, damit der Ferdinand Dein Geld kriegt" (44). Ferdinand's father had already suggested to Christel that she might marry his son, and Lewald's character describes her reaction in vivid fashion: "[ihr] ging der Schreck durch alle Glieder" (34).

The *ALR*, however, appears to forbid self-serving solutions of the sort that Christel's guardian proposes: "Ein Vormund soll während seiner Vormundschaft, ohne vorhergegangene Untersuchung und Genehmigung des vormundschaftlichen Gerichts, weder sich selbst, noch seine Kinder, mit seinen Pflegebefohlnen verehlichen" (II 1 §14). Should the guardian marry himself or his child to his ward without the court's permission, however, a new guardian will be appointed, the marriage investigated and perhaps declared invalid, and the decision left up to the ward as to how much of her property she will give to her husband after attaining her majority (II 1 §989–96). As we will see, however, the court's "permission" was none too difficult to obtain in Christel's case. Koch notes that for an investigation of a proposed marriage a special guardian "can" be appointed, as "should" always happen in cases where the ward's affairs are linked to the guardian's (6, note 14). The weakness of the statute's language points to the likelihood of its violation. The clause pertaining to the court's investigation and permission further leaves open the possibility of male guardians enriching themselves and their families at the expense of their wards. The framers of the legal code were aware that property could prove a temptation: the numerous provisions concerning the rights and restrictions of husbands with respect to the fortunes of wives who are still wards (II 18 §736–99) support the interpretation of the paragraph discouraging marriage between wards and the family members of guardians as one concerned with the transfer of property. These provisions also indicate that the law expects the guardian to scrutinize the financial transactions of the ward's husband with a suspicious eye, which was clearly unlikely in a case in which the guardian was also the father-in-law. Did the framers perhaps place too much faith in the extent of a court's willingness to investigate and reject the petition of such a guardian? Lewald's text indicates that, at the point of his marriage, Ferdinand has made his dissipation evident to the lady of the manor and greatly exaggerated his stories of success in the theater. Despite insistent evidence that the guardian's son merely wants to acquire the resources to continue his dissolute life, the schoolmaster obtains "permission" for the marriage by writing a letter to announce "daß [Christel] heirathen und Geld zur Einrichtung haben wollte" (68). The court responds by sending five hundred "Thaler," which Ferdinand pockets as they leave for the city, an action that is representative of their married life. Tellingly, another law that might have helped Christel is never at issue in Lewald's narrative: that law enables a guardian to retain contractually some portion of a female ward's property for her before her marriage (II 18 §738). Its omission underscores the fact that the constellation of characters and their competing interests make such disinterestedness on the part of the father of the groom unlikely, to say the least.

Christel, presumably unfamiliar with the *ALR* paragraph that concerns her, is unenthusiastic about her new partner, although her first response to Wilhelm's revelation of the schoolmaster's motivation is "Im Grunde hatte ich nichts gegen den Ferdinand, und heirathen mußte ich doch" (44). She prefers Wilhelm, who also wants to marry her, but is cowed by his father's noisy rejection of her as a potential daughter-in-law. He wants Wilhelm to marry the daughter of a rich farmer who once lived in the area. The uproar Wilhelm's father raises makes Christel the subject of village gossip, and when she must go to the communal well, she slinks toward it, "als hätte ich ein Verbrechen begangen. Es weiß keiner, wie einem Frauenzimmer zu Muthe ist, das Etwas auf sich gehalten hat, und soll nun so dastehen in aller Leute Munde" (58). Her relationship with Wilhelm founders because she keeps her promise to her foster parents not to communicate with him, although he thinks she should ignore the gossip. Christel's dependence, not to mention her "sanftes Aeußere," her "stilles Wesen," and her horror at being the subject of scandal, makes such defiance an unlikely prospect. While Wilhelm is away doing his three-year army service, his mother convinces him that Christel has taken up with Ferdinand. Wilhelm then rejects her when she writes.

Although Christel concludes that she would not have to marry, thanks to her income, she succumbs to Ferdinand's ailing mother's assertion, "Ledig kannst Du nicht bleiben, ledig kann er nicht bleiben" (64), and her own anger at Wilhelm's rejection. She accepts Ferdinand because marriage to him represents the only escape from what has become an untenable situation in the village; she goes through with the wedding, despite the warnings of the lady of the manor, because she fears the gossip that would follow a broken engagement. Lewald's text thus suggests that the norms and behavioral codes represented by "Heirathen mußte ich doch" and "Ledig kannst du nicht bleiben," as well as the shame associated with being "in aller Leute Munde," take precedence over a legal provision that might have preserved Christel's money and her options, had these norms not argued against its enforcement.

Christel's marriage, however, is a match made in hell. Ferdinand spends most of his time with a singer, an evil "older woman," and their sole means of support is the quarterly interest from Christel's money. They have "Noth und Zank und Trunkenheit und Schulden" at home (77), and Christel tells the sympathetic female narrator that she would not have endured it if she had had an alternative (73). When Ferdinand takes the money he has persuaded her to borrow against the principal, she says, "Ich konnte Nichts dagegen thun als mich bei ihm beschweren, er war einmal mein Mann" (78). These comments, as well as the earlier statements as to the inevitability of her marrying, reinforce a carefully constructed picture of the limited options to which at least some women were subject, and this character's subsequent legal "education" is used to illustrate the constraints to which all women were potentially subject.

When Christel finally decides that she wants a divorce, Ferdinand informs her that because she is not yet twenty-four she cannot obtain it without permission from her guardian, his father, who will never agree to it. His response recalls that of the anonymous "Justizbeamter" who threw his wife to the ground and read her the rights the legal code had given him and taken from her. His father invokes not only the legal code, but conventional morality, wifely duty, and religious mandates in his subsequent refusal of her request:

> Er antwortete mir sehr beweglich, ich sah, wie ihm dabei zu Muthe war; von der Scheidung wollte er jedoch Nichts wissen. Er gab mir zu bedenken, was aus dem Ferdinand werden sollte, wenn er ganz dem schlechten Frauenzimmer in die Hände fiele; er ermahnte mich zur Geduld, verwies mich auf den lieben Gott, auf die vielen Menschen, die gesündigt hatten und in sich gegangen waren, und ganz zuletzt hieß es, er als Vater könnte es nicht verantworten, in die Scheidung einzuwilligen, so lange er noch etwas über mich zu sagen hätte. Was ich nachher thäte, das wäre meine Sache, das müßte ich mit meinem Gewissen abmachen und mit meinem himmlischen Vater. (80–81)

Christel succumbs to this multifaceted assault, particularly since Ferdinand behaves less objectionably than usual before the "Termin, in dem [Christel] mündig gesprochen werden sollte," but she wants to know how to protect her money in order to provide for herself in her old age. The concept of "Gütergemeinschaft" becomes the next legal blow dealt her by the narrative:

> Ich war also wie vor den Kopf geschlagen, als ich hörte, daß ich mein Geld nicht festsetzen könnte ohne meines Mannes Willen, denn wir hatten Gütergemeinschaft; was mein wäre, wäre sein, was ich erwürbe, gehörte auch ihm, wenn er nicht als Verschwender bekannt gemacht würde. Ich konnte es mir gar nicht denken, daß Alles so gegen die Frauen eingerichtet wäre, die ohnehin schon immer die Unterdrückten sind, und als ich dem Advokaten das zu verstehen gab, meinte er, ich thäte ihm leid, es sei schlimm für mich, gegen das Gesetz sei jedoch Nichts zu machen. Ich möchte mir überlegen, ob ich meinen Mann wollte als Verschwender erklären lassen, dann sei mir gleich und ganz geholfen; es käme dann in die Blätter, Niemand borgte ihm mehr, und ich behielte das Meine.
>
> Das war am Montag; Mittwoch war der Termin. Ich stand nun und sollte wählen: entweder die Scheidung einklagen, oder den Eltern und meinem Manne, denn das war und blieb er doch einmal, den Schimpf anthun, daß ihr Name auf solche Art durch die Blätter ging. (81–82)

Lewald's construction of this character, so apt a representative of the gendered "oppressed" to whom Christel refers and whom the defender of the painter "X" had also evoked, leaves the reader little doubt as to the character's so-called choice. That she refuses to protect her own interests for the sake of an unrelated family that clearly considers her desires subordinate to its own and that she stays with Ferdinand even after it occurs to her that he might try to kill her for her money underscores the author's portrait of Christel's noble, self-sacrificing nature. Lest we miss the point, Lewald has the narrator add her praise of Christel's lack of interest in vengeance: although Ferdinand steals the money she receives on coming of age and runs off with the singer, "sie hatte keinen Zorn, kein Rachegefühl, nur ihre leidensvolle Miene, ihre sanfte Klage." Christel even blames herself for marrying Ferdinand for the wrong reasons and against the advice of the "gnädige Frau" (84).

Lewald also introduces a legal inaccuracy, which works to emphasize Christel's self-sacrificing nobility. Once she has been abandoned, she returns to her village to live with Ferdinand's parents. There she and Wilhelm are reunited when his wife dies. Wilhelm wants her to advertise for Ferdinand and, when he does not appear, have him declared dead, but she hesitates to do something so awful to poor Ferdinand "merely" that she might be happy herself (92). She in fact did not have that legal option. The *ALR* mandated a ten-year waiting period from the time of the last sighting until an individual could be declared legally dead (II 18 §823, §828), a restriction that allowed a prodigal of either gender considerable latitude. The greater mobility of men, however, supports the likelihood that this provision primarily disadvantaged women who had been abandoned and whose plans for remarriage and perhaps economic improvement were subordinate to any late claim the negligent husband might return to make. As such, this law would seem to constitute a likely contribution to Lewald's argument that the law as it stands makes "Alles so gegen die Frauen eingerichtet," but she has made that point with Christel's experience as a ward and as a dispossessed property owner. Christel's reluctance to use a law she in any case does not yet have at her disposal serves instead to support her character as deserving of legal intervention and change.

As it stands, the court can only give her the empty advice to be careful with her money when she receives it (76–77). While the law also offers her the options of divorce or family scandal, the narrative indicates that the price for either is too high, because they both entail the loss of the approval of others. The construction of women's legal options is thus at odds with their social construction. The options are a sham that benefits the men by whom the law is made. The text does not argue for a redefinition of laudable feminine behavior to include the kind of "Durchsetzungsvermögen" that would have enabled Christel to reject her own socialization and the connections that have consistently worked to her legal disadvantage. Rather, it makes her the model of the worthy "oppressed" for whose sake law should be rewritten. Her situation stands in contrast to Wilhelm's: Wilhelm's father opposes his son's marriage to Christel once she is widowed, but Wilhelm can avail himself of both his financial independence and the resistance to others' will that his gender permits him. Significantly, his financial assets consist of his "Muttertheil," his inheritance from his mother, and all the property brought into the marriage by his wife, the woman whose dowry had made her such a compelling bridal candidate to his father. The same laws that make women powerless in this text work to the conspicuous advantage of male characters, as do social expectations, which are points not lost on Lewald's reader.

MacKinnon offers an insightful and useful explanation for the discrepancy in the benefits available to men and women. The liberal state, she argues, promotes "negative liberty": one is free to be left alone (164). Men, on the other hand, are "socially granted the positive freedom to do whatever [they] want" to women, which means that "civil society, the domain in which women are distinctively subordinated and deprived of power, has been placed beyond reach of legal guarantees. Women are oppressed socially, prior to law, without express state acts, often in intimate contexts" (164–65). The law as it stands cannot help Christel preserve her property from the social rule that insists that she not embarrass her husband and his family by revealing his failure to live up to the definition of a "Hausherr." Social codes and constraints work in tandem with the law in order to ensure the continuation of a family in which a woman's possibilities for self-determination are always limited.

## IV

At issue in Lewald's "Kein Haus. Eine Dorfgeschichte" is the intersection of family law and other legal complexes, such as the proscriptions against free movement, marriage restrictions, and the changing construction of unwed mothers under the law. Even after the demise of the feudal system, peasants were hindered in their ability to move. The obligation of the "Gutsherr" to provide for "his" peasants was no longer in force, and communities, which were the entities primarily responsible for the support of the poor, attempted to protect themselves with laws restricting individuals from settling by requiring "Nachweis eines nachhaltig gesicherten Nahrungsstandes, der Entrichtung von Zuzugsgeldern und guten Leumunds-Zeugnissen" (Gerhard 21–22). As a result, almost half the population of the German territories before 1848 lived "'zwischen Staat und Stand' in Armut und Elend" (Gerhard 22). Prussian law attempted to alleviate these problems in 1842, but the freedom to move was effected only by a law that the Norddeutsche Bund passed in 1867 (Gerhard 22). Related to the laws restricting movement were the "polizeiliche oder gemeindliche Heiratsbeschränkungen" that were also intended to reduce community costs for support. The Norddeutsche Bund finally eliminated these in 1868, but the communities' experience with these restrictions prior to that had proven them ineffective: the costs for care of the poor were actually much higher in territories with marriage restrictions than in those without them (Gerhard 115–16). This discrepancy suggests that community acceptance of poor families led to an increased desire on the part of those families to meet community standards of self-sufficiency.

The invalidation in 1854 of the *ALR*'s provisions regarding the rights of unwed mothers and their children added to the misery of the female poor (Gerhard 176). The *ALR* had in effect assumed the "innocence" of the "unbescholtene" unwed mother and had insisted that fathers or their parents support her and her child.[17] Even when the father could object that "die Geschwächte auch Andern den Beyschlaf gestattet habe," he was still required to pay at least "Niederkunfts- und Taufkosten," as well as six weeks of "Verpflegung," as long as the woman in question was not a prostitute (II 1 §1036, §1028). The "Revisor" had supported these provisions over the objections of some, arguing that women, weaker by nature, should not be held solely accountable for a mistake (Gerhard 176). He also wrote what was still the dominant opinion in 1830, that "wilde Ehe" should be tolerated as a lesser evil, "stillschweigend und unter großen Einschränkungen," because it was preferable to the "Zusammen- und Wiederauseinanderlaufen beider Geschlechter," and that cohabitation of this sort should be given legal recognition (qtd. in Gerhard 435). By 1854, lawmakers would argue that a man's progress toward "maturity" almost necessitated the peccadillo of unplanned fatherhood. They maintained that the law enabled any "Allerwelts-Hure" to make a financial claim,[18] and that the rights of unwed mothers in fact promoted their "immorality" by making pregnancy a source of income (Gerhard 176).[19] The first law's construction of unwed mothers allowed them to retain their "Unbescholtenheit" even while pregnant—although it cast a suspicious eye on the women who found themselves in the same predicament twice (II 1 §1041)—while the revision cast them as guilty, opportunistic whores. The new consequences of a pregnant woman's "guilt" reflect the legislators' economic interest in such a construction: only the unavoidable costs of delivery will be paid, and only in the case of "Notzucht" can she receive compensation (Gerhard 176–77).

These laws and others reflected increasing middle-class indignation at the difference in the lives of the lower classes, a difference that the middle class termed immorality and criminalized, despite the fact that significant economic and legal barriers to marriage existed for the poor (Gerhard

113). These barriers, such as church costs (Gerhard 113) and local and countrywide restrictions (Gerhard 20), were rooted in the community's fear that it would be left to bear the costs of supporting offspring; "[s]o bestand…noch lange eine Verbindung zwischen Armen-, Niederlassungs- und Heiratsrecht" (Blasius 82). The "wilde Ehe" that outraged the middle class and their legislators was, as Dirk Blasius maintains, "oft nicht eine bewußt gewählte Lebensform, sondern eine aus rechtlicher Not veranlaßte Verbindung zweier Menschen" (84).[20]

Lewald focuses her criticism in "Kein Haus" on the variety of laws that prevent the (worthy) poor from marrying. Her story shares the middle-class view that marriage is the only moral possibility, and she constructs her peasant protagonists as worthy in part because of their unquestioning acceptance of this view. Despite her orchestration of a general consensus on this issue on the part of the narrator, the protagonists, and the plot, however, Lewald is a remarkably sanguine midwife at the birth of not one, but two, illegitimate children: she provides an elaborate narrative excuse for the first and allows the second to be conceived under cover of benign authorial silence. She reserves her criticism for the tight-fisted, self-seeking community and the hypocritical "morality" of the ruling powers.

The sympathetic female narrator of "Kein Haus" hears Jakob and Anne's story from Jakob's sister. Unable to work at the neighborhood estate, Jakob had taken a job in another village as the "Gemeindehirt." Here the community provides him with a room and payment in kind. He eventually meets Anne, a servant in a neighboring village; they fall in love and want to marry. In order to marry in this community, however, a man must either own a house, be in someone's service, or rent from someone who will take responsibility for the family. If the bridegroom cannot meet these conditions, the entire community must give its consent to the marriage. Out of the miserly and, the text suggests, mistaken belief that it might have to provide for the offspring in the future, the community refuses its permission. Anne finds a job in Jakob's village, but they, and especially she, become increasingly despondent about their inability to marry. One night she leaves the village to visit him in the field where he is tending the sheep: "Da fiel es ihr ein, wie das Alles noch viel schöner sein müßte, wenn der Jakob und sie Mann und Frau wären, wenn sie *von Rechts wegen* [my emphasis] zu ihm gehen könnte, statt sich nun weg zu schleichen von Hause, mit Angst und Noth wie ein Dieb" (41). She falls into his arms when she finds him, and a pregnancy results. Jakob wants nothing more than to marry Anne, "damit alles in Ordnung käme" (42), but their only option is cohabitation. Anne moves into Jakob's hut, and the community looks the other way, because it is not liable for the support of children it has not officially sanctioned. Schneider focuses her discussion of Lewald's story on its indictment of marriage restrictions. As she points out, the pregnancy highlights the absurdity of these, as they were intended to prevent the population growth that was viewed as the primary cause of poverty (*Zeitroman* 98).

The child is born and Anne and Jakob try again to get permission to marry so that the child will not experience the stigma of illegitimacy. Although they fail, Jakob has the boy baptized under his name. Anne is pregnant again when the new constable visits to take the census and discovers that she and Jakob are not married, and that she is not even from the principality in which the village is located. He threatens to send her back to the village in which she was born, which occasions a new attempt to obtain the community's permission to marry. The villagers respond by insisting that the constable will forget about the family. They are, however, mistaken:

> Es war ein neuer Landrath in's Amt gekommen, einer von den Frommen, der hatte seinen Sinn gesetzt gegen all' die unehelichen Kinder in den Dörfern. Und statt den Bauern zu befehlen, daß sie Leuten, die sich ordentlich nähren konnten, Nichts in den Weg legen sollten bei der Heirath, wollte der Landrath die alte Zucht herstellen, wie sie es nannten, und bessere Sitten einführen; und wer ihm nicht beistand von den Schulzen, dem sollte sein Amt genommen werden. (52)

The district magistrate wishes to use the law to further his own version of "morality," and the constable uses it to uphold his own version of order: when he returns and insists on taking the pregnant Anne away, he tells the villagers, who are momentarily sympathetic to her plight, "Nicht die Barmherzigkeit, die Gerechtigkeit und die Ordnung sollen aufrecht erhalten werden" (54).

The constable's words point to the fundamental irreconcilability of the law as it stands and compassion for the pregnant "wives" and mothers whose human ties the legal discourse does not acknowledge. Gerhard identifies a similar silence in her discussion of the "Gesindeordnung" that ruled the servant class after the end of feudalism: "die Bestimmung-

en...schweigen über die individuelle, alltägliche Not, deren gesellschaft-
liche Ursachen nicht erkannt oder geleugnet wurden" (56). Individual
human misery finds no expression in the law. In her criticism of the district
magistrate, Lewald offers her solution to the "individuelle Not" caused by
the law's conspicuously blind eye. The villagers, however, not only will not
allow Jakob and Anne to marry, they create obstacles even to their
reunion: they delay Jakob's search for Anne and, when he finally locates
her, rarely allow him to visit her. Each of the two principalities involved
had attempted to make her the responsibility of the other. We see her last,
ill and starving, living in a barn in the village where she was born, after
having spent the interim in the workhouse. Jakob visits her there and
brings her their son, because he fears she will kill herself if she has nothing
to live for. His fears are justified: when her baby is born the night she is
told that she will have to move to the poorhouse, she drowns herself and
the two children. Jakob goes mad at the news, loses his job, and moves in
with Anne's former employer, who has in the meantime hired his sister.

Lewald constructs Jakob and Anne as eminently worthy characters
who want to participate in a legal system that excludes them. Although, in
their desire to marry and have a family, they obey what the text suggests
are "natural laws," man-made law not only prohibits their union, but forces
them into the marginalizing behavior of sex without marriage—outside the
village limits—that results in Anne's banishment. Living on the margin,
she gives birth in a barn. The obvious analogy to the Virgin Mary, another
worthy unwed mother, further elevates this estimable character.
Conversely, the law's representatives and adherents are consistently
portrayed as hypocritical, self-serving, and uncompassionate, interested
primarily in preserving their own prerogatives, which tars the law itself
with the same associations. The couple's characterization provides
effective—and affecting—support for Lewald's argument that the
deserving poor be allowed to marry: they are economically and
psychologically vulnerable, honest, hard-working, good parents, and
almost completely unable to defend themselves.

Anne is particularly defenseless because she bears the children, and the
text stresses her vulnerability throughout. Lewald's narrative intimates
that Anne's gender, and the weakness it entails, makes the various
punishments the couple endures disproportionately hard on her: *her* work
suffers when they must conduct their courtship at night; *she* goes to see

him the night she conceives; *she* fears public censure when she gets
pregnant because she has not been allowed to marry; *she* is sent to the
workhouse,[21] where a zealous clergyman convinces her that she deserves
her suffering because she has sinned, although God knows "wie gerne [sie]
ehrliche Wege gegangen wären" (58); and *she*, not he, makes the desperate
choice of suicide and murder as her only alternative. Anne's agonized
account of her suffering underscores the unfair apportioning of blame:

> Und hätte ich den Jungen nicht, hätte ich das Andere nicht, das leben will, ich
> hätt' es längst gebüßt, und es wär Alles gut. Dich haben sie nicht gejagt wie ein
> Stück Wild aus einem Land in's andere, am hellen Tage vor aller Leute Augen,
> aber mich! aber mich! und gestoßen und geschimpft haben sie mich auf offener
> Landstraße. Mir ist's ordentlich recht, daß ich nicht unter Menschen bin,
> sondern so allein liege. Da sieht mich Keiner! Da kennt mich Keiner! Herr
> Gott! wie soll ich noch leben unter anderer Leute Augen? (59)

Anne's withdrawal and her shame at the public humiliation she has
experienced not only emphasize the victimization in which they originated,
but contribute to her consistent characterization as laudable. She is
introduced as "ein großes schönes Frauenzimmer," despite her
"Pockennarben," who is "handfest und gut in der Arbeit" (15). The lovers
manage to support themselves and even save money in large part because
she is a "tüchtiges Frauenzimmer" (47). Her very "Tüchtigkeit" becomes
in fact a contributing factor in her suicide: she does not want to go to the
poorhouse with the "Missethäter" (64–65). In other words, she retains her
sense of and respect for the social order and its rules to the end, although
it proves fatal to her. Her former employer reiterates the incongruity of
Anne's character and her fate: "So'n braves Frauenzimmer und im
Arbeitshaus!" (57) and "in ihrer Todesangst und Noth ist sie, so wie sie
war, mit beiden Kindern in den Teich gegangen. Und so ein braves
Frauenzimmer!" (66). The text portrays Jakob as no less worthy, and it
illustrates this worthiness in part by giving the couple's child his name.
"*Von Rechts wegen* [my emphasis] hätte der Junge müssen auf ihren Namen
getauft werden, der Jakob nahm ihn aber auf den seinen. Es ist mein
Kind, sagte er, und das soll er bleiben vor Gott und Menschen" (46),
although, according to the *ALR*, illegitimate children take their mother's
name (II 2 §640). Thus Lewald makes another symbolic legal "mistake" in
order to prove a point about her characters: Jakob is a good family father,
even when the law does not compel or even allow him to be.

Together Anne and Jakob are "ordentliche Menschen, brav und willig," whose characterization and situation make Lewald's point about the injustice of the laws responsible for Anne's death and for the misery of others like her. "Und mancher Schlechte hat's so gut! — Aber freilich! es geht vielen Anderen auch nicht besser wie der Anne und dem Jakob. Der Arme hat's schwer in der Welt!" concludes the woman for whom Anne had first worked (67–68), and the narrator asserts, "Der Gedanke an das Unglück dieser Menschen, *das leider in seiner Art nicht vereinzelt da stand* [my emphasis], beschäftigte mich unablässig" (63). Lewald's narrative acts as a potential force for the change that her simple characters no longer consider possible: before she has heard the story, the narrator tells Jakob's sister that she might be able to help him, and the sister responds, "Helfen?…helfen können Sie nicht, das ist nun einmal so! Aber sagen will ich's Ihnen wohl, denn es muß 'nen Stein erbarmen" (8). When she has heard it all, the narrator informs the reader that the sister had simply related the facts, but "grade diese Art und Weise hatte etwas tief Ergreifendes" (58). In other words, this tragic story depends not on narrative artistry, but on the suffering it captures. Since even a "stone" could not withold its pity, the reader will of course be moved and, like the narrator, seized with the desire to aid the many victims of the legal circumstances Lewald describes. Another Lewald text that includes marriage restrictions in its plot argues more explicitly for activism on behalf of those suffering under the law: "Wo der Arm staatlicher Justiz nicht hinreicht, muß menschliches Rechtsgefühl den Richter machen" (*Prinz Louis Ferdinand*, qtd. in Schneider, *Zeitroman* 101). Laws must be changed and Lewald tells the reader how: the recalcitrant peasants must be prohibited from denying the deserving poor the right to marry (52).

The community's desire to protect itself legally from the poor and the increasing judicial hostility toward unwed mothers collide in this text with the eminently middle-class values of this peasant couple. The consequences of the collision indicate that the legal code and its agents are unable to acknowledge worth when they encounter it. The text insists that Anne and Jakob would never have been a burden to the community and that they were more horrified about their child's illegitimacy than their neighbors. The moralistic dudgeon of the "Landrath" was superfluous and misdirected: their problem could not be solved by enforcing the "alte Zucht" und "bessere Sitten" that they, too, respected. They in fact were the victims of an economic policy that found it expedient to blame widespread poverty not on the circumstances that had robbed the rural poor of the ability to support themselves, but on the "Leichtigkeit" with which people could marry and settle despite lack of employment, "mit all ihren traurigen Folgen für das Familienleben" (Gerhard 141–42). This process necessarily scapegoated women, Lewald argues, because they bear the children for whom the economy cannot provide. The text intimates that even when couples are not allowed to marry, "natural laws" will mandate their union and reproduction, after which man-made laws and social codes will conspire to burden the "wife" and mother disproportionately. Lawmakers can term them "Allerwelts-Huren" and, like Anne, they can be left to conclude their "guilt": "Ja, es sind ihrer zu viel! man soll keine Menschen in die Welt setzen! es sind zu viel, Gott der Herr will's nicht, ich muß das büßen!" (65). Anne does penance by drowning herself, one of many ("nicht vereinzelte") unwed mothers sacrificed to an economic solution masquerading as legislated morality.

V

The entry on "Frauen" in an encyclopedia from 1818 asserts, "Die Frauen sind die Repräsentanten der Liebe wie die Männer des Rechts im allgemeinsten Sinne" (qtd. in Gerhard 138). Lewald's texts demonstrate that men are the representatives of the law in the narrower sense as well, and that male control of laws and legal entities works to women's disadvantage, particularly in the realm specifically assigned to them: marriage and the family. As nineteenth-century domestic ideology worked to expand the importance of that realm, male anxiety about the loss of power outside the home led to the desire for increased control over the "Repräsentanten der Liebe" within it. The definition of bourgeois masculinity depended heavily on the characteristics of the "Hausherr." Accordingly, a woman's subordination to the family father's will had to be visible and codified, her "superior" morality, wifely duty, and maternal instincts legislated and enforced.

Gerhard suggests that the culmination of these nineteenth-century legal efforts was the *BGB* (see, for instance, 167, 173, and 177). The provisions with which Gottfried Planck defended the new legal code to the Göttinger Frauenverein in 1899 support her assertions. A woman, he announced, now had the right to enter into transactions relating to the management of household affairs in her husband's name; "ja das Bürgerliche Gesetzbuch geht sogar soweit, zu bestimmen, daß, wenn die Frau ein Geschäft dieser Art abschließt, angenommen werden soll, daß es im Namen des Mannes abgeschlossen ist" (Planck 11). The reader almost suspects sarcasm. At a time (1890–1908) when the women's movement was nearing its peak with respect to agitation and organization (Frederiksen 7), the legal code confined women to the house as the only realm in which they had legal authority, in which "power" was legitimated by a husband's name and the fact that the wife's now legally protected purchases were "Eß- und Trinkwaaren...Hausgeräth und Kleidung." Fearful, perhaps, that his female listeners would take their new "Schlüsselgewalt" too much to heart, Planck reminded them that carrying on a marriage requires that one partner have the deciding vote and that the *BGB* supports the "christliche und deutsche Auffassung der Ehe, nach welcher der Mann das Haupt der Ehe ist." The husband is the partner legally entitled to make decisions; however, Planck asserted, it will of course often be the other way around (11). Once again, his statement suggests, women were advised to employ extralegal means such as "nächtliche Umarmungen." Further, where there was no ostensible law mandating wifely obedience, social codes would continue to step into the breach. In his address, Planck argued that the new legal code would prevent "Mißbrauch des [ehelichen] Rechtes." If, for instance, a husband wishes to emigrate to a country with an unhealthy climate or where he has no certain means of providing for his family, his wife should not be obliged to follow him. However, "[e]s ist schön, wenn sie es doch thut" (8–9).

Laws and judicial decisions of the nineteenth century increasingly limited women's already negligible rights to divorce, to retain control of property, and to receive support for illegitimate children. Lewald's texts resist the legislated disempowerment of women with the creation of worthy, moral female protagonists at the questionable mercy of the law. These characters have proven themselves apt representatives of the domestic ideal. The author therefore challenges the legal system to give them the protection that she believes they deserve.

Lewald here addresses the situation of women who fail to find protection in marriage or cannot marry a particular man. As Chapter Three demonstrates, in her essays and in other fictional texts she takes up the additional plight of women who are trained for nothing except marriage and who will find this lack of education detrimental even within the domestic circle. In these texts she advocates better education for girls and women, in direct opposition to contemporaries who feared that knowledge might lead women away from the path of feminine destiny.

# CHAPTER THREE

## "Behandelt uns wie Männer, damit wir tüchtige Frauen werden können":[1] Lewald and Her Contemporaries on Women's Education

When the school Fanny Lewald had been attending closed unexpectedly, her education ended at thirteen, a year earlier than she and her parents had anticipated. Lewald had been a talented student. She reports in her autobiography that she learned easily and received praise both at school and at home for her ability (*ML* I: 57). She was also one of the class "Paradepferde" in the school's public examinations (*ML* I: 86). Despite her success in the classroom, however, her education also proved to be a source of frustration. When she was nine, for instance, a visiting "Konsistorialrat" had tested her in various subjects and concluded by saying, "Nu! Dein Kopf hätt' auch besser auf 'nem Jungen gesessen!" Lewald had concurred with his opinion:

> [O]hne es zu wissen, was er getan, hatte der treffliche Mann einen meiner geheimen Schmerzen berührt—ich beneidete es schon lange allen Knaben, daß sie Knaben waren und studieren konnten, und ich hatte eine Art von Geringschätzung gegen die Frauen....Von jeher hatten Fremde, wenn sie meine Fähigkeiten lobten, mit einer Art von Bedauern hinzugefügt: "wie schade, daß das kein Junge ist!" (*ML* I: 87–88)

Wanting to learn "wie ein Mann," she clung to the memory of a story she had once heard about a female professor in Bologna, which, however, "noch dazu bei[trug], [sie] vollends zu verwirren" (*ML* I: 89). The abrupt end of her formal education was followed not by a professorship, but by almost twenty years of reluctant housekeeping that she characterized in the second volume of her autobiography as "Leidensjahre." These years confirmed her early anxiety about her domestic future and her envy of her brothers' educational options.

Lewald's experience of an education that both rewarded and constrained her supports James Albisetti's contention that nineteenth-century girls' schools "could stimulate in young girls an early awareness of, and a protest against, their 'second-class citizenship' rather than a submissive conformity to the 'German ideal of womanhood'" (xiv). Lewald's own protest against prevailing educational norms took various forms and mounted a modest challenge to the feminine ideal by manipulating it in the service of her critique. Her fictional and nonfictional texts demonstrate points of contention and of concurrence with contemporary educational models for girls. The protagonists of Lewald's stories and novels generally adhere to conventional codes of behavior, and the familiarity of these codes becomes a part of the author's argument. Her essays and her own life, which was always an integral part of her arguments for better "Mädchenerziehung," on the other hand, suggest an awareness of the more radical potential of education. The essays and her autobiography take an aggressive stance on women's right to formal education, "da wir Steuern zahlen wie die Männer." Here, for instance, she calls for "Realschulen," conceding that "Frauen-Universitäten" can wait, and underscores her demand on behalf of female taxpayers with "Es ist keine Wohltat, die man uns zu erzeigen hat, es ist ein Recht, daß man uns einräumen muß und wird" (*Für und wider* 146). Her fiction argues the case more covertly, suggesting that women educated in nothing other than stereotypically "feminine" pursuits and vanities may succumb to seduction and that schooling makes women more, not less, suited for happy marriages. Despite their divergent form and tone, however, these texts share an underlying philosophy that posits the utter necessity of education to women, married or not.[2] The essay "Einige Gedanken über Mädchenerziehung" (1843) makes her earliest published argument in favor of better education for girls, and the open letters collected in *Für und wider die Frauen* (1870) adroitly demonstrate the benefits to both men and women of women's education. The story "In Ragaz" (1880) sounds a warning to husbands who fail to ensure that their wives are adequately occupied intellectually, while the novel *Nella. Eine Weihnachtsgeschichte* (1870) highlights the advantages of education to women and their families.

As Brigitta van Rheinberg states, Lewald "beschäftigte sich während ihres ganzen Lebens mit dem Problem der mangelhaften Mädchenerziehung. Sie hatte klar erkannt, daß hier der Schlüssel zur Lösung vieler Probleme lag" (185). Lewald recorded her protests on the particular subject of women's education[3] in her autobiography and in various essays written over the course of her lifetime. These texts, however, as well as her fictional narratives, also evince an enduring approval of the contemporary feminine ideal. Real or fictional, the educated women to whom Lewald gives a voice prefer marriage to independence:

> Mir ist...kein Mädchen vorgekommen, das nicht, selbst bei großer künstlerischer Begabung und nach beträchtlichen Erfolgen in seinem künstlerischen Berufe, gern bereit gewesen wäre, auf seine Unabhängigkeit zu verzichten, wenn sich ihm das Glück geboten hat, als Gattin eines geliebten Mannes in ein von ihm versorgtes Haus eintreten zu können.

Her own example, and that of various talented female friends, proves that the husbands and families of such women need not have cause for complaint (*Für und wider* 171), presumably meaning that these wives assent fully to the demands of the household and their traditional roles within it.

With this argument, Lewald's work and life participate in the contemporary debates on women's education that were a main feature of the nineteenth-century German women's movement. Ulrike Helmer points out that this movement understood "Frauenemanzipation" as a contribution to the "Vervollkommnung der bürgerlichen Gesellschaft und nicht als Entfaltung autonomer Subjektivität" ("Einleitung" 8). She argues that the feminists' demands for employment options for women did not stem from the desire for greater independence but for the option of "Selbstversorgung im Härtefall." Marriage remained the higher good ("Einleitung" 9). The radical feminists—whom the cigar-smoking, free-living Louise Aston represented most notoriously—were regarded by moderate counterparts such as Louise Otto as "Feindin[nen] eines Strebens, welches sich eine Hebung der deutschen Frau zur Aufgabe gemacht hat" ("Einleitung" 8; see also Albisetti 100–01 and Rheinberg 183–84). Educational goals that included making women better wives and mothers were thus not anathema to most proponents of the early women's movement. Lewald herself argued that a deficient education produces women "welche den großen oder auch nur den ernsten Gedanken eines verständigen Mannes zu folgen, einem vernünftigen Manne die passende Gefährtin, einem heranwachsenden Geschlechte eine würdige und besonnene Führerin zu werden [nicht] fähig sind" (*Für und wider* 137). The first of her novels to make the latter argument was *Eine Lebensfrage* (1845). Here the author illustrates her point with the shallow Caroline, whose lack of education makes her shrewish, incompatible with her long-suffering husband Alfred, and overly dependent on the scheming parish priest. Alfred forms an attachment to the educated and refined Therese, for whom he eventually divorces Caroline.

Life imitated art less than a year later when Lewald met and fell in love with Adolf Stahr, a father of five who was married to a woman whom he now found unacceptably child-like. To my knowledge, no one has accused Marie Stahr of religious excess or even of shrewishness—beyond a nine-year reluctance to agree to a divorce that was hardly to her advantage—but the ineducability of Lewald's Caroline hovers at the edges of Stahr's description of his own unsatisfactory marriage. In a statement that, as Rheinberg puts it, Lewald "ihn aussprechen ließ" in her *Römisches Tagebuch*,[4] Stahr seems in part to reference Lewald's characters and to fit his own narrative into the framework of hers:

> [Meine Frau] ist rein und gut wie ein Kind—aber sie ist eben auch ein Kind….Und gerade ihre kindliche Beschränktheit, ihre kindliche Harmlosigkeit haben mich entzückt. Es war mir in meiner eigenen unreifen Unerfahrenheit eine Freude, mich ihr in jedem Augenblick so hoch überlegen zu fühlen—was mir zur Qual geworden ist, ihre Unfähigkeit, sich zu entwickeln, das bewunderte ich an ihr, das habe ich für schöne abgeschlossene Naturbestimmtheit angesehen! Ich habe ihn schon lange erkannt, schon oft gebüßt, jenen männlichen Hochmuth und diesen Irrtum. Schwer gebüßt! (qtd. in Rheinberg 122–23)

Lewald allows several male protagonists to make a version of the same "masculine" mistake and sometimes to arrive at a similar recognition of the advantages of wives who have been educated to provide adequate emotional and intellectual companionship.

Lewald's essays, on the other hand, dispense with the relative subtlety of her fiction. Here she often addresses her comments on women's schooling and employment directly to men. The character of her examination of and challenge to the prevailing discourse on education and femininity thus differs from the approach she took to the medical and legal representation of women. This difference suggests that Lewald felt that she possessed a legitimate claim to speak openly on this issue as opposed to others. The subject of Jewish emancipation, for instance, is one on which her comments in essay form might have been taken less seriously, if indeed she had been able to publish them at all. In 1847 she tried and failed to get an essay, "Über die Ehe zwischen Juden und Christen," published in various journals (Schneider, *Zeitroman* 85). Although her subject was marriage, editors perhaps felt that their readers would not accept Lewald's authority on this issue. In reference to her *Jenny* (1843), Lewald states that she had intended that novel to make a literary contribution to the battle for Jewish emancipation that Heinrich Simon, a male relative, was fighting by legal means.[5] In other words, she cannot assist the cause with public speeches or legal briefs, but she can create literary characters whose fates will make the same case for Jewish civil rights.[6] The same year, however, she had published her first essay on girls' education, calling the subject "ein in unsern Tagen gar häufig besprochener Gegenstand." Despite the attention already devoted by others to that topic, she maintains that it is "immer gut, sein Scherflein beizutragen zu einer guten Sache, und seine Überzeugung auszusprechen, da wo man sich dazu gedrungen fühlt" ("Mädchenerziehung" 380).

One might locate part of the impetus to articulate her thoughts on this particular "good cause" in the relatively high number of those who had made their own verbal contributions. Although, as Albisetti notes, the literature on female education "increased dramatically" in the mid-1860s (93), even in previous centuries women such as Dorothea Leporin Erxleben and Mary Wollstonecraft had deemed themselves entitled to speak on the subject of the education of their own sex.[7] The publication and public discussion of their texts indicates that others, too, acknowledged this "entitlement." Even Fichte, for instance, arguing against the phenomenon of women writers, "judged that women should restrict themselves to producing works about the education and morality of their own sex" (Albisetti 12). And why not? While there were no female lawyers in mid-nineteenth-century Germany, many of the middle-class women who were actually employed were working as teachers or governesses. And the vast majority of women, like Lewald, were former schoolgirls.

I

By the end of the eighteenth century, the rulers of almost all the German states had instituted compulsory elementary education. Reading, writing, arithmetic, religion, and singing comprised the very basic curriculum in the eight-year "Volksschulen" (Craig 186–89).[8] In addition to these schools, the first seventy years of the nineteenth century saw a huge increase in the number of higher girls' schools ("höhere Töchterschulen"), which provided a kind of secondary education for girls until age fifteen or sixteen (Albisetti 307). Albisetti argues that the increase in the number of these schools "reflect[ed]…a changing view of the proper education and upbringing for the daughters of Germany's expanding middle classes" (23).[9] Despite the new availability of an extended education, however, most girls continued to leave even the higher girls' schools at fourteen. Most boys, on the other hand, stayed in school at least until they were sixteen (Albisetti 50–51). The premature "graduation" of daughters suggests parental skepticism as to the seriousness of the educational endeavor for girls, as do some of the problems girls' schools had in common: irregular attendance and exemption from courses of which parents disapproved (Albisetti 41–42).

Institutional options varied from the private, which were more common, to the public, from the day school to the "Pensionat." These boarding schools drew particular criticism from conservatives like Wilhelm Heinrich Riehl, because they "removed daughters from parental control," but others argued that the necessity of a secondary school education was paramount (Albisetti 94–95). As an example, Albisetti cites Lewald's defense of "communal education" for girls (95): "Die Schule bietet gerade ihnen, deren Dasein sonst ganz in der Familie verfließt, die eigentliche Vorbildung für das Leben in der Welt und unter den fremden Menschen." It also prevents them from being "verwöhnt" by private teachers (*ML* I: 67).

Schools also conformed to the prevailing view that boys and girls should be educated separately. August Spilleke, the director of the Königliche Friedrich-Wilhelm-Gymnasium, the Realschule, and the girls' school connected with it in Berlin, for instance, hurries to correct the misconception under which some of the public seem to labor: because the boys' and girls' schools under his direction are in the same building, they may not be "gehörig von einander geschieden." He insists, however, that this is "völlig falsch," "da selbst die Eingänge zu beiden Schulen gänzlich von einander getrennt sind, und vollends zwischen den Lehrzimmern auch nicht die entfernteste Communication Statt findet" ("Prüfung" 28). Sylvina Zander lists some of the arguments against co-education still current in 1906: the possibility of "Gefährdung der Sittlichkeit" in the case of the older children and the difficulty of maintaining discipline, since boys require a "straffe Hand," whereas "bei den Mädchen…'auf das Gemüth' gewirkt werden [muß]" (254). This difference in approach had its roots in the different goals of boys' and girls' education.

As a consequence of the Enlightenment, the second half of the eighteenth century brought a veritable flurry of treatises on the subject of formal education specifically for girls. Interest in educating the other half of humanity, Elisabeth Blochmann argues, was superseded in these works by concern for the stability of the family, and hence for the state and society (13), which was endangered by changes in the structure of the "ganze Haus," by women's exposure to the literature of the Enlightenment and "Empfindsamkeit," and by new models of resistant femininity such as Richardson's Clarissa (14–15). Even Kant had cautiously concluded that "[u]ntil we have studied feminine nature better, it is best to leave the education of girls to their mothers, and to let them off from books" (qtd. in Albisetti 15).

The conservative bourgeois response to the new question of women's education was victorious and remained influential into the next century: it sought to determine "Richtung, Ausmaß und Gehalt der Bildung, ja auch ihre Form" in accordance with the "Bestimmung des Weibes" (E. Blochmann16). This ambiguous term, as Albisetti points out, can suggest that a woman's life as such is a function of either "definition, destiny, [or] vocation" (10). This life had hitherto unsuspected implications. Joachim Heinrich Campe's influential *Väterlicher Rath für meine Tochter* (1789), for instance, was written from the perspective of the rising middle class, which took as one of its signifiers its "Familiensinn" and its corollary assumption that "Ordnung und Stabilität der Gesellschaft" are dependent on family values.[10] These are in turn dependent on women's recognition and affirmation of their "Bestimmung als Gattin, Hausfrau und Mutter" (E. Blochmann 31). Women's unique vocation was hence an important part of discussions on the subject of women's education and played a decisive role in justifying and preserving educational limitations. Campe and others began to worry that excessive reading, among other distractions, might divert women from their "cultural function" (E. Blochmann 34), since "Gelehrsamkeit und Schöngeisterei" are irreconcilable with women's vocation (E. Blochmann 35).

During Lewald's school years, her mother embodied this anxiety on the subject of her daughter's potential "miseducation." Her own father had considered education for women superfluous. As a result, Lewald writes, her mother was largely uneducated: "sie schrieb und rechnete nur notdürftig und hatte nicht das Geringste von wissenschaftlichem Unterricht gehabt" (*ML* I: 7). This lack was a source of continuing regret for her mother, and no small part of the ambivalence with which Lewald and her mother regarded one another stemmed from the fact that when the daughter was eight years old, she was better educated than her mother (*ML* I: 88). Her mother, however, alternated between admiration of her daughter and concern that her academic interests were taking precedence over domestic skills that were more important.

But if girls had to be educated, what form should that education take? The school inspector Wilhelm von Türk visited Karoline Rudolphi's school in 1804. In a report on various schools published in 1806, he stated that if he had a daughter whom he loved above all else, he would entrust her to Rudolphi's care, which he praised as follows:

> Mir ist es bei der weiblichen Erziehung weder um glänzende Talente, noch um das, was man Welt nennt, noch weniger um Gelehrsamkeit zu thun, sondern um die häuslichen Tugenden und besonders um jene zarte Weiblichkeit, um jene kindliche Reinheit und Unschuld, die dem Mädchen selbst die sicherste Schutzwehr gegen alle Künste der Verführung, gegen alle nachtheiligen Einwirkungen neuer und ungewohnter Eindrücke der Sinnen-Welt gewährt und dem Manne, dem ein solches Weib zu Theil wird, sein eigenes und das Glück seiner Kinder sichert. Jene zarte Weiblichkeit, jenen kindlichen Sinn, glaubte ich an den Zöglingen der edlen Rudolphi zu bemerken. (139–40)

One wonders what that "zarte Weiblichkeit" looked like and how it was produced. The criticism of Betty Gleim suggests an answer. Gleim was the director of what Elisabeth Blochmann calls "[w]ohl die bedeutendste Mädchenschule" that was founded in that period (111). She also edited a reader that was one of the few textbooks used at Lewald's school (*ML* I: 62; 292, note 37). Gleim had visited Rudolphi's school in 1810 and described it in her diary: "Der Unterricht—Geographie—war spielend und süßlich; es wurde sehr viel Stoff ohne sonderliche Ordnung herbeigetragen; ernste Geistesarbeit wurde nicht verlangt. Die Schülerinnen…zeigten sich denn auch sehr gleichgültig und passiv" (qtd. in E. Blochmann 71).[11] "Gleichgültig und passiv" lend themselves, however, to another interpretation. J.C. Heyse, a Gymnasium and girls' school director who was an ardent admirer of Rudolphi, saw "edle Weiblichkeit" as "Sanftmut, Unschuld, Reinheit [und] Bescheidenheit," in opposition to the "Vergnügungssucht" he feared was typical of contemporary life (E. Blochmann 104).

Gleim and Heyse's variant representations of what was potentially the same student population find an echo in Lewald's fabled ambivalence. The characteristics Heyse lauds are those with which Lewald repeatedly outfits her heroines, and yet it is not difficult to read at least "Sanftmut" and "Bescheidenheit" as the indifference and passivity that Gleim censured. Nevertheless, Lewald's autobiographical sketch of the school she had attended just a few years after Gleim's visit to Rudolphi's institution suggests that she, too, might have looked askance at Rudolphi's methods and their outcome. The director of Lewald's school, for instance, once pulled a student of his, a "sehr träges, schlaffes und schon halb erwachsenes Mädchen," from her chair and shouted, "Ich bin kein Lehrer für Dumme! ich kann nur gescheite Kinder unterrichten!" Lewald's response to this spectacle was a shy sympathy with the teacher (*ML* I: 61).

As Gleim's criticism of Türk's favorite school demonstrates, the methodology employed in girls' schools and the characterization of the ideal female student were not undisputed. Further, Campe and others of his ilk were not the only voices participating in discussions of women's abilities and purpose. And yet, despite the lack of agreement on a number of points, the majority opinion was that women in general, although there were exceptions, had a single vocation determined by nature, which could be enhanced by a certain type of education that included habituating girls to the domestic environment and its demands.

Or perhaps, as Elisabeth Blochmann argues, domestic skills were all that leapt to mind, thanks to the prevalence of a gendered division of labor rooted in tradition, when the founding fathers of middle-class girls' schools wondered what their pupils should be taught (121). In any case, the girls' schools she describes were zealous in their promotion of needlework, which stood in for the many domestic tasks that did not lend themselves to practice in the schoolroom (122). It could claim as many as 12–18 hours of the school week (E. Blochmann 100–11). It also cultivated a "'taste for the quiet, domestic life' with its attention to small details" (Albisetti 21) that was the backdrop for any performance of women's vocation. In 1826, the Lübeck school director Johann Heinrich Meier asserted that needlework fostered "ächt weibliche Wirksamkeit." The hours devoted to it ensured that virtues such as "Ausdauer, Arbeitslust und Arbeitsdrang… 'stark, wie ein Naturtrieb' werden: 'auf Gewöhnung, allein auf Gewöhnung kommt es hier an'" (qtd. in Zander 126). Endurance and diligence were as desirable in women as a taste for seclusion and calm. Yet despite the many pupils who were reportedly "unlustig" when it came to this subject (Zander 126), demonstrating that biology did not necessarily predispose girls to the domesticity for which "Handarbeit" was both surrogate and guarantor, needlework remained an unquestioned part of the curriculum in the girls' schools for many years. As if to prove the pedagogues' point, Lewald's father made it the primary activity of his daughter's day after she had left school. Lewald had herself "proven" that she would otherwise have had nothing to do:

> Die ersten Wochen nach dem Verlassen der Schule gingen mit allerlei Versuchsbeschäftigungen hin. Die Mutter wußte mich nicht recht zu verwenden, ich trieb mich also ziemlich planlos in den Stuben umher, bis ich irgend ein Buch erwischte und mich in einen Winkel hinsetzte, um zu lesen. Das lag jedoch gar nicht in meines Vaters Absichten. (*ML* I: 140)

Her father then drafted a daily schedule for her that included three and a half to five and a half hours of "Handarbeit" a day, Monday through Saturday. He recognized her actual interests and predispositions in his contractual promise that, in compensation for her acquiescence to these terms, she would receive other lessons and "good books" (*ML* I: 140–41).

Needlework had taken up a substantial part of Lewald's school day as well. Other subjects, she writes, included "Lesen, Schreiben, Rechnen, Religion, Geographie, Geschichte, [Unterricht] in der deutschen und in der französischen Sprache, und sehr schlechten Unterricht im Gesang und im Zeichnen. Naturwissenschaften und Literaturgeschichte wurden gar nicht gelehrt" (*ML* I: 61–62). The school director Spilleke reported in 1827 on the subjects taught at his Gymnasium and Realschule, both all-male, as well as at his "Töchterschule." His account both suggests that Lewald's school was typical and provides an instructive comparison of the educational situation of boys and girls. The report describes everything covered in the eight classes of the Gymnasium, discusses the guidelines for the personal reading of these pupils, lists the regulations introduced that year by the authorities relevant to Gymnasien, gives a head count by class for the Gymnasium's students, and describes each of the 16 most recent graduates along the following lines: "Otto Hellwig, aus Berlin gebürtig, 17 Jahre alt, 5 Jahr auf dem Gymnasio, 2 Jahr in Prima; erhielt No. I. und wird in Berlin Jura studiren" ("Prüfung" 1–14). He then thanks the school's benefactors and moves on to the Realschule, which had seven classes, the content of which he describes. The content of the girls' classes follows, as well as a head count for the Realschule and the girls' school ("Prüfung" 17–25). The way in which Spilleke organizes his report suggests that the Realschule and the girls' school share similarities, one of which was the apparent unimportance of what the graduates did after completing their education there. Another was the relative lack of prestige of each school. Spilleke complains that parents unreasonably choose to send their sons to the Gymnasium rather than the Realschule even when they will begin to work immediately following graduation, thanks to the "wahrhaft magische Kraft" of the word "Gymnasium" ("Prüfung" 25). He argues that such parents seem to think that the Realschule educates only those who will take up a simple trade or some entirely mechanical occupation, but that a look at the curriculum should convince them otherwise. The students are, after all, being instructed in mineralogy, physics, chemistry, mathematics, French, English, and so on ("Prüfung" 26).

Here the similarity with the girls' school ends. Boys did not always complete the seven classes available to them, but those who stayed through at least the third class, when instruction in Latin began, received a more extensive education than any girl, who, as of 1826, had the option of completing up to five classes. Male and female outcomes were therefore different, as were starting points. The boys' first year began with ten to twelve hours of German, four hours of French, two hours of religion, four hours of arithmetic, six hours of writing, and two hours of drawing ("Prüfung" 21–22). The girls, on the other hand, began with eight hours of German, two hours of French, an indeterminate amount of religion, four hours of arithmetic, four hours of writing, two hours of drawing, and eight hours of needlework ("Prüfung" 24–25). The last year of school for boys at the Realschule included German, French, Latin, English, religion, mathematics, experimental chemistry, natural history, history, geography, writing, drawing, and singing ("Prüfung" 17–18). A girl's last year included German, French, religion, history, geography, arithmetic, "Naturlehre,"[12] writing, drawing, singing, and needlework (a constant feature throughout her schooling at eight hours a week; only German received as much attention and then only in the first two classes) ("Prüfung" 22). Unsurprisingly, a sixteen-year-old boy knew much more than his fourteen-year-old sister, but even two six-year-olds of different sexes were dissimilarly prepared. Needlework exacted a price, but, as noted above, it was critical to the female educational project.

Religion, too, was conceived of as a subject that contributed more to the character of girls than the sum of the knowledge imparted in the classroom. In Johann Heinrich Meier's school in Lübeck, the girls were read Bible stories, "vor allem Jesu Reden, Sprüche und Wandel..., die dann—möglichst auswendig gekonnt—zur Richtschnur eigenen Handelns werden sollten." The actual Bible was withheld from the pupils, presumably because of its sexual content (Zander 122). Albisetti suggests that the presence of large numbers of pastors and theology students on the staff of girls' schools underscores the primacy of religious instruction at these schools and partially explains the opposition to attempts to reshape the curriculum along the lines of boys' institutions. The theologians would believe that "women's position in German society was not only 'natural' but ordained by God" (40–41). In a speech commemorating the dedication of a new school building for the girls' school, Spilleke emphasizes the necessity of cultivating piety in female pupils. Piety confers purity and harmony; without it, women are predisposed to "ein trauriges, innerlich ödes und zerrissenes [Leben]" because they have nothing other than their domestic circle and their emotions. Men without piety, on the other hand, may yet find "einen gewissen Haltpunkt" in their more varied, worldly existence. For this reason religious instruction should be the focal point— "von welchem alles ausgeht, auf welchen alles zurückgeführt...werden muß"—of female education ("Rede" 15–16). Boys, too, should receive religious instruction, but theirs should be directed toward their analytical, critical desire to "know," he maintains, whereas women need and want the pure ideal that the life of Christ can provide. "Darum sei Christus allein in seiner ganzen göttlichen Erscheinung der Anfang und das Ende des Religionsunterrichts für die weibliche Jugend." This approach yields girls notable for their "Anspruchslosigkeit, Freundlichkeit, Geduld [und] Ergebung" (Spilleke, "Rede" 17–18).

Even when girls and boys studied the same subjects, gendered pedagogical considerations determined the instructional content and approach. The teaching of history was a case in point: Albisetti postulates a "belief that girls could develop their moral sensitivity only through exposure to positive models, not by negative examples or rational deduction." Educators should expose girls only to the "'sunny side' of history," to "great men and great events," and to "biographies of 'truly noble men, women, and mothers'" (19). Spilleke agreed and argued that natural science instruction should be expurgated for girls as well. In fact, it should focus on the "stille Pflanzenwelt," which was an apt model for their own lives within the domestic circle ("Rede" 21).

From a twentieth-century perspective, the incessant assertions of women's unsuitability for anything other than lives as wives and mothers are positively tedious, and yet all of the rhetorical effort expended on the subject of women's vocation suggests that the speakers either encountered or anticipated resistance. Over the course of the nineteenth century, the schools that were "created to educate women to their 'Bestimmung'" (Albisetti 22) in large part nourished and/or succumbed to that resistance. As Elisabeth Blochmann argues, no matter how single-mindedly these schools approached their task, they were of additional, unintentional benefit to their pupils. Formal education not only deferred the beginning of girls' exclusive employment in the household, it gave them at least the possibility of intellectual development and a better understanding of "Lebenszusammenhänge" (121). Beyond those relatively modest accomplishments, the schools contributed to loosening the bonds for which they were nominally educating the students in their charge: "auch die Mädchen [traten] durch die Schule in einen neuen sozialen Zusammenhang...der ihre Loyalität forderte und allmählich gewann" (122). Steffi Cornelius makes a similar argument in her claim that the previous twenty years of female education in the higher girls' schools prepared the women of Württemberg to identify with the national goals of the revolution of 1848: "durch sie wurde die Isolation häuslicher Erziehung aufgebrochen, und der gemeinsame Schulunterricht bürgerlicher Mädchen ließ ein neues Bewußtsein gemeinsamer sozialer Identität und Geschichte entstehen," which in turn contributed to the political formation of the middle class (200). One might also argue that the German women's movement after 1865, which had as one of its goals the improvement of girls' education (Frederiksen 12), was itself the result of the education that its leaders had received. Albisetti believes, for instance, that "new opportunities combined with the discrimination and prejudices" experienced by the now increasing numbers of women teachers led to their participation in the women's movement (58). These women owed their careers to the higher girls' schools and the nineteenth-century willingness to consider at least limited female intellectual development.

Individual parents, too, could be surprisingly ambitious for their daughters, sometimes to the annoyance of educators[13] and apparently independently of the cultural proscriptions and norms they may otherwise have supported. Parental ambition, whatever its motivation, presumably conveyed the message to daughters that schooling could lead to the improvement of their position both within and outside the family. Lewald's autobiographical narrative, with its focus on the ambivalent pride of her mother and her sense of intellectual community with her father, vividly demonstrates this phenomenon. This message ran counter to the goals of the schools themselves, which were attempting to fashion a uniform product, valuable precisely because it was so inconspicuous. Paradigmatic of this desire was, for instance, this regulation of the Luisenstiftung: "Das Tagewerk sei, wie es einer frommen, heiteren und durch Verträglichkeit glückseligen Familie geziemt, mit Vermeidung alles dessen, was den Hang zum Sonderbaren hervorbringen könnte" (qtd. in E. Blochmann 118).

Market forces, however, often compelled the schools' acquiescence. Public examinations of schoolchildren constituted one such point of contention. Pedagogues generally argued that such examinations of their female pupils undermined those pupils' femininity by nourishing "ambition" and "rewarding...effort" and were events at which "talented girls manifest[ed] a disagreeable tendency to push themselves forward, less talented to retreat into the shadows" (qtd. in Albisetti 45). Parents, however, insisted on the examinations (Albisetti 46), although they were presumably as opposed to female ambition and effort in the abstract as the pedagogues. While the examinations may also have served as an opportunity to evaluate the quality of the school itself, these complaints foreground the disconcerting opportunity for recognition of individual girls as "better," a prospect not unappealing to parents. Further, parents of "less talented" girls apparently resisted that designation, despite its irrelevance to the exercise of women's vocation. Albisetti notes that when a Hamburg school "tried in 1880 to divide its pupils into a 'higher' and 'middle' school on the basis of ability, parents of many girls assigned to the less prestigious track" sent them to other schools (42). The competition among private schools for students meant that they also acceded to parents' interest in additions to the curriculum, such as "other languages, history of art and literature, mythology." The time spent on needlework dropped as a result (Albisetti 46) and Albisetti mentions no parental complaints about this reduction. Parents who had earlier valued institutionalized domesticity had begun to find other accomplishments gratifying, useful, and/or marketable, accomplishments that, unlike needlework, girls generally could not learn at home. One assumes that the change in parental values supported the loosening of domestic bonds described above, further complicating what had been a more or less general consensus on the goals and the form of girls' education.

## II

Although Lewald relished her own domestic prowess, she, too, found other occupations she could justify. Despite her repeated assertions that "ihr das Hausfrauendasein 'eine dritte und [ihr] wesentliche Existenz' sei" (Rheinberg 140), it was, after all, only a third life. She gained a different satisfaction from writing and from the influence her writing enjoyed. Helmer notes that Lewald wrote "in aller Bescheidenheit von einer 'großen Wirkung' ihrer Schriften" and mentioned the many letters she had received in response to her work ("Einleitung" 12). In the dedication to John Stuart Mill of her essays on women's education and employment, Lewald states that she is a woman who "seit nahezu einem Menschenalter in ihrer literarischen und privaten Tätigkeit dieselbe hochwichtige Aufgabe [wie er] in ihrem Vaterlande nach Kräften zu fördern nicht ohne Erfolg bestrebt gewesen ist" (*Für und wider* 100). In a letter dated 1 March 1870, Mill thanked her for the copy of the book she had sent him, saying, "It is a real honor to have my name inscribed at the beginning of such a volume" (1703). A week earlier he had sent a list of titles in French and English on the "situation sociale des femmes" to Georg Brandes, a Danish scholar, saying that he did not know what had been published in Germany other than the work of Lewald, "que vous connaissez" (1700).

In her first essay on the subject of women, "Einige Gedanken über Mädchenerziehung" (1843), Lewald argues that although marriage is the "naturgemäße Beruf" of women, not every woman "must" marry. The only hindrances she mentions specifically, however, are a lack of fortune, a match that is not "passend," and a woman's own affections (382). Although she makes "Schicksal" nominally responsible for unmarried women (382), the hindrances she lists depend in large part on the inclination of the bride in question: marriage may be woman's "natural profession," but she can be as discriminating as she likes when it comes to entering that particular work force. Women should be educated for the eventuality that they do not marry (382–83) — and for the eventuality that they do, since a reasonably well-educated woman makes a better wife and mother (383–84). Lewald claims, in other words, as do most women arguing at the time in favor of education, that schooling enhances "Bestimmung," but she attaches conditions to that vocation that may prevent its realization. She thereby suggests that a female life without marriage is preferable to a marriage without "eigne Ueberzeugung" (382). Lewald had demonstrated her own conviction on this point: she was thirty-two at the time and still living at home, after having refused a distasteful suitor (*ML* II: 136).

She argues further in this early essay that education not only produces companionable spouses and insightful mothers, it curtails the development of negative characteristics to which women are so regrettably prey, such as "Kleinigkeitsgeist…, Kleinstädterei und Klatscherei" (387). Lewald's rather cranky opinion of most of her own sex has been well documented,[14] but she here manipulates popular stereotypes of feminine pettiness and idleness to gain support for her position that women should be educated and thereby occupied, both mentally and physically. The subject of occupation, however, gives her an opening to counteract the related stereotype of feminine weakness: "Thätigkeit, rasches, unermüdliches aber bescheidenes Wirken, ist die Hauptsache für unser Geschlecht…. Darum müssen wir viel von uns verlangen, und wir können es, denn das Weib vermag unendlich viel" (392).

An all-capable woman whose stage is the household and whose effect is mitigated by "Bescheidenheit" may not have disconcerted anyone in

1843. Almost twenty years later, however, Lewald raises the specter of independent and ambitious schoolgirls: "Wollen wir uns [in der Masse; hier: in der Schule] erhalten, so müssen wir suchen uns derselben anzupassen, wollen wir uns bemerkbar machen, müssen wir uns auszeichnen. Unsere Fügsamkeit wird geübt, unsere Selbständigkeit erweckt, unser Ehrgeiz angeregt" (*ML* I: 66). These girls are, as Elisabeth Blochmann suggests more generally about educated nineteenth-century girls (122), free to choose the objects of their platonic affection, to form new loyalties, and to make decisions about their own aversions (*ML* I: 66–67). Lewald couches this description in a discussion of the effect of schooling on children in general. Although she does not gender these "Kinder," she nevertheless compels her reader to read them as female, because she here describes the beginning of her own education. Here the difference between her fiction and her nonfiction in the construction of femininity becomes pronounced: no matter how capable Lewald's fictional heroines may be, she does not construct them as "independent" and "ambitious."[15] "Real" women, however, can be both, and these qualities are used to interest readers in their fates in much the same manner in which modesty and self-sacrifice are employed in the fictional texts—that is, to argue that the women who possess these qualities are worthy of notice, assistance, and/or admiration.

The use of "human" or even "masculine," rather than "feminine," characteristics to describe the women in her essays may indicate a mixed readership for Lewald's nonfiction, rather than the female majority that presumably read her novels. She addressed her "Osterbriefe," for instance, to the "fathers, brothers, and future husbands" of working-class women and, as mentioned above, dedicated her letters "Für und wider die Frauen" to John Stuart Mill. In one of these letters she emphasizes her certainty that among the readers of the newspaper in which they appear there are "Hunderte und Hunderte von Männern, von jungen Lehrern, Assessoren, Dozenten u.s.w." who can confirm the particular point she makes (173). She claims in another of the letters that she had written her autobiography, as well as her "Osterbriefe," "nur mit der bestimmten Absicht..., es den Frauen und den Männern, beiden, klar zu machen, was für die Erziehung der Frauen geschehen müsse" in order that women may assume the place in society to which every rational being is entitled (101). Men, after all, were in a better position to respond to some of the demands she made.

Like Louise Otto, she saw in them political helpers rather than opponents (Helmer, "Einleitung" 10). Lewald's satisfaction with this situation, however, seems to have had limits. She mentions a discussion she had had with several men about the possibility of girls being accepted as "Lehrlinge" in various trades. Each thought it was legally forbidden, although, as Lewald points out, it technically was not. If it were, she states, "so wären auch in diesem Punkte die Frauen mit der einstigen Änderung dieses Gesetzes auf den guten Willen der männlichen Gesetzgeber angewiesen, und wer von dem guten Willen anderer in diesen wichtigsten Angelegenheiten abhängt, ist eben ein *Unfreier und ein Höriger* [her emphasis]." Her solution, however, still depends on male goodwill:

> Es wäre dankenswert und wichtig, wenn ein der Gewerbetätigkeit der Frauen geneigter Mann, der zugleich ein gründlicher Kenner dieses Teils der Gesetzgebung wäre, den Frauen Aufschluß darüber geben wollte, worauf sie unter den bestehenden Gesetzen und Verordnungen mit ihren Bestrebungen zu rechnen und zu fußen haben. (*Für und wider* 184)

In any case, by characterizing schoolgirls as independent and ambitious, Lewald may have intended to inspire identification on the part of male readers, as well as to contribute to a redrawing of the boundaries of the "feminine" in print.

Reader expectations perhaps played a role as well. The novels Lewald wrote, for instance, demanded representations of virtue embodied in heroines so tractable they sometimes bordered on limp. Exclusive reference to this flabby excellence might have strained credibility in a forum in which even school directors admitted that the girls consigned to their care were not always as malleable and as pure as one might hope:

> Nicht immer ist in den Kindern welche uns anvertraut werden, das Heilige mit gleich zarter Sorge gepflegt worden, nicht überall findet sich der Boden des Herzens noch ganz rein, nicht überall erscheint uns an ihnen jene Hingebung, jene Liebe, jene Sanftmuth, jener Gehorsam, durch welchen erst jedes Wort der Lehre Eingang finden kann in die Seele. (Spilleke, "Rede" 24)

Lewald herself preferred the "neue bürgerliche Ideal der tatkräftigen, realistischen und zielstrebigen Frau" to the fragile and lovely indolence associated with the nobility (Helmer, "Einleitung" 7–8). Nevertheless, Rheinberg argues, the feminine ideal propagated by Lewald and other women who participated in the nineteenth-century women's movement was "stark an den traditionell weiblichen Tugenden 'Opfermut,' 'Hingabe' und 'Liebe' orientiert. Allerdings mit der Variante, daß diese Tugenden nun für den Dienst an der Allgemeinheit eingesetzt werden sollten" (204). Lewald censures, for instance, women who devote themselves to expensive trifles: how do these luxuries pertain to their love for their husbands and the "hingebende Sorge und Aufopferung für die Familie...als deren Mutter und Mitbegründerin die Frau dasteht?" (*Für und wider* 171). While Lewald's writings may have contributed to a redrawing of feminine boundaries, they were not designed to tear up the gender map.

The women who populate the fourteen letters of *Für und wider die Frauen* illustrate Lewald's view that women should receive an education that will enable them to work and that they are entitled to employment. This capability will make them more desirable marriage partners because husbands can be certain that their wives married out of affection, rather than to acquire a breadwinner, and if women do not marry, they will not encumber their fathers or siblings. Although Lewald reiterates in these essays her conviction that marriage to a beloved husband in a home that he provides (171) is always preferable to a life of independent employment, this view coexists uneasily with her recurring criticism of the "Beschränkung des freien Gebrauchs der angeborenen Fähigkeiten zu eigener Förderung" to which women are subject (109). One example of the two views attempting to cohabit in the same sentence occurs in a complaint about the old "Schreckbild der 'emanzipierten Frau,'" which casts its shadow on all those women, "die sich die Freiheit nehmen, ihre Talente auszubilden, ihre Fähigkeiten zu entwickeln und sich furchtlos und ihrer selbst gewiß in dem Leben und in der Welt zu bewegen, sich selbst zu ernähren und für sich selber einzustehen—wenn kein anderer da ist, welcher sie dieser Mühen überhebt" (165). Here the last clause sounds like an afterthought and as such appears to subvert its own nominal point.

Lewald reconciled these contradictions in her own life by marrying and continuing to write. She and Stahr each paid half the costs of the household. As Schneider points out, Lewald denied her heroines precisely this independence: they renounce their careers after marriage (*FL* 90). Stahr's tenuous health, however, must have functioned as partial justification for Lewald's continued employment: after his return from Italy, he had given up teaching for health reasons (Rheinberg 125) and was compelled to cobble together a living for his family through the writing of newspaper articles, essays, and reviews (Schneider, *FL* 87–88).

He was hardly in a position to become the sole provider of a second family. In this respect, Lewald's own life and marriage attest to one of the points she makes in *Für und wider die Frauen*. There are men, she argues, who "trotz aller ihrer Tüchtigkeit…oftmals nicht daran denken können, sich einen eigenen Herd zu gründen, weil ihr Erwerb zum Unterhalt für eine Familie nicht ausreichend ist." They may find a woman with whom they could otherwise be happy, but because she has been trained for nothing but housekeeping and thrift and can contribute nothing to the family income (unlike Lewald herself), her "eigentliche[r] weibliche[r] Beruf" comes to nothing (173).

Such women turn up repeatedly in these letters on women's rights to education and employment. Lewald tells the reader that she can add nothing new to the theoretical works on the subject, but those who do not have access to all these texts or who prefer practice to theory may find it useful "wenn eine Frau ihnen aus dem ziemlich weit reichenden Kreise ihrer persönlichen Erfahrungen immer und immer wieder die Beispiele vorhält, welche für diese gute Sache sprechen" (138–39). In other words, she has chosen her examples carefully and fully intends them to support the arguments of the women's movement. She further assures the reader of the validity of her observations: they are the fruit of much and varied experience.

Her cast includes both middle- and working-class women, whose character options are dependent on their class membership. Her working-class women are almost invariably the noble poor. One woman is elderly and ill; she staves off starvation with poorly paid knitting. Several others are young women from the country, desperate to defend their honor against the attempts made by unscrupulous bar owners to exploit them (150–53). Her middle-class women, on the other hand, are often deplorable. Their inactivity and deficient education have reduced them to the status of toys (137), and they are so limited that they ridicule those of their sex (140) who do not want to live a similarly "sanftes Haremsleben" (179). They spend their empty days cultivating migraines (171) and living beyond the means of their fathers and husbands, sometimes driving these men to white-collar crime (199). Further, their ignorance is so profound that they have no desire to learn (172, 177–78). Lewald's text contrasts one representative hypocrite whom the author "von dem Beruf der Gattin und der Mutter salbungs- und gefühlvoll predigen hörte," while having her children raised and her household run by servants, to the family's "unschöne, alternde" music teacher, who longs to have a child like the one her frivolous employer fails to appreciate. Where, the author asks, is true femininity? Do we find it

> bei der Gattin und Mutter, die ihre Muße für Nichtigkeiten verwendete, oder bei dem armen emanzipierten Mädchen, das wie ein Mann um des Lebens Notdurft kämpfte, das früh und spät zu Fuß und unbegleitet durch die entlegensten Straßen gehen mußte, das von seiner schweren Arbeit dem Staate seiner Steuer redlich zahlte und das in aller seiner Arbeit und Sorge noch das Herz hatte, für ein Kind arbeiten und leben zu wollen? (170)

Lewald knows that her question is rhetorical: her readers are supposed to have already found the answer in the "seelenvollen Augen" of the teacher, "den Knaben an ihr Herz drückend und küssend" (170).

This hard-working, taxpaying, child-loving, unmarried, underpaid teacher is paradigmatic of the middle-class female alternative Lewald also presents in these letters, the "tatkräftigen, realistischen und zielstrebigen" women to whom Helmer referred ("Einleitung" 7). These women long for an education in order to free themselves and their families from the burden of supporting an unmarried daughter. They are the pitiable, long-suffering hostages of a father's misguided sense of his own honor, unable to work because their employment would encroach on the authority of the "Familienoberhaupt." This authority is based on a solvency that enables him to support the women of the family in idle plenty (111–12). There is the "sehr geschickte" daughter of a brave but sickly mother and a drunken father, who becomes such a talented bookbinder that she can outstitch even very skillful journeymen. Her sensible and appreciative benefactor wants to make a master bookbinder of her (124–25). The "kleine, reizende, geistreiche" Auguste achieves her goals even without a benefactor: once a poor and dependent lady companion, she "rises," as far as Lewald is concerned, to become the owner of a shop that sells undergarments and that makes her the scourge of her horrified circle of former acquaintances (134–36). There are also potential "medizinische Genies" or "große kaufmännische Talente" whose position, Lewald claims, is "in gewissem Sinne" worse than that of the American slaves: while the slave can always be certain of having an owner, a woman may wait in vain for a husband (109–10). These women are "unbescholtene, ehrbare, einem ernsten Streben hingegebene Frauenzimmer" who should not be hindered in their desire to study (185).

And these examples are persuasive. They work in part because they are affecting portraits of "deserving" women of modest, helpful desires, opposed by other examples of women with whom few readers were likely to identify willingly, and in part because Lewald makes clear her commitment to a traditional model of femininity. She censures women who violate "ihre beschworenen Pflichten und...die Sitte" (165), underscores the respectability of the worthy women she presents to the reader, and maintains that women should subordinate themselves to their "tüchtigen" husbands voluntarily (195). These arguments serve to mitigate the otherwise shocking effect of the message that women must have options. Traditional values and conventional morality, in other words, are not under siege: women want to subordinate themselves to a beloved husband; should no husband appear, these educated, self-supporting women will not violate gendered codes of moral behavior. She assumes the best of her male readers, asking "Was hat Euch eine Frau, die kein eigenes Geistesleben führt, die nichts Rechtes weiß und nichts Rechtes kann, was hat sie Euch hinzugeben als eben ihren Körper? Und begehrt Ihr von der Ehe nichts als Befriedigung Eures sinnlichen Verlangens?" and apparently expecting the response to be "No." Should the reader hesitate, however, she reminds him that women are destined not merely for sexual exploitation: "Bedürft Ihr nicht der ernsten Erzieherin für Eure Söhne, der vorsichtigen Beraterin für Eure Tochter, der klugen Verwalterin Eures Erwerbes?" (172–73). By linking education to the creation of exemplary wives, mothers, and housekeepers, Lewald makes girls' education not only acceptable, but necessary to traditional family structures.

## III

Betty Gleim had argued in 1810 that intellectual development, far from distracting women from their vocation, would help prevent the "innere Leere and Langeweile...die Unfähigkeit, sich selbst zu beschäftigen...die Begierde, sich zu zeigen; die Eitelkeit, die Putzsucht, die Gefallsucht" that not only make many women so discontent in their own homes, but cause them to seek their pleasure elsewhere (qtd. in E. Blochmann 112). In this respect, a substantive education actually supports the exercise of "Bestimmung." Seventy years later, Lewald made the same point in her "In Ragaz" (1880), which recounts the story of a crisis in the marriage of a

French couple, Delmar and Rose. This tale also demonstrates Lewald's contention that it is "der Müßiggang und die Geistesleere, welche eine große Anzahl Frauen zu einem spielenden Spielzeug heruntergedrückt haben" (*Für und wider* 137) and indirectly criticizes schools like the one Karoline Rudolphi directed. The institution shares the blame with the husband who fails to continue its educational task.

For Lewald, men are "Erzieher, Aufklärer, Lehrer der Frau" (Helmer, "Nachwort" 276); they have a duty to assist in the further development of their wives, sisters, and daughters (Rheinberg 179). As she puts it, "die Erziehung der Frauen wird zum großen Teil, wenn nicht durch die Männer selbst, so durch unsere Liebe für sie bewirkt" (*ML* I: 199). Lewald herself enjoyed honoring Stahr as her superior in erudition and information, contrasting his "klassische Bildung des 'wirklichen Wissens'" with her own "rudimentäre des 'zufälligen Könnens'" (Schneider, *FL* 61). Rheinberg maintains that Lewald found a "lebenslangen Lehrer" in Stahr (116). Although his tendency to instruct or correct her irritated her occasionally during their early acquaintance, she felt "daß [sie] ihm etwas wert sein mußte, weil er sich so bemühte, [sie] aufzuklären und [ihr] Urteil zu berichtigen" (qtd. in Rheinberg 121). Her gratitude to Stahr echoes her gratitude to Leopold Bock, her first fiancé. In addition to mentioning the "great benefit" she gained from his direction of her reading, Lewald credits Leopold with improving her character:

> eben diese Liebe, eben dieser Glaube an mich erhoben mich allmählich; und was die Jahre hindurch fortgesetzte Bemühung meines Vaters doch nicht in dem nötigen Maße erreicht hatte, mir—abgesehen von der Entwicklung des Verstandes—einen wahrhaft sittlichen innern Halt und meinem Gemütsleben die rechte Entfaltung zu geben, das vollbrachte die vertrauende Liebe eines reinen Männerherzens in sehr kurzer Zeit. (*ML* I: 192–93)

Lewald's view was not new. Marie von Clausewitz hinted at its prevalence in 1812:

> Unsere wahre Vollendung erhalten wir erst durch die Hand der Liebe. Ich brauche wohl kaum zu sagen, daß ich dies alles in einem höheren Sinn nehme und keineswegs der Meinung bin, daß ein Mann seine Frau wie ein unmündiges Kind erziehen müsse; diese Ansicht ist mir im Gegenteil immer ein Greuel gewesen, und ich kann mir nicht denken, daß daraus je ein schönes und würdiges und für beide Teile befriedigendes Verhältnis entstehen kann. (qtd. in E. Blochmann 46)

Lewald's "In Ragaz" argues, however, that men who fail to guide their wives at all put them at risk. The heroine of this story has received an inadequate education, both at school and from her husband, and this lack endangers first her marriage and then her life.

The narrative opens with Delmar's first attack of gout, which inspires him to take a wife and start a family. Attractive, wealthy, and forty-three, his circle considers him a very desirable prospective husband. When a female friend suggests her seventeen-year-old niece, Rose, as an appropriate match, her picture elicits Delmar's ecstatic "Welch' eine Anmuth, welch' eine Kindlichkeit!" (8). Rose's "Kindlichkeit" is her most enduring feature, and she becomes her husband's first and only child: "Er wollte ihr Geliebter und ihr Erzieher, ihr Gatte und ihr Vater, mit einem Wort ihr Ein und Alles sein" (14). Lewald's text indicates, however, that Delmar fails to raise his young wife properly. Fresh from a convent education that, although it had given her a smattering of English and Italian (17), had focused primarily on producing "kleine Heilige" (13), Rose finds an overindulgent father in Delmar. Her barren body and her lack of a maternal urge, which she happily attributes to her selfishness (15–16), intimate that her childlike mind and manner are warning signs and that her husband indulges both at his peril.

Although Rose and Delmar enjoy fifteen years of marital harmony, the narrative eventually makes good on its ominous hint. Delmar's gout necessitates regular journeys to Baden-Baden, where Rose finds herself "in ihrem Elemente" (17). Here she can use the foreign phrases she had learned in school and relish the effect of her own charms: "Sie kam sich in diesem buntscheckigen Sprachenaufputz stets sehr reizend vor. Sie liebte es, die Wirkung ihrer Anmuth in weiterem und immer neuem Kreise zu erproben" (18). Although the reader raises an eyebrow at this revelation, Delmar does not: he enjoys taking his lovely and devoted young wife to Germany every year, where they see the old friends who "seiner Rose den Hof machten und ihr den Willen thaten, wie er selber" (18). In 1870, however, Baden-Baden is no longer an appropriate destination for this French couple. Because the Germans have won the "von den Franzosen unheilvoll heraufbeschworenen Krieg" (20), Delmar and Rose go to Switzerland instead. Their hotel rooms remind Rose of rooms in the convent in which she was educated (26–27), and this similarity frames an event that acts as implicit condemnation of the chronically deficient

"Erziehung" she has experienced throughout life.

Fleeting references to the convent and what it offers its pupils are interspersed in the text with discussions of Delmar's permissive "education" of his childlike wife. He had begun with good intentions: "Er wollte ihre guten Anlagen entwickeln, ihre Vorstellungen berichtigen, um sie und sich vor den Gefahren zu beschützen, welche der Jugend und der Schönheit drohen." The text suggests, however, that what superseded these was a second desire: "aber soweit es immer möglich war, sollte sie sie selber bleiben" (14). Lewald's text makes in response the stern point that women are not children and that they must be shaped and molded for adult responsibility by a benevolent husband and teacher. The convent school had accomplished its task of producing qualities that "in der Ehe und in der Welt, in welcher man lebte, doch einmal nicht erhalten bleiben konnten" (13), and it was Delmar's duty to nurture other qualities that would make an honorable woman of the innocent girl. In this respect, the text suggests that a woman's life is one very long day of instruction. Formal schooling provides no more than basic knowledge; a husband at the domestic blackboard supplies the rest. Delmar's reluctance to do anything but humor his child-bride, however, exacerbates the legacy of the inadequate convent school where Rose had been taught to "lächeln und zu gehorchen" (73). She becomes a woman whose favorite occupation is registering her own pleasing effect on others.

Delmar, now nearly sixty, finds an old school friend at the spa, leaving his bored young wife to befriend a melancholy Swiss woman, Fides, and her husband, Joseph. Fides and Joseph have known and loved each other since childhood. The orphaned daughter of a goatherd, she had grown up in Joseph's father's house. Joseph became a physician and, against his parents' wishes, married Fides. They were reconciled with his parents after Joseph cured his mother of an illness. They also had two sons, both of whom have recently died.

Educationally speaking, they are a paradigmatic couple: Fides learns through her husband and for him. Shy and sad as a child, she had made no progress in school until Joseph began to tutor her. Reading and writing were mediated through him, as are subsequent lessons in life. Before they married, she had worked for friends of his who gave her, in addition to the job, "Unterricht und Lehre" (63). In contrast to Rose, Fides fills her days at home with activity: she manages the house and the farm and acts as her husband's pharmacist (115), a skill she presumably learned from him. She plans to spend the winter filling in the gaps in her education in order to offer her husband the intellectual companionship he would otherwise have found in their growing boys (132). Even after years of marriage, Joseph maintains his firm grip on Fides's character development: contemplating an action, he decides against it because it would encourage Fides "sich in ähnlichen Fällen in ähnlicher Weise nachzugeben und gehen zu lassen" (141).

Fides's story fascinates Rose, and she consumes her new friend's life as though it were a novel: she was "von der einfachen Erzählung mehr gefesselt, als je von einem erdichteten Roman" (59). Describing the story later, Delmar says, "[M]eine Frau ist hingenommen von dieser neuen Dorfgeschichte aus dem Leben" (68). Rose realizes that she herself has never experienced any passion, and, at an embarrassing loss when Fides asks her about her own life, she casts that fact as her tragedy in her response (72–73). She begins to spend most of her time with Fides and Joseph; "zum Zeitvertreib," she determines to draw the latter's attentions to herself (82). Eventually she persuades herself that she is even in love with her friend's husband and that Delmar's age justifies her emotional infidelity.

The narrative repeatedly shifts position on the relevance of the age difference. Although her years and Delmar's are a persistent theme, Rose's reprehensibility as a heroine seems to discount her own attempts to excuse herself. The narrative, however, has charged Delmar with the responsibility for Rose's character. She entered into marriage a good-natured schoolgirl with "keine[m] unbeugsamen Willen," whom the nuns at her convent school had found more "behandelbar" than all her classmates (10), and she has become a self-absorbed coquette who enjoys her new inner turmoil simply because it occupies her (86). Delmar's lapse, therefore, does not primarily consist of marrying a much younger woman, but of failing to use his age and experience to mold her appropriately. He has a tardy and short-lived moment of insight early in their stay in Ragaz: "Rose war trotz aller ihrer Anmut ein verzogenes Kind, und er trug daran die Schuld" (86). Later, however, he insists that he and Rose "[sich] immer gut dabei befunden [haben], daß [er] ihr freie Hand ließ" (120). Joseph, however, concurs with Delmar's earlier assessment when he muses that "mit einem anderen, ihr gleichaltrigen und strengeren Manne

Rose vielleicht mehr hätte werden können, als das liebenswürdige, selbstische und eigenwillige Kind, das sie *geblieben* war [my emphasis]" (140).

Delmar's old friends discern Rose's intentions and suspect Joseph of complicity; they warn both Delmar and Fides. Fides tells her husband what she has heard. He takes offense at his humble, submissive wife's apparent lack of faith in him and announces that they will leave for home that day. Rose seeks him out in order to make a farewell declaration of her love, imagining that they will share a romantic moment of renunciation and then be left to their lingering memories. Joseph's polite rejection leaves her humiliated and, of course, in the grip of a "Nervenfieber" (169). Rose and Delmar return to France, where rumors of suicide accompany her subsequent death. As she had once said,

> Gott...hat [mich] auf die Welt kommen lassen, damit ich mich an ihr erfreue und den Anderen gefalle. Sehe ich, daß mir dies gelingt, so hab ich ein gut Gewissen, denn ich erfülle meinen Beruf. Freut sich meiner niemand, so komme ich mir unnütz vor...und der Tag, an welchem ich mir sagen müßte, daß ich nicht mehr zu gefallen vermöge, würde mein letzter Tag sein. (23)

Lewald's narrative censures such pathological "femininity," arguing that women's "profession" mandates somewhat more substantial contributions and that men must form these nascent professionals into women like Fides who know how to occupy themselves with serious wifely pursuits. Rose's last reported statement is "Der Zeitvertreib, das ist die Sünde! Das ist der Tod! der Tod!" (170). Her author argues for the kind of meaningful intellectual and physical employment that makes the distractions of flirtation unnecessary. Only the education for such employment makes "tüchtige Frauen" (*Für und wider* 146) of the female "children" given to schools and to husbands to raise.

## IV

Some women, of course, required "employment" not only for character development but for subsistence. While most professions were closed to women, teaching, especially small children, was an occupation that one might represent as women's work (M. Blochmann 36). The teacher did not simply impart "technische Geschicklichkeiten," she disseminated femininity: "von deren weiblicher Charakterbildung [kann] man sich auch sonst großen Gewinn für die Kultur der zarten Gemüter unserer Töchter mit Recht vesprechen" (qtd. in E. Blochmann 118). Female teachers themselves argued for recognition of their unique ability to serve as a "Vorbild...von echter Weiblichkeit, von Offenheit und Wahrheitsliebe, von treuer Pflichterfüllung, von offenem Sinne für alles Gute, Schöne und Edle" (Marie Calm, qtd. in M. Blochmann 42). It was also, as Helene Lange would argue in 1890, "gute deutsche Sitte" that "Frauen vorwiegend durch Frauen erzogen werden" (qtd. in M. Blochmann 81). Not that the presence of women at the front of the classroom was undisputed, however. Many insisted that such learnedness in women was unnatural and that female teachers would become a "Karikatur des Weiblichen." "Gerate sie im Unterricht einmal aus der Fassung," for instance, "so stehe sie 'sogleich in den Verzerrungsmasken einer Furie da,' während der Lehrer, der seinen Unmut 'zu titanhafter Entrüstung' steigere, immer noch eine 'imposante Erscheinung' sei" (M. Blochmann 31). Other factors complicated the ideological positions on "femininity" that inform each of these viewpoints: there were periodic shortages of male teachers (Albisetti 50, 67), parents were sometimes reluctant to send their daughters to schools staffed by men (Albisetti 41), unmarried women required some means of support, and, although the life of an unmarried female teacher could look unattractive to girls being educated to be wives and mothers, her very career undermined the otherwise omnipresent insistence on women's alleged sole vocation.

With the novel *Nella. Eine Weihnachtsgeschichte*, Lewald responds to those who would argue against the utility of girls' schools and against a curriculum that prepares women to provide for themselves as teachers. She contests the alleged detriment of education to families and to a woman's "Bestimmung" by suggesting that the most advanced education available to women can be an absolute prerequisite to their domestic success. Her novel insists on the advantages of education to women and their families, reconciling these advantages with Lewald's conditional support of the contemporary feminine ideal. Nella, the educated female protagonist, remains an exemplary and devoted daughter despite her schooling. Further, her education alone makes it possible for her to become the wife, rather than the mistress, of the man with whom she has had a bond since childhood. She is a working-class girl who receives an education that prepares her either to support herself as a teacher or to marry into the "Besitz-" and "Bildungsbürgertum" of her future in-laws.

The author employs contemporary educational structures and professions typically pursued by educated women in a plot that insists that adequate schooling will not disrupt the social order as far as class and gender hierarchies are concerned. Rather, the traditional order can benefit from its confirmation by worthy newcomers.

Nella's future father-in-law, Peter Aegidius Vandermehren, is the latest in a long line of factory owners, the first of whom had worked themselves up from relatively low origins. He marries Livia, a governess whom he had met in his travels and who had impressed him with her beauty, the "Schärfe ihres Verstandes und...ein Zug von tüchtiger Beharrlichkeit," which reminds him of his own (13). Though without any fortune of her own, she was the daughter of a renowned professor, and in the early years of her marriage she wields the "großen and schönen Gedanken" that allegedly had been paramount in her father's house as an effective weapon against Vandermehren's sense of his own superiority to her (28). They have a son, Aurel, whose birth occasions the founding of a school for the male and female children of the factory workers. Gertrud, the wife of one of Vandermehren's workers, becomes Aurel's wet nurse. Gertrud and her husband enjoy reading, maintain a charmingly clean little home, and later have a daughter, Nella. Aurel and Nella grow into childhood playmates, although the jealous Livia subtly opposes their friendship. At eleven, Nella hears for the first time from her father that the factory owner's family is not "[ihres] Gleichen" and that she "nicht hin[gehört]" (71). Somewhat later she says to her surprised father and teacher, "[I]ch möchte höher hinaus." Her father is irritated, but the teacher responds, "Lerne nur ordentlich!...nachher wird man ja sehen, wozu man Dich gebrauchen kann!" (108). She subsequently witnesses the suicide of the factory worker Franz Savion and the director's daughter Emma, who had been denied her father's permission to marry because of their class differences (despite Franz's shirt collar, which "sauberer aussah, als der seiner sämmtlichen Genossen" [102]). Franz may have been inspired by an unnamed George Sand novel, in which "[d]ie Liebe eines jungen Mannes von geringer Herkunft zu einer vornehmen Schönen...eine Hauptrolle [spielte]" (110). Further, Nella's father and teacher know that Franz "sich viel mit dem Lesen sozialistischer Schriften beschäftigte" (106). As the teacher once concluded, "[Franz] versteht sein Fach, an Gaben hat's ihm Gott nicht fehlen lassen, und er ist ein schöner Mensch.

Aber er ist an die falschen Propheten gekommen, und das bringt man mit aller Vernunft nicht mehr aus ihm heraus" (109). Franz and Emma's attempt to overcome class barriers is premature; their failure reflects Lewald's opinion of those "false prophets" to whom Franz has turned.[16] The narrative leaves it to Nella—whose education has been more substantial than Franz's French novels and socialist tracts—to cross the chasm separating her from the factory owner's son.

Vandermehren's district elects him its representative, and he and Livia spend much of their time in Berlin, while Aurel studies languages at a boarding school in Switzerland with a tutor who covers the remaining subjects. Livia schemes to send Nella away because she resents Aurel's continuing affection for her. Nella is the "begabteste und lernbegierigste" of all the students at the local school (147), which works to Livia's advantage. The teacher has asked for an assistant who can address the female factory workers' deficient skills in "weiblichen Arbeiten" by giving the younger children preparation for the sewing and knitting courses. He would prefer a teacher who had been trained at one of the Fröbel schools (146). Livia suggests educating one of the school's own pupils for the position. As the most talented of these, Nella is the logical choice. Friedrich Fröbel (1782–1852) was a pedagogue who had been influenced by Rousseau and Pestalozzi and had founded the first kindergartens.[17] His adherents were active in the attempt in the 1860s to improve women's education for motherhood (Albisetti 99). Livia and the schoolteacher have chosen a candidate whose education will indeed prepare her for motherhood, although not solely by training her in instructional techniques for small children. Contrary to Livia's expectations, the beneficiaries of Nella's education will be Aurel and his children.

Livia sends Nella to a well-regarded boarding school far from home run by an old friend of hers and receives regular reports on Nella's exceptional progress. Her physical and intellectual development is rapid, she is popular with students and teachers alike, and her truthfulness and her seriousness endear her to the director. The director believes that she will make an excellent teacher and governess, thanks not only to her significant progress in the "Wissenschaften," foreign languages, and music, but to her "rasche, entschlossene Selbstüberwindung, derer man nicht entbehren darf, wenn man bestimmt ist, unter der Abhängigkeit von Fremden seinen Weg durch das Leben zu gehen" (159–60). She convinces

Nella that many people, particularly women, "von der Vorsehung nicht zum Glücke bestimmt, und also berufen wären, ihre Zufriedenheit in entsagendem Wirken und das Wohl der Andern zu begründen" and that Nella, too, belongs to this unhappy sisterhood (182). The director's cheerless view of the life of a governess corresponds to Livia's early account of her own existence before she married, and the sympathetic reader may question the value of an education that prepares women for such misery. Yet the narrative eventually counters its own portrayal with a plot development that underscores the positive aspects of the education Nella has received. Although teaching was virtually the only occupation open to women, it offered at least the choice of the "strangers" on whom one would depend, as well as the opportunity to escape other, less tenable situations. In a moment of crisis, Nella avails herself of this limited option in order to save her parents, demonstrating both the value of education for girls and a filial devotion unaltered by such education.

Still in Switzerland, Aurel sees a picture that his cousin has painted of the now strikingly beautiful Nella and writes to her. The director inspects mail not sent by family members, however, a precaution Aurel does not anticipate. His lack of suspicion suggests, assuming that Lewald intended plausibility, that epistolary chaperones were reading between the lines only at girls' schools and that Aurel's own mail had never been subject to institutional scrutiny. The director dictates a cold response, which Aurel, believing it to be Nella's own formulation, reads as proof that she has become a "pedantische Gouvernante" (203) who had written to him "als wäre sie schon eine alte Jungfer" (232). With this bit of dialogue, Lewald participates in the maintenance of a female stereotype, the prudish spinster schoolteacher. The narrator refers to the school's director as one of the "alten Mädchen, die für sich selbst auf Liebesglück verzichtet haben" (181), and Aurel, the male protagonist, can "read" that desiccated self-denial in the letter the director writes for Nella.

Several years later, Aurel returns home, where his parents have built a castle on the heights above their old mansion—which had been near the factory—and arranged for their own accession to the nobility. This development horrifies Aurel, who is a proud, upstanding "Bürger." He visits Gertrud, reads all of Nella's letters to her parents, and realizes that he loves her. He enters his father's business, proves himself a worthy successor, and sees Nella, now a teacher at the boarding school, when she returns home on a visit. Their familial origins are irrelevant now, and their gendered character traits complement one another perfectly: "ein herrlicheres junges Paar hatte selten Brust an Brust geruht; Er, voll entwickelt in stolzer freier Männlichkeit; Sie, schön erblüht im Reize weiblicher bewußter Zurückhaltung" (265). Nella returns Aurel's love, but his parents and her father oppose their relationship. While Aurel is away on a business trip, Vandermehren fires Nella's father as part of an attempt to get rid of Nella. She offers to leave voluntarily, so that her aging parents will not be forced out of their home. She has that option because her education qualifies her to take a job as a governess with the family of a Russian general living in the Crimea. Because of her education and her experience, she can contemplate a relocation that would mean death to her parents, to whom "jenseit dieser Berge die Fremde an[fängt]" (325). When Aurel discovers what his parents have done, he leaves his family in order to start his own business and to search for Nella. His mother, whose maternal heart is broken, finally persuades Vandermehren to permit the marriage. The family reunites on Christmas Eve.

Nella becomes a source of pride for her in-laws when the new "schöne Baronin" visits them in Berlin. Her own mother then stays in the castle to care for her grandchildren. The two sets of parents preserve the class differences that Nella overcame through education: Nella's factory-worker parents, though welcome in Schloß Vandermehren, choose to stay in their old home. This conciliatory outcome indicates to readers that educating particularly talented members of the lower classes is a risk-free proposition as far as the traditional world order is concerned. Aurel himself remains firmly anchored in the middle class, despite the family's embarrassing new title. Although his father may want to distance himself physically and socially from the factory that enriched him and his forebears, Aurel and Lewald, his creator, proclaim their own preference with the choice of tidy, book-loving, working-class parents-in-law—who like their own comfortable cottage.

Lewald appears at first to repeat the ambivalence of her resolution of the question of class differences in her characterization of women's education. Although education, as Livia once puts it, brings "Unterricht und Aufklärung" to the masses (35); although the author makes women the primary providers of that enlightenment, at least to children and female adolescents; and although only Nella's boarding school education qualifies her for marriage to Aurel, Lewald's view of the options education gives women seems bleak aside from the fact that it offers options at all. The employment for which an education can prepare them is clearly second best: it is not the happiness that providence has reserved for more fortunate women. On the day on which Nella passes her exams with high marks and enters the ranks of the school's teachers, "[kommt] ein unaussprechliches Gefühl der Angst, der Unfreiheit und der Verzagtheit über sie" (183). As discussed above, Lewald repeatedly affirmed the secondary nature of paid employment for women in her fiction and nonfiction.

Yet although a career in education does not adequately substitute for marriage, learning itself gives women significant advantages. Lewald's *Nella* uses an incident at the local school to suggest that although education may expose women to the ridicule of the ignorant, it ultimately strengthens them. In this incident, early in the novel, Aurel's schoolmates mock a new innovation: "auch die Mädchen in der Aureliusschule turnen"; the spectacle is "ein reiner Jokus" (58–59). The request of one boy for tickets, "wenn die Mädchen ihr Schauturnen haben und Rad schlagen werden" (59), suggests that contemporary objections to girls' physical education included the presumptive salacious response of observers. In his *Schooling German Girls and Women*, Albisetti in fact notes that parents resisted the introduction of special clothing for such exercise at the turn of the century because they "objected to their daughters' legs being exposed" (49). Lewald, however, gives Aurel the task of defending the practice: "Meine Eltern haben es angeordnet, weil es die Mädchen kräftiger machen soll" (59). The author's supportive introduction of this controversial discipline for girls into her text demonstrates her own pedagogical progressiveness and her cognizance of educational trends. In her study of girls' education in Lübeck, Zander states that doctors were the first to suggest physical exercise for girls, but that their suggestions were ignored until the second half of the nineteenth century. As one of the earliest school systems to do so, Lübeck mandated gymnastics for the girls' elementary schools in 1876. Zander notes that Prussia did not have similar requirements until 1905 (240–41).

Lewald's text argues that education strengthens the social position of women as well. The narrative points to the more sordid side of life for uneducated women in Vandermehren's assertion that Livia should never have sent Nella away to school: "Ohne diese Bildung hätte Aurel vielleicht irgend eine Affaire mit dem Mädchen haben können; an eine Heirat mit ihr zu denken, würde ihm nicht eingefallen sein" (295). Lewald's characterization of Nella and Aurel suggests otherwise, but the dialogue she writes for Vandermehren indicates that education makes women generally less vulnerable to sexual exploitation. She makes that point elsewhere as well. Girls who are left without an "Ernährer" and have not been educated for a career, for instance, "nur zu oft dahin [geraten], sich je nach ihrem Stande, ein für allemal an den Ersten Besten oder sich alltäglich zu verkaufen und in diesem letzteren Falle meist ein Ende zu nehmen, von welchem die Phantasie es aus keuscher Selbstsucht in der Regel sehr geraten findet, das Auge abzuwenden" (*Für und wider* 110).

Finally, education can actually make women more appealing and therefore more likely to find a husband and employment in the domestic sphere. Although Aurel had been fond of Nella as a child, he falls in love with her only after reading the letters she had written to her parents from her boarding school: "Er wurde es nicht müde, die Briefe immer auf das Neue anzusehen. Alles rührte, Alles entzückte ihn an denselben. Bald lächelte er über die noch ungeübten Federzüge in den ersten Briefen, um daneben Nella's jetzige fast männlich sichere Handschrift zu bewundern" (237). Her education has given Nella an expressive ability that separates her from her origins (not to mention a confidence only categorizable as "masculine"). Her parents, too, can read that difference and worry that they have lost her: "Kannst du mit ihr reden, wie sie schreibt? Es klingt sehr gut, es klingt gerade wie aus den Büchern" (187). Nella acknowledges the debt Aurel's love owes to her educational opportunities in the farewell letter she writes before leaving for the Crimea. As she puts it, "Ich kann nicht Unfrieden bringen in das Haus Deiner Eltern, denen ich danke, was ich bin, denen ich danke, daß Du mich zu lieben vermochtest" (329). Lewald wrote a love story and she makes the obligatory nod to the power of love: after reading Aurel's first letter to her, Nella leaves the director's room "weit über ihren bisherigen Zustand hinausgehoben mit dem Bewußtsein ihrer Liebe" (180). The rest of her novel, however, details the far more significant role that education played in moving Nella into the Vandermehren mansion and reassures the reader that "Bildung" does not detract from any of the "feminine" qualities that make exemplary wives, mothers, daughters, and daughters-in-law. Far from it: Nella's education has made an unassuming, universally admired woman of an unassuming, intelligent girl. In other words, Nella's schooling has enhanced her natural abilities, while preserving the traditional feminine ideal, and has enabled her to realize her "Bestimmung" with the appropriate man. And she opts for that vocation, rather than for a career as a teacher. What more could the average critic of girls' education want?

V

That critic might, for example, prefer a less subversive "advocate." Although the outlines of the plot of *Nella* appear to conform to traditional notions of femininity and female possibility, the author employs her story to contest the outmoded social structures that would deny (deserving) members of the working class entrance to the "Bürgertum" above it. Through education, Nella gains admittance to the middle class, the class Lewald preferred by far to any other. The intellectual advancement her awed parents can read in her letters mirrors the improvement in her social position. In this respect, Lewald contests in her novel the outmoded social structures that hinder female educational advancement as well. Lewald makes this point most overtly in her essays. These are also a forum in which she narrativizes the fates of the brave and earnest daughters of the deluded men who would deny them the opportunity to provide for themselves should they fail to make an appropriate match. The crossing of the boundaries of genre marks the philosophical consistency of her fiction and nonfiction. Despite the apparent conventionality of her fictional heroines, they go to the barricades with the "real" women who make the author's persuasive argument for the necessity of adequate education for girls.

Rheinberg states that Lewald's own life served as an example of a successful "Frauenemanzipation," which she herself recognized (178) and which was consonant with her pride in her own domesticity and her support of a version of the traditional feminine ideal. She incarnated her own theories not least because she was the product of a "Mädchenerziehung" that gave her the desire for more and better education. In both her fictional and her nonfictional texts she makes an apparent attempt to allay the fears—in part by raising other specters—of those who opposed educational improvements for women who were destined to be wives and mothers. Nevertheless, the inherent contradiction of educating girls solely for the domestic environment is a visible crack in the story of a woman "saved" from a career as a governess in exile; it yawns wider in the tale of a childless, wayward former pupil of a convent; and it gapes alarmingly in Lewald's ambiguous claim that a woman should be free to develop her talents and her abilities, and to confront life and its demands with fearless self-assurance—unless a man should offer to do that for her (*Für und wider* 165). Although Lewald partially attributes her own achievements to the men who had "guided" her, her texts and her life suggest that conservative fears were justified: one may be able to take the girl out of the school at thirteen, but taking the school out of the girl may prove difficult.

In the texts discussed in this chapter, Lewald argues that education for women will not lessen their desire to marry and that it makes good marriages better. Other narratives, however, subtly undermine the contemporary assumption that marriage and family life as such both benefit and satisfy all women. These narratives are the subject of Chapter Four.

# CHAPTER FOUR

# "Daß dir ziehe Glück ins Haus / Schaue nicht zu weit hinaus!":[1] Lewald and Domestic Ideology

On her first trip to Germany in the winter of 1854/1855, George Eliot was introduced to Fanny Lewald and Adolf Stahr. As Gabriele Schneider points out, there were a number of parallels between the lives of the two women, which included their unconventional domestic arrangements (*FL* 78–79). In July 1854, Eliot had begun living with George Henry Lewes, a married man who was unable to obtain a divorce. Their twenty-four-year relationship ended with his death in 1878 (Rose 206). Lewald and Stahr waited nine years for his wife's consent to a divorce. Since 1852 they had lived near one another in Berlin. Writing to a friend soon after Stahr's arrival, Lewald explains that they do not share an apartment because Stahr opposes it: they lack the "Gewerbeschein." "Indes," she continues, "er kommt schon Morgens 8 Uhr zum Frühstück u[nd] bleibt in seiner für ihn eingerichteten Arbeitsstube bis zur Nacht bei mir" (qtd. in Rheinberg 136). Eliot and Lewes were never able to legalize their union and spent their years together in contented seclusion, since Eliot "could not be received in society" (Rose 220). Lewald and Stahr, on the other hand, married at last on 6 February 1855. Three years later Lewald wrote in her diary, "Ich genieße jetzt unsere bürgerliche Ehe als ein großes Glück, jetzt muß ich zugeben, daß das sichere Beruhen, die Übereinstimmung mit dem Hergebrachten auch sehr süß sind" (qtd. in Rheinberg 140). As uncommon as her life as a writer (and "other woman") had been, Lewald appeared to exercise her "Bestimmung," the alleged vocation of women for domestic life, with pleasure. She took pride in creating a cozy and home-like environment wherever she and Stahr traveled, enjoyed caring for her family members, and found satisfaction in household management: "So legte sie beispielsweise äußersten Wert auf eine korrekte Haushaltsabrechnung, die sie dann Stahr alljährlich zum Jahresende präsentierte" (Rheinberg 140).

The "presentation" of the household accounts to Stahr, who paid only half of the household expenses (Schneider, *FL* 90), points to Lewald's capacity for gestures that belie, and thereby facilitate, less conventional behavior. Rheinberg claims, for instance, that Lewald was the dominant spouse and notes that Stahr's niece once said that Lewald was "klug genug, es den Gatten nicht merken zu lassen" (145). This tactic may illuminate an aspect of Lewald's narrative strategy. In several fictional accounts of marriage and family, Lewald unites the symbolic commonplace with a potentially inconvenient or even uncomfortable subtext. Her *Clementine* (1843) offers the reader a worthy heroine who marries out of a sense of duty to both her family and her unknown suitor, then renounces an illicit love—and is unhappy. In *Schloß Tannenburg* (1859), the author undermines her portrayal of an allegedly ideal family by appearing to ask (to paraphrase a reviewer of Alissa Walser's "Geschenkt") "where a brother's love ends and incest begins" (Krüger-Fürhoff 71).[2] Although the reader knows that no taboos have been transgressed, the question itself invites a re-reading of the ideal as such. Finally, in "Der Magnetberg" (1880), Lewald reiterates her frequent statement that women are happiest when married (although Clementine's experience would appear to contradict this assertion). Nevertheless, her plot suggests that women must first experience destitution in order to appreciate domestic life. Written over the course of almost forty years, a timespan that included the rise of the German women's movement, these texts display an increasing suspicion of the ideal. Clementine's unhappy sacrifice, for instance, gives way to the transient rebellion of the female protagonist of "Der Magnetberg."

Lewald was by all accounts a happy homemaker, and yet her visions of domestic harmony are sometimes oddly out of tune. Does she write a darker version of her own atypical, yet happy, marriage? Does she write for readers who had experienced the disjuncture between the real and ideal family firsthand? Are her texts meant as a contribution to the definitions of "femininity" and to the evolving vision of "family" in the nineteenth century? In her discussion of the change in domestic paradigms that began in the eighteenth century, Heidi Rosenbaum argues that the dissemination in literature of new models of "family" is predicated on the assumption that readers will find some aspect of their own experience reflected in the text (262–63). Karen Pawluk Danford suggests that literary reflections of the family could be ambiguous:

> Realist writers were faced with the dilemma of reconciling actual social circumstances and the social beliefs of the middle classes which focused on the family as the moral foundation of society. In addition, and on a deeper level, they confronted the role of the family as both a source of idyll in that it provides the images of relationships which would seem to satisfy the human longing for community and security, and a source of tragedy in that precisely these powerful intimate and authoritarian relationships come into conflict with individual desires and self-expression. (143)[3]

By the mid-nineteenth century, if Lewald's texts are any guide, readers' experience included some doubt about the alleged satisfaction to be gained from women's "vocation" and an awareness of the potential pathology of family life. It also incorporated a recognition of the bleak alternatives to life within the domestic circle in an age that made the domesticity of women a defining characteristic of the middle class. The modern family, a creation of the late eighteenth and nineteenth century, was predicated in large part on women's peculiar "Bestimmung": to be wives, mothers, and housekeepers. Family sociologists, the writers of conduct books for girls, and experts on housekeeping undertook the task of explicating this vocation. Lewald's narratives offer a skeptical response to the theorists' cheery advocacy of the domestic ideal.

## I

What was the ideal and when and why did it arise? Ute Gerhard notes that the *Conversations-Lexikon für gebildete Stände* of 1818 had no entry under "Familie." Thirty years later, another encyclopedia, *Wigand's*, produced pages on the subject. In these it struggled to bring three definitions of the family[4] under one ideological umbrella, describing it as the "Basis, welche dem bürgerlichen und staatlichen Leben zur festen Unterlage dient" (qtd. in Gerhard 76). An additional flood of new literature poured into the breach, and Gerhard argues that this quantitative difference suggests that the concept of the family was still in flux in the first half of the nineteenth century (77). The "ganze Haus" was being transformed into a "heile Welt," and "[d]ie bürgerliche Familie, deren Seele die Frau ist, hat begonnen, als Oase des Friedens in einer unheimlicher werdenden Welt empfunden zu werden.... Die Einhegung der Frau in diesem Bereich hat eine neue Motivierung empfangen" (E. Blochmann 68). The new texts consecrated the middle-class family model as the universal ideal, a designation that, Gerhard claims, continues to function to consign all women to the domestic environment (74) as "Gattin, Mutter und Hausfrau."[5] Lewald's female characters are the sometimes reluctant beneficiaries of a hundred years of family theory, as texts and practices from both the eighteenth and the nineteenth century shaped the family model that Lewald interrogates in her work.

The domestic environment was separated early from other social realms and groups. Gerhard cites Philippe Ariès's contention that the eighteenth-century family had used architecture and etiquette, among other things, to withdraw from the outside world: "Durch die Spezialisierung der Wohnräume und die Veränderung der Umgangsformen wurde ein neues Bedürfnis nach Isolierung, nach Privatleben befriedigt. Die Familie reduzierte sich auf Eltern und Kinder; Diener, Klienten und Freunde wurden ausgeschlossen" (90). Families added doors and corridors and designated smaller spaces for special purposes, such as studies, nurseries, bedrooms, and living rooms, that promoted separation even within the domestic environment (Rosenbaum 303). This separation mirrored new divisions within what had previously been a community of "Hausgenossen": Rosenbaum notes that the "normative Familienliteratur" of the late eighteenth century rarely mentions servants or even grandparents (301).

The family paradigm that originated in the mid-eighteenth century and was enshrined by the culture of the nineteenth is inextricably linked to the parallel rise of the middle class. Its manifestations must therefore be viewed through the filter of class consciousness. Rosenbaum argues that a politically demoralized "Bildungsbürgertum" was the first to emphasize its family values as a marker of its difference from—and moral superiority to—the nobility (258–61). She examines the dominant bourgeois family during two half-centuries: the "Bildungsbürger" of the late eighteenth century and the "Besitzbürger" who eclipsed their educated predecessors in the second half of the nineteenth century. The two groups differed in their relative prosperity and in their position on aristocratic conventions, but the ostentatious embrace of "family life" was a defining characteristic of both groups (310–11, 340–43).

Lewald's upright "Bürger" almost always conform to the earlier model of the middle class, and occasionally explicitly reject the new bourgeois coziness with luxury-loving aristocrats. Although the eighteenth-century family ideal, which relatively few adherents sought to realize, often differed significantly from reality, it reached a peak during the Biedermeier period when a "wahrer Familienkult" arose (Rosenbaum 252). Novel aspects of the bourgeois family model included "love" as the impetus to marriage, child-raising as a primary focus, and a family sphere separate from other realms (Rosenbaum 251). These features derived from the peculiar socioeconomic position of "Bildungsbürger": as "höhere Beamte sowie Vertreter der freien Berufe," men increasingly left the house to work, while women, who were not employed outside the home, tended to the house and garden. The financial situation of this class was modest, but relatively secure (Rosenbaum 251–52). Class membership was based neither on birth, as in the case of the nobility, nor on profession, as in the case of farmers and artisans, but on one's own economic or intellectual achievements. This awareness fueled the individualism that further characterized the middle class (Rosenbaum 258) and soon influenced the representation of marriages as unions of particular partners (Rosenbaum 261). Children, then, were the product of a unique connection and as such required special solicitude. Care was provided by tutors and servants conscientiously selected by parents (Rosenbaum 268). The separation of spheres, the exclusion of women from paid employment, and the emotionalization of the family led to an intensification of the maternal relationship. Women were established as child-raising "specialists" (Rosenbaum 282–83), for which, Rosenbaum argues, they were often repaid with loving gratitude by sons and ambivalence by daughters. Here Rosenbaum cites the example of the conflicted relationship between Fanny Lewald and her mother as evidence of this phenomenon (359).

Most of this description of the family as such will not be unfamiliar to twentieth-century readers. Nineteenth-century "Bürgertum" was inordinately successful in imposing its family model permanently on other social groups. Gerhard argues that the middle class, whose new economic might was accompanied by the birth of the proletariat, attempted to defuse the threat from "below" through the indoctrination of its own "Familienmoral" (140), a project on which Lewald, in novels and stories such as *Nella* and "Kein Haus," certainly collaborated. My investigation in this chapter focuses on bourgeois family norms, both because of their primacy in nineteenth-century German culture and because Lewald's texts invariably manifest them.

As Gerhard points out, the definition and consolidation of the role of women in the family is an essential part of bourgeois family ideology (139–40). The "Sinn für häusliche Glückseligkeit"—in addition to individual achievement, reason, knowledge, naturalness, and honesty, among others—represents an essential element of the bourgeois catalog of virtues (Gerhard 125). Rosenbaum claims that only in a domestic sphere from which the work world and the public sphere were excluded could the middle-class family ideal, a family free of social ties and influences, establish itself (305). This family was nevertheless subject to external discursive representations and to manipulation by the patriarchal structures to which it owed its existence. The German conduct books written for girls and women in the late eighteenth century were authored, to my knowledge, almost exclusively by men. In 1807 Johann Ludwig Ewald wonders coyly in his first chapter whether it would not have been better to have a woman offer the advice contained in his *Die Kunst ein gutes Mädchen, eine gute Gattin, Mutter und Hausfrau zu werden*, but concludes that only a man is able to say what sort of feminine behavior has an effect on men: what inspires their love and what repels them (17–18). And, because the new "Ehe- und Familienideal mit seiner Betonung von Zuneigung, Gemüt und Innigkeit" was a weapon in the arsenal mustered by the bourgeoisie in its battle against the multifaceted preeminence of the nobility, the ideal itself had a political dimension (Rosenbaum 284). Wilhelm Heinrich Riehl's mid-century conquest of the "house," on behalf of German "Hausväter" and for the sake of national stability, made the alleged personal explicitly political. As he put it, "Die Familie ist der Schwer- und Angelpunkt unseres sozialpolitischen weil unseres nationalen Lebens. Der deutsche Staat änderte sich und die deutsche Gesellschaft — und die deutsche Familie blieb doch im wesentlichen was sie war" (xiii). Danford notes that although Riehl "is often considered hopelessly conservative, deluded, and unscientific, his ideas represent, to a degree, the national liberal bourgeois stance on issues of morality, property, and the family as well as the German state" (18). Although Riehl denied that the family was a model for the state,[6] the analogy of the family to the state was otherwise ubiquitous. Joachim Heinrich Campe, for instance, solemnly assured his girl readers that the well-being of the state rested in large part in the hands of women—"was dem ersten Gehör nach unglaublich klingt"—because they raise future citizens (373). Because the domestic situation was characterized by "[e]nge Häuslichkeit, verstärkte Abhängigkeit, Funktionsverlust und Isolation," Gerhard remarks that it is not surprising, "daß es eines ungeheuren ideologischen Aufwands bedurfte, der Frau die neue Situation schmackhaft zu machen. Denn immer wieder waren es Männer, die so genau wußten, wo 'sie sich allein glücklich fühlt'" (95). There was, however, enough at stake for bourgeois self-definition to make the effort to convince women of their unique vocation worthwhile.

Early apologists, however, tended to acknowledge the constriction of the domestic environment. Campe had been more than straightforward in his *Väterlicher Rat für meine Tochter* (1789), which promulgated its unvarnished truths through ten editions until 1832: he views women's vocation as an "'ungünstiges Verhältnis,' als einen, 'nach unserer jetzigen Weltverfassung, abhängigen und auf geistige sowohl als körperliche Schwächung abzielenden Zustand.'" His modest goal is to instill in girls "'jene glückliche Gemüthsart'…, die das 'vorzüglichste Mittel sei, die Unannehmlichkeiten der ganzen weiblichen Lage zu vermindern'" (qtd. in Gerhard 130). Ewald offers his presumably adolescent female readers a similarly sober portrayal of their lives as women. Girls must master renunciation, his conduct book intones in 1807, "weil in der Natur und *in unserer Einrichtung* [my emphasis], gerade ihrem Geschlechte, so viele Fesseln angelegt sind, die jede unter ihnen willig trägt, und tragen muß, wenn sie sich nicht verächtlich machen will" (67). Religion aids women in meeting the demands of their profession: without it, how can they "sich so beherrschen, so entbehren, still dulden, verleugnen, sich willenslos unterwerfen…immer so thätig seyn…ohne Schein und oft ohne Genuß" (149)?

By the second half of the century, however, theorists like Riehl were unwilling to admit that women's weaknesses, virtues, and vocation had any other source but nature (Gerhard 131). The fundamental inequality rooted in gendered physiology (5) and mentality (12–13), Riehl argues, is divinely mandated: "Indem...Gott der Herr Mann und Weib schuf, hat er die Ungleichheit und die Abhängigkeit als eine Grundbedingung aller menschlichen Entwicklung gesetzt" (3). As this quotation suggests, Riehl derives his evidence of the "natural" form of the family in large part from Christian mythology. Folk customs and proverbs also play a significant role in making his case, as does grammar: "Der Staat ist männlichen Geschlechtes...wo bleiben da die Frauen? Sie sollen bleiben in der 'Familie,' die ja die vorwiegende Signatur der Weiblichkeit schon in ihrem Geschlechtsartikel aufzeigt" (9). This assignment means their complete identification with the head of the household: "[das Weib] wird nur vollgültig, indem es sich eins weiß mit einem Mann; es existiert nicht für sich, sondern nur in und mit der Familie" (20). Ewald had been far more generous, arguing that all humans are, first and foremost, "ein Wesen für sich" and meant to develop *um sein selbstwillen* [his emphasis]." Women are "Menschenwesen, ehe sie Göttinnen [sic], Mütter und Hausfrauen sind" (173). Ewald's rhetoric is reminiscent of the ideological conflicts evident in the paragraphs of the *ALR*, in which the spirit of the Enlightenment wars with traditional hierarchies. Writing in 1854, however, Riehl was untroubled by the female nonentity, an indifference that supports Ingeborg Weber-Kellermann's assertion that the position of wives and mothers had never been as subordinate and dependent as it was during the second half of the nineteenth century (qtd. in Gerhard 149).

Riehl's *Die Familie*, first published in 1854, went through seventeen editions until 1935 (Gerhard 149).[7] His vision of domestic arrangements was clearly popular, but with whom? Riehl states in the preface to the first edition that he wants, in addition to scholars, another sort of readership for his book: German women (viii). In the preface to the ninth edition, he claims that his work is drawn from life and intended to affect life (xi). Women may well have read his "Idyll vom deutschen Hause" (viii), but any who sought guidance on their own contributions to a personal domestic idyll would have been disappointed. Riehl periodically reiterates the subordinate nature of femininity and the perverseness of calls for the emancipation of women[8] in the first half of his book, but is vague on what women should actually do in the domestic environment. Riehl's more concrete suggestions include: "Die Frauen sollen aber überhaupt sorgen, daß das heilige Feuer des häuslichen Herdes niemals erlischt, das heißt, ihr

Beruf ist es ganz besonders, die Sitte des Hauses zu pflegen, zu schirmen und fortzubilden" (13) and "Unsere Religionsbegriffe lernen wir bei den Männern; beten aber lernen wir bei der Mutter. Die Mutter lehrt uns die Selbstbeschränkung, der Vater öffnet uns den ersten Blick in die Welt" (23). His chapter on women's emancipation (57–94), on the hand, is more informative. There he charges women with weakening art, music, and drama (as consumers) and literature (as consumers and producers). Women's dubious contributions to cultural life are generally noxious, he argues, attributing the rise of the women's movement largely to the new (and, he hints, undeserved) respectability of the actress (64). He trots out Louise Aston and her cigars in an argument against the perversity of women in politics (75). He returns more explicitly to the family in his assertion that only the unavailability of divorce protects women from the "Fessellosigkeit" of men (75) and that women have a "natürliche" and "konservative" vocation: "zum Erhalten und Pflegen der überlieferten Sitten, zur Bewahrung des Hauses, zur Hebung eines Geistes der Selbstbeschränkung, des Maßes und der Opferwilligkeit" (84). Women without families should find a relative to take them in as an "alte Tante" (78).

With this dubious solution to the plight of unmarried women, Riehl indicates the primary focus of his book, which makes in fact a conservative plea for a return to the golden age of the "ganze Haus." Men have abdicated their rights and responsibilities as "Hausväter," he argues, and retrieving the authority attendant upon these should be their primary project. Parents produce their families and thus have authority over them. However, although not compelled by external oppression, "sondern weil sie es ihrer Natur nach gar nicht anders kann und mag, tritt die Frau unter die Autorität des Mannes" (128). The specifics of women's position within the family — except as "subjects" of their husbands — disappear entirely from this part of his text. Women become, at most, someone who sits in state in either the kitchen (in the case of the farmer's wife, who appears to be the eyes, ears, and heart of the kitchen) (190) or the "Familienzimmer" (the bourgeois) (196). As such they are almost synonymous with the room itself.

The respect of children and servants for the paterfamilias inculcates respect for other institutions, such as the state, the law, and the church (136), and these institutions, of course, should do their part as well. The "contract" conception of marriage, for instance, which Riehl compares with the so-called temporary marriages — that is, prostitution — available to travelers in Persia, must be eliminated. The "family" will fail in its educative and representative function unless its bonds are irrevocable, and those who are unhappy in their marriages should sacrifice themselves to the greater good of the institution (240–44). Riehl does not gender his sacrificial lambs, but his advice read in conjunction with cultural probabilities tells us that he addresses himself to women: the partner who is still "christlich und sittlich gesinnt...soll nie aufhören zu arbeiten, daß er den andern zu sich herüberziehe. Dadurch wird auch eine solche unglückliche Ehe nicht ohne Weihe und Segen bleiben" (244). The church, too, must reassert its rights to intervene in the lives of parishioners. Riehl lauds the example of a village pastor who restored reverence and moral behavior to his flock, primarily by shaming women:

> Er läßt z.B. kein gefallenes Mädchen zum Abendmahl zu, wenn sie nicht...vor versammeltem Presbyterium in der Kirche ihre Schuld bekannt, Reue gezeigt und Besserung gelobt. Bräute, welche nicht mehr Jungfrauen waren, und es trotzdem wagten, mit einem Kranz auf dem Kopfe vor dem Altar zu erscheinen, exkommunizierte er. (253)

The men involved do not appear in his account.

National customs, both positive and negative, reflect German family values. One vice, "Kneipen," for instance, affirms the German propensity for family life. "Verkommene, verkneipte, zu wirklichen Trunkenbolden herabgesunkene Stammgäste" are really just men who are looking for home in all the wrong places. "Aus lauter Familienbedürftigkeit," which they attempt to satisfy with their "Zechgenossen," they forget their actual families at home (278–79). These families, of course, include the women who cannot divorce them, but here again women are peculiarly invisible in Riehl's argument. There is something for everyone in Riehl's brand of muscular domesticity, which aims to restore the authority of the "house," except the women who are its silent, even ghostly inhabitants.

While Riehl's book makes the connection between masculinity and the domestic environment explicit, other writers promoted instead the notion that the home was a feminine space in which influential women shaped the lives of their families for good or ill. Campe's book of "fatherly advice" summarizes feminine "Bestimmung" as follows:

Ihr seyd wahrlich nicht dazu bestimmt, nur große Kinder, tändelnde Puppen, Närrinnen oder gar Furien zu seyn; ihr seyd vielmehr geschaffen...um *beglückende Gattinnen, bildende Mütter* und *weise Vorsteherinnen des innern Hauswesens* zu werden; Gattinnen, die der ganzen zweiten Hälfte des menschlichen Geschlechts, der männlichen, welche die größern Beschwerden, Sorgen und Mühseligkeiten zu tragen hat, durch zärtliche Theilnehmung, Liebe, Pflege und Fürsorge das Leben versüßen sollen; Mütter, welche nicht bloß Kinder gebähren, sondern auch die ersten Keime jeder schönen menschlichen Tugend in ihnen pflegen, die ersten Knospen ihrer Seelenfähigkeiten weislich zur Entwicklung fördern sollen; Vorsteherinnen des Hauswesens, welche durch Aufmerksamkeit, Ordnung, Reinlichkeit, Fleiß, Sparsamkeit, wirtschaftliche Kenntnisse und Geschicklichkeiten, den Wohlstand, die Ehre, die häusliche Ruhe und Glückseligkeit des erwerbenden Gatten sicher stellen, ihm die Sorgen der Nahrung erleichtern, und sein Haus zu einer Wohnung des Friedens, der Freude und der Glückseligkeit machen sollen. (372)

His representation of the joys and the vicissitudes of domestic life does not differ from Ewald's, who, like Campe, emphasizes the centrality of women's role to the household. A man's happiness is largely dependent on his wife: "Er kann viel oder wenig thun, wird mehr oder versinkt, ist ein guter Vater oder ein schlechter Vater, ein guter Hauswirth oder ein Verschwender, je nachdem ihm seine Gattinn mehr oder weniger glücklich macht" (Ewald 76). Men may have the "greater cares," but women contribute much to their ability to endure them. Women can in fact bankrupt their hapless husbands: if they are poor housewives and their spouses fail to notice, the disorder will increase to the point of ruin. The children's fortunes will be lost, the family members will be estranged from one another, and the children will infect their own households with the bad habits they have learned at home (Ewald 85–86). The pressure and the corollary recognition would seem to have been enormous, yet Ewald notes sadly that, because what is best and most noble often goes unacknowledged, girls cannot expect much gratitude (86–87).

Subsequent descriptions of the role of "Gattin, Mutter und Hausfrau" varied little with respect to the desirable characteristics of the ideal spouse, mother, and housewife. Girls' education had previously been limited to "ein bißchen Lesen, Schreiben und Rechnen für den Hausgebrauch" (Rosenbaum 278). The goal of late eighteenth- and early nineteenth-century educational reforms was to improve a woman's exercise of her particular vocation. Better education enabled her to teach her young children and to make moderately interesting conversation with her husband, particularly about his literary interests. The improvements were not without risk, however: improper education might make women unsuited to their vocation (Rosenbaum 278–79). Campe argues that a "gelehrtes Tischgespräch" with his wife will not compensate a man for an overcooked dinner or for the neglect of his laundry and his children (qtd. in Gerhard 128). While the expectation of competent housekeeping did not disappear in later decades, it must have coexisted more or less uneasily with the new ideal of the "intellectual relationship" that Rosenbaum describes: a "Minimum an Gefühl" was a virtual necessity for both partners, who would communicate not only about domestic affairs, but perhaps about literature as well. This requirement implied both more education as well as a new position for wives within marriage (Rosenbaum 264–65). Lewald usually solves this dilemma by privileging characters who reconcile these elements. Her wifely protagonists are excellent mothers and housekeepers who are reasonably well-educated and reasonably desirous of learning more.

In the second half of the nineteenth century, middle-class women were still confined to the domestic sphere, but the environment itself had changed. Households no longer produced most of the goods they consumed, which reduced the organizational demands on housewives. Those with many servants did little if any actual housework, while less prosperous wives needed at least one servant in order to imply that they did none. This charade points to the representative function of the bourgeois housewife: her lack of useful occupation confirmed her husband's status as a competent provider (Rosenbaum 340–42). She was, however, still expected to act as "Gattin, Mutter und Hausfrau," and she could still turn to publishers for help.

Gerhard notes Henriette Davidis's "unvergleichlicher Lese- und Verkaufserfolg" after the mid-nineteenth century (66). Her *Die Hausfrau: Eine Mitgabe für angehende Hausfrauen* (1861) appeared in at least sixteen editions. The foreword to the first edition suggests that by the 1860s the well-read wife indeed enjoyed a certain vogue:

> Wohl ist es herrlich, sich über das Alltägliche zu erheben, am Wahren, Schönen und Geistvollen unserer reichen Litteratur sich zu erfreuen, aus ihr Stoff zu sammeln für Geist und Gemüt; aber es wird dieser Sinn bei den Männern doch dann erst die rechte Anerkennung finden, wenn er sich mit der Aufmerksamkeit auf die unabweisbaren Ansprüche des praktischen Lebens verbindet und als

Mitgabe zu einer angenehmen Häuslichkeit hervortritt. (v–vi)

In fact, she argues, mothers are neglecting their daughters' practical preparation for housekeeping in favor of developing their intellectual gifts (vi). Davidis energetically redresses that neglect. Her text suggests that no detail is too small to contribute to "angenehme Häuslichkeit," from the most hygienic method to wash out chamberpots (75), to the exact amount of butter to be rationed to the servants each week (369), to the best color for tablecloths in the living room (68).

Attention to these details makes a wife significant in her own household, Davidis argues, and she should attempt to maintain control even during illness. For "[h]at aber die Frau ihr häusliches Regiment einmal in eine fremde Hand gelegt, so verliert sie sehr leicht das nötige Interesse dafür und mit diesem auch ihr Ansehen im Hause" (17). Davidis moves on to instructions for ruling the household from the sickroom and leaves unexplored her own intriguing acknowledgement that housekeeping might be fundamentally uninteresting, despite the fact that it alone confers status on women in their own homes. Lewald's autobiography provides confirmation of the latter assertion. When Lewald was fourteen, her mother had given birth to her last child. For a time, Lewald took over the management of the household despite her own and her mother's misgivings. Her efforts are successful, however, and she "genoß…zum ersten Male die Kräftigung, welche selbständiges Handeln uns mit seiner Verantwortlichkeit auferlegt." Her employment comes to an end when her mother recovers, although, she claims, her father preferred that she continue and both her mother's health and her own development might have profited from accession to his wishes. What could explain her mother's obstinacy?

> [D]ie Mutter, welche in der Bewältigung des Haushaltes ihre eigentliche Stärke und ihr eigentliches Element besaß, konnte den Gedanken nicht ertragen, daß sie, wenn sie mich die Wirtschaft weiter selbständig fortführen ließ, ihre Überlegenheit über mich *auch* in diesem Punkt allmählich verlieren könnte [my emphasis]. (*ML* I: 161)

The reader feels a certain sympathy for her mother's point. Davidis asserts that household management from one's bed requires "eine außerordentliche Willenskraft und unverdroßene[n] Eifer" (17), but Lewald here, presumably unintentionally, demonstrates that it may have been worth the effort.

Davidis's book does not preach mere cleanliness and domestic control. Rather, she promises her readers love and recognition in exchange for industry and wifely self-denial. She illustrates her point with the story of a woman so graciously selfless and so diligently supportive, she seems almost the product of imagination. Her similarity to fictional heroines in fact indicates a certain fluidity of boundaries between the didactic and the literary texts written for women. The husband of this well-educated, formerly elegant woman had suffered business reversals, losing her fortune as well in the process. Davidis visits them in their now modest home, in which the wife does all the housework herself and wears cotton dresses made from the fabric produced in the small factory her husband has since built. She is as neat and clean and cheerful as the rooms of their simple home, and when she leaves to make coffee for their guest, her husband gratefully proclaims, "Was eine Frau vermag, das habe ich erfahren—mein Mut war gebrochen, sie war aber meine Kraft, mein Rat und mein Glück" (25–26). The reader is touched despite her irritated awareness that this tale is part and parcel of the "enormous ideological expenditure" to which Gerhard attributes women's eventual acceptance of their domestic definition (95).

Davidis begins her book of household hints with an unexpected chapter on marital advice to young women (1–23). The emphasis of her list suggests that three issues were of paramount importance to young wives: money, management of recalcitrant servants, and marital discord due to a husband's tyranny. Davidis returns repeatedly, for instance, to the proposition that wives should be informed of the state of the family finances and should be given a fixed amount for household expenses (rather than having to request money for each purchase), not least because it will give them "mehr Vergnügen am Hauswesen" (7). In effect, a wife's dependence should be masked with a certain degree of knowledge and cash flow.

A wife does have dominion over a small group of subjects, however, as the servants are her special charge. A housewife must be tireless in her efforts to ferret out disobedience, presumption, sloth, and shoddy work on the part of what Davidis suggests is a thieving class. She should also suffer the chicanery of the servants in silence, unless it becomes mandatory that her husband "durch eine ernstliche Zurechtweisung die Autorität der Frau unterstützt" (21). Davidis mentions, however, only one such instance: should one servant attempt to incite the others to rebellion against "die Herrschaft," the man of the house should "eingreif[en] und die betreffende Person vor den übrigen Dienstleuten, die zu diesem Zweck ins Wohnzimmer berufen werden, zur Rede stell[en] und sie ungesäumt ihres Dienstes ent[lassen]" (60). She envisions this scene with a vividness that she otherwise reserves for chamberpots, suggesting the gravity of such rebellion. The husband's responsibility in the face of household mutiny additionally suggests that he is the actual captain of the domestic ship.

Further, husbands may exercise their rights in sometimes alarming fashion. Davidis's text inspires reader curiosity not only about the behavior of the servants. Husbands, too, appear to be a mysteriously captious household presence. The institution of a fixed allowance for a wife's household and clothing costs, for instance, can prevent "unzählige böse Worte, ungerechte Vorwürfe und Kränkungen" (7), since the "sanfte Bräutigam...sich vielleicht als ein strenger Ehemann oder als ein Brausekopf [zeigt], den schon bei geringen Anlässen der Zorn übermannt" (19). This comment intimates that domestic tyranny was both common and unpredictable. Karin Hausen's reading of contemporary autobiographies suggests that nineteenth-century engagements tended to be both short and based on a fairly limited acquaintance. Further, men availed themselves of the opportunity to visit a prospective fiancée in her home, while the bride generally had not seen her husband at his parents' home or at work before the marriage (93). Visiting her family for an evening, a suitor might well have appeared pleasant enough to the woman who would find herself bound for life to what seems, based on Davidis's representation, a rather capricious being. Even the "besten und gutmütigsten" husbands tend toward "Aufwallungen, die *in manchen Fällen* mit unangenehmen Vorkommnissen im Berufsleben im Zusammenhang stehen [my emphasis]." Wives who respond with patience and humility will rise in the esteem of their now abashed, although not openly apologetic, husbands (Davidis 19). These warnings suggest that absolute power corrupts absolutely. Since wives were largely unable to alter the terms under which they lived, it was enough for women in typical marital circumstances to know that they should endure their husbands' often inexplicable anger in silence.

Beyond this anger, "besondere Verhältnisse" occasionally arise.

Although, Davidis avers, it is ordinarily unseemly for wives to exercise authority in the family, there are situations that make this reversal unavoidable: situations in which "der Mann, schlaff und nachlässig, durch unordentliches Wirthschaften den Wohlstand bald zu Grunde richten würde, wenn die Frau aus unzeitiger Schonung sich dem Willen des Gatten rückhaltlos unterwerfen wollte." Yet, although she should take charge, she should do so considerately and should attempt to conceal her dominance from others, "damit der Mann nicht unmündig erscheine, und sein Ehrgefühl nicht ganz zu Grunde gehe" (26).[9] However, she continues, the situation could be worse. Davidis apparently hints here at an extramarital affair serious enough to have come to the wife's attention. She gives no detailed suggestions for a response, but does advise that, if at all possible, "so weiche sie nicht von ihrem Platz; wenigstens thue sie keine unüberlegten, zu raschen Schritte und sei, wenn sie eine Sinnesänderung sieht, im Vergeben und Vergessen unermüdlich." Religion will help: she should pray for the strength to endure her lot with patience (27).

Almost a hundred years earlier, Ewald had dispensed similar advice, which suggests that certain standards of ideal feminine behavior were unwavering. Girls and women should execute their duties faithfully—even to "mürrische, ungerechte Eltern," "treulose und gefühllose Gatten," and "verwöhnte, verdorbene Kinder" (52). This particular representation of the family seems unusually dark, and Ewald also admits that men who are sensual, dissipated, and luxury-loving are sometimes at fault in an unhappy marriage (258). Otherwise, however, what should the wives of gamblers, philanderers, and speculators do (310–11)? Do not complain to your friends or encourage their critical comments (314–15), he advises his readers. Use love to win him back (322). After all, his infidelity and other vices usually have a source: he is unhappy or bored at home. Find out why and improve yourself (329–32).

In 1861, Davidis had opened her first chapter with the disheartening news that "[e]s…so viele unglückliche Ehen, so viel Mangel an häuslichem Glück [gibt]" that she feels compelled to begin with some marital advice. In the sixteenth edition, which appeared almost forty years later, the author mitigates the same opening statement with this hopeful clause: "Wenn auch schöne Eintracht im Ehestande nicht so selten ist" (1). Was her cautious optimism warranted? Perhaps not. Her statement, like her anecdote about the cheerful, cotton-wearing wife of a bankrupt, may have been a more or less unwitting participant in the effort that Gerhard describes to convince wives and mothers that they really were happiest at home (95). Yet while Davidis takes heart at the happy marriages that are "not that rare" and otherwise advises patience and forgiveness, and while Ewald urges women with unfaithful husbands to wait for their return and to regard themselves as the source of their husbands' betrayal, Lewald raises a skeptical eyebrow at the notion that a reprehensible husband can be improved by a patient wife. The cases of Madame Berent in *Eine Lebensfrage*, Christel in "Das große Loos," and Urika in *Treue Liebe* intimate that depraved men will not change, no matter how tirelessly their wives forgive them. These wives are models of forbearance, yet their husbands enter and exit the narrative as rotters. Even in the cases of women attached to less blatant wrongdoers—and some virtual saints—Lewald nevertheless manages to suggest that the "Idyll vom deutschen Hause" may be unsatisfying, monotonous, and/or too narrowly conceived.

## II

In *Clementine* (1843), Lewald explores the disadvantages of the "marriage of convenience," adding her voice to those of other novelists of the early 1840s who delineated the suffering of women in such marriages (Hausen 93).[10] She also questions the myth of the universal satisfaction to be gained from the mere exercise of women's vocation. A "Gattin, Hausfrau und Mutter" may find her work rewarding, but a superior woman must do that work in the context of a passionate attachment to a husband who is at leisure to befriend, instruct, and appreciate his wife. Such marriages, Lewald's novel suggests, are rare. The fiancé will raise expectations of companionship that the husband will disappoint. A husband's sphere is demanding, significant, and interesting; a wife's consists of waiting for her husband to enliven a few of the evening hours in the domestic circle. Waiting and housekeeping are feminine tasks, and the reader might expect that a dutiful performance would reap rewards for the female protagonist. The text, however, points out repeatedly that although Clementine admirably fulfills others' expectations, she gains little beyond the dubious satisfaction of self-denial. Is it enough?

Contemporary accounts of the success of marriages of convenience are mixed. Lewald's own aunt had succumbed to family suasion and married a man Lewald describes as "vermögend, aber ungebildet" and "in Erscheinung, Sprache und Manier gleich unangenehm" (*ML* I: 163–64). She never reports on the specifics of his unpleasantness. Rather, she heightens reader curiosity with the aunt's bitter remark:

> Es ist Unsinn zu behaupten, daß eine Frau sich an etwas gewöhnen könne, was ihr abstoßend ist. Habe ich mich denn an mein Los gewöhnt? Ich wußte, daß ich mein Todesurteil unterzeichnete, als ich mich verheiratete, und ich habe es ihnen gesagt. Aber sie haben mir alle zugeredet, alle—nun bedauern sie mich alle. (*ML* I: 164)

Johanna Schopenhauer, on the other hand, reports satisfaction in her unequal marriage, which began in 1784. Her prosperous husband was twenty years older than his eighteen-year-old bride, and their expectations were modest: "Glühende Liebe heuchelte ich ihm ebenso wenig, als er Anspruch darauf machte, aber wir fühlten beide, wie er mit jedem Tag mir werther wurde" (qtd. in Rosenbaum 287). "Das ist die 'vernünftige' Liebe," Rosenbaum explains. "Weder Abneigung noch heftige Zuneigung existierten zwischen den Partnern, sondern vielmehr wohltemperierte Gefühle füreinander" (287). Although "love" was a new precondition for the ideal bourgeois marriage, "rational" love was the order of the day (Rosenbaum 285). Parents, Rosenbaum maintains, found support in literature that acted as a corrective to the passions whipped up by "Sturm und Drang." She describes a fictional scene from 1791 in which a mother informs her oldest daughter that an old family friend has asked for her hand. After some discussion, the daughter interjects weakly that she feels none of the "brennende, heftige Leidenschaft" that poets and novelists report, whereupon the mother insists that consuming passions are an inadequate foundation for marriage. Love based on reason, virtue, and mutual respect is far more durable (286).

Dialogue of this sort does not strain credulity in its late eighteenth-century context, but did the marriage of convenience become less plausible in the years that followed? The short answer to this question, Rosenbaum suggests, is no. The relative prosperity of suitors retained significance for women because marriage was virtually the only occupation permitted them. A sizeable dowry was also not unwelcome to men, such as civil servants, living on a fixed income or desirous of increasing their creditworthiness. Despite the new importance of "inclination," financial concerns thus remained primary well into the nineteenth century for both sexes (287). The "Besitzbürger," who were the dominant representatives of the middle class in the second half of the nineteenth century, had always regarded marriage as a transaction that promoted business connections (Rosenbaum 332–33). Even this group, however, was gradually "infected" by the sentimentalized marriage models of "Bildungsbürgertum," a contagion that freed sons, but not daughters, to consider a prospective spouse's *additional* charms. Rosenbaum points out, however, that financial considerations remained important, even if they were no longer solely at issue (333–34). The fictional family of Lewald's beleaguered heroine, whose story falls squarely between the two periods Rosenbaum investigates, can thus rely on the support of many of the novel's readers even though Clementine's "Versorgung" is not at issue. Lewald's father certainly approved of his daughter's first novel (*ML* III: 19). Clementine's reluctance to marry an unloved suitor and her desire for a more companionable marriage, however, were also contemporary phenomena.

Clementine Frei (who, upon her marriage, will become markedly *un*free) at first resists her family's pressure to marry Meining, the distinguished physician who is the most recent of her many suitors. Years earlier she had been disappointed in her love for Robert Thalberg, who had exercised great influence on her intellectual development (5). She now prefers to live with her memories, caring for her sister's children. Her aunt and sister, both of whom found contentment in marriages to men who were virtual strangers to them on their wedding day, convince her that she has an obligation to marry because she has an obligation to make others happy. As her aunt puts it:

> Du bist unglücklich geworden durch Deine Liebe und durch Robert's Wankelmuth…das entbindet Dich nicht von der Pflicht, Dich mit Bewußtsein, aus freier Wahl für das Wohl Anderer zu opfern. Das Weib ist geschaffen, sich liebend hinzugeben und zu beglücken; thust Du das?…Du, vor Vielen dazu berufen, einem Manne das Leben zu verschönen, mit dem unerschöpflichen Reichtum an Liebe und Nachsicht, Du willst das nicht…. Du hältst so viel darauf, die Achtung vor Dir selbst nicht zu verlieren, weil Dir das leichter wird, als die unsere zu verdienen…wir…würden Dich achten, wenn Du dem Glücke eines Anderen, eines braven Mannes, Deine Neigungen zu opfern im Stande wärest. Zwingen kann man Dich nicht, Du bist reich und unabhängig in jeder Beziehung; aber ich wende mich an Dein richtiges Urtheil, an Deine Wahrheitsliebe und an Dein Herz. (18–20)

The story's outcome reveals the irony of the aunt's appeal to Clementine's "good judgment" and "love of truth," but it achieves its goal: Clementine capitulates and marries Meining, who is more than twenty years her senior. The sister's comment on the age difference ("er ist freilich fünfzig Jahre alt, Du bist aber schon siebenundzwanzig, was kann denn passender sein?" [3]) seems earnestly intended in its context, yet the narrative suggests that the gap contributed in part to the protagonists' marital problems (34). As she did almost forty years later in "In Ragaz," Lewald hints that men who are old enough to be the fathers of their fiancées do themselves and their future wives a disservice. Meining knows that Clementine has had a previous attachment. She wants to share the details of that attachment with him, but he forbids her to tell him the name of the man she had loved. Events, of course, confirm the wisdom of Clementine's desire for candor.

The narrator tells us that Clementine's sister, Marie, is the sort of woman that the majority of men want: she "liebte ihren [Mann] von Herzen, betete ihre beiden Kinder an [und] sorgte treulich für ihr Haus." Her husband, a professor, spends his days teaching or working in his study. Davidis describes a man's study as a kind of shrine to masculine work. "Wo des Mannes Beruf es erfordert," she writes, "da sei vor allem für ein freundliches, helles, bequemes und ruhiges Studier- oder Schreibzimmer gesorgt." A wife should not subject that study to ordinary cleaning rituals, use it for her own purposes, or allow the children to make noise in its vicinity (71–72). Marie's husband emerges from his separate space for meals, during which he listens "mit der größten Theilnahme" to Marie's domestic tales. When not telling these tales, she takes walks or receives visits from like-minded friends (9). Marie is, in other words, a stereotypical spouse, mother, and housewife on the order of most of the women who populate nineteenth-century treatises on women's vocation, and she and her husband are thoroughly content with one another. Rosenbaum claims that men and women shared an interest in excluding the work world from the private sphere. Men regarded the home as a refuge; women wanted to preserve that space from contact with a world outside their comprehension (305). Marie's character supports that contention: her husband's meals with the family are a type of domestic tourism, whereby he makes a point of "doing as the Romans do," but she visits his study only to report on Clementine's response to the familial arm-twisting (4). Lewald employs her character to acknowledge that, indeed, many women are content in the domestic sphere that even a contemporary encyclopedia referred to as "engbeschränkt,"[11] but those who are must ally themselves with a fictional wife who married at sixteen and whose world consists of her children, her servants, and her matchmaking.

Clementine, on the other hand, finds her life as a newlywed oddly unsatisfying. Her situation illustrates Gerhard's assertion that isolation characterized the lives of bourgeois housewives (95). The text makes Meining's self-absorption evident from the outset: "Dieses Mädchen in seinem Hause walten zu sehen, von ihrem Geiste seine Mußestunden verschönen zu lassen, ihrer milden Pflege in kranken Tagen zu genießen und sie, der er von Herzen zugethan war, ihren Kummer vergessen zu machen, war bald sein Lieblingswunsch geworden" (13). Even her broken heart becomes the playing field of an imagined personal triumph. Once he has won her, however, his practice and his scholarship reclaim his attention, leaving her isolated in their home.

Their home life reads like a dissenting opinion to Davidis's "Ein Wort an junge Frauen," the introduction to her housekeeping guide. Despite Davidis's assertions that household management consumes the greater part of the housewife's day even in homes with many servants, Clementine finds that her housekeeping duties occupy no more than an hour each morning. (And despite the alleged centrality of wifely duties to both family and state, the reader never discovers what activities that hour encompasses, suggesting, perhaps, that they are too dull to merit even a paragraph.) Meining, on the other hand, has a full schedule: he spends the morning with patients, returns to the house for lunch but then requires an hour of rest before the afternoon's labors, follows these with his work on a medical textbook, and pleads exhaustion at dinner. At this point he permits himself to curse the profession he has no intention of renouncing, "der…ihm den ruhigen Genuß seiner Häuslichkeit unmöglich mache" (29–30). His inability to enjoy domestic comforts stands in stark contrast to the promises with which Davidis tempts the readers of her manual. Although she acknowledges that the "Übermaß von Aufmerksamkeiten" of courtship ends with marriage and therefore that "eine gewisse Ernüchterung, nicht selten eine Enttäuschung bei der jungen Frau ein[tritt], die erst nach und nach den Mann verstehen und seinem wahren Wesen nach begreifen lernt" (18–19), she otherwise hints that good housekeeping is the way to a husband's now sober heart. A wife's primary goal should be that of winning her husband over to "angenehme Häuslichkeit" (9):

> Eine kluge und wahrhaft liebende Gattin wird dem Manne beim Eintritt ins Haus stets einen angenehmen Eindruck zu gewähren suchen. Kehrt derselbe aus dem Berufsleben in seine Häuslichkeit zurück, so muß er im Wohnzimmer einen gemütlichen Aufenthalt, Ordnung und Reinlichkeit in der ganzen Umgebung und—eine reinliche, freundliche und gemütliche Hausfrau finden. (22)

Encountering the domestic environment—and the woman who manages it—presumably becomes one with appreciating it/her, yet Clementine's husband remains drawn to the outside world of professional significance and unmoved by the charms of a cozy living room.

Davidis argues further that faithful observation of housewifely duties contributes greatly to preventing strife and relieving a husband's cares (5). Never entrust a servant, she adjures the brides who are her readers, with the critical job of dusting a husband's desk. Consider this task a kind of "Liebesdienst," whereby a wife may maintain the order of a husband's thoughts by preserving the learned disorder of his papers. Once a husband is persuaded that he "hierbei ruhig sein und sich auf sein sorgsames Frauchen verlassen darf, so wird sicherlich bei seiner Rückkehr ein reines Zimmer, mehr noch eine fürsorgliche Gattin ihm eine willkommene und angenehme Erscheinung sein" (72). Here Davidis virtually conflates the housekeeper and the housekeeping, making it difficult to determine the worthier object of affection. The solution to a household lacking in husbandly affection becomes a carefully wielded feather duster. That same care can be a wife's contribution to her husband's weighty thoughts: "Und gewiß wird dies ganz anders zu seinem Wohlbefinden dienen, als wenn er in einer unreinen Umgebung und Atmosphäre geistig schaffen muß" (72).

Clementine, however, had imagined a rather different sort of intellectual converse with her new husband. Unlike her sister, she feels worthy of sharing her husband's mental life and longs for evenings in which he would enjoy talking over his day with her, listening to her views and "correcting" them (31). Even Davidis finds such interchange worthwhile. She suggests in an aside to husbands who may have picked up her book that women living with men who are immersed in cerebral work may want to improve themselves in order better to understand their husbands. A husband should encourage such desires by giving his wife, "soweit es ihr Verständnis ermöglicht," insight into his own intellectual interests and by helping her to return to her interrupted studies. She justifies this endeavor with the assertion that the marriage will become a "wahrhaft geistige Vermählung...bei der Geben und Empfangen gleich große Befriedigung gewährt" (13–14). The suggestion is an unusual one in a book that otherwise asserts repeatedly that "Reinlichkeit" is what men want in a wife. Davidis yields here to the century's new recognition of intellectual communion in marriage, although Meining does not. Clementine's more cerebral evenings with Meining are rare, and she begins to suspect that her husband requires only a "sorgliche Frau, eine freundliche Gesellschafterin" and that her intellectual abilities are irrelevant to him (31–32). Any housekeeper could replace her in his affections (34). Lewald's critique of the domestic trinity of "spouse, mother, and housewife" centers on this irrelevance and the unhappiness it engenders in the worthy Clementine.

A job offer for Meining in Berlin, Clementine's birthplace, performs the apparent function of "deus ex machina." Their new life demands a higher social profile and, once again, Clementine proves an ideal, if inwardly melancholy, spouse. Meining's appreciation of his wife increases because she finds favor with an even larger circle (60), and the reader frowns at his superficiality mere pages before Robert Thalberg reenters Clementine's life. The timing seems propitious: the narrator has demonstrated both Meining's inability to appreciate and instruct his young wife and Clementine's noble attempts to esteem him despite his self-absorption. The reader is ready for a change.

Robert Thalberg, however, proves a questionable savior. He has not married, although he has had at least one illicit affair (with an actress) since leaving Clementine, the sweetheart of his youth. He gradually rediscovers his love for the woman who is now Meining's wife and ignores the advice of a male friend to preserve both her honor and his own by leaving Berlin. Meining, who, thanks to his prohibition, does not recognize his new acquaintance as his wife's former suitor, invites Robert to visit them often. Unable to avoid him, Clementine eventually acknowledges to herself that she still loves Robert and suffers at great length over her emotional betrayal of her husband.

Their discussions as a group, however, reveal the long-suffering Clementine's views on "freedom" for women and portend doom for any relationship outside her marriage. When Robert states that women must be able to share men's ideas on freedom, without desiring it for themselves, for whom it is an "Unding," Clementine seconds this opinion heartily. And, although she believes that she would have been as able a professional as any man, had she had the necessary education, her position as a woman must and should preclude any "emancipation" other than what she achieves through love and marriage. Further, she would "rather die" than divorce (80–84).

This belief prevails even when Robert falls still more violently in love with Clementine after having watched her play with the neighbors' children. The scene with these children is typical of Lewald's treatment of the maternal aspect of the domestic trinity. She employs children primarily as props that function to characterize her female protagonists quickly. Her mothers or would-be mothers are written in the spirit of the age: just as the culture reads evidence of "good" maternal behavior as indicative of a "good" woman (and vice versa), Lewald uses the few children that appear in her narratives as signposts that point the way to a conclusion about the mother herself. In *Eine Lebensfrage*, for instance, she discredits Alfred's peevish wife, Caroline, with her inability to guide her son's moral development; in an essay in *Für und wider die Frauen* she brands as general hypocrites the mothers who leave their adorable children to the servants' care, while extolling the virtues of their "feminine profession"; and in *Treue Liebe* she demonstrates that Urika's body indeed knows best: the author gives her worthy character a son as soon as she extricates herself from the wandering life she loathes and the husband she no longer loves. Struck by the maternal instincts Clementine indicates in her play with the children, Robert urges her to leave Meining and marry him. He envisions her as "[sein] Weib, mit [seinem] Kinde, in den Zimmern [seines] Schlosses" (93)—in other words, exercising her feminine vocation under his protection.

Clementine never seriously contemplates leaving her husband. She tells Robert that she could never destroy Meining's peace and honor, although she regards the fact that she became Meining's wife "mit getheiltem Herzen" as a wrong that has destroyed her life and caused all her suffering (137–38). Nevertheless, the text demonstrates a peculiar ambivalence toward Robert's proposal. On the one hand, the maternal Clementine would find her wish for children fulfilled with Robert; Meining's aversion to their "noise" appears to preclude that addition to their family. Clementine's family pressured her into marriage with an unloved suitor, and she genteelly resents the coercion; divorce would redress that wrong. Robert was Clementine's first "teacher" and evinces an apparent desire for the kind of intellectual companionship her marriage lacks, while Meining's new appreciation of her gifts derives from the recognition she receives from others in Berlin. Would Robert, however, really be a more enlightened husband than Meining? Robert, too, believes that the "wahre Stellung des Weibes eine abhängige sein muß" (82). Although Clementine concurs in this opinion, she has earlier indicated that she has no option to do otherwise: she will not confront the choices that confound men, because "[ihr] bestimmter Weg vorgezeichnet ist" (79). Robert defines her repeatedly as "his," but he also defines her as "rein" when she rejects his various advances. Clementine asks whether he could love a woman who had proven herself capable of forgetting her spouse (138). She and the reader suspect that being "his" and retaining her purity for him are mutually exclusive. Finally, Robert has squandered an earlier opportunity to win Clementine. A veritable chorus of textual voices insists that he should not be given another chance. The narrative protests that his passion for a faithless actress hardly excuses his neglect of the noble girl who loved him; Clementine's aunt and sister and Robert's friend each mention his abandonment at least once, while Robert flagellates himself mercilessly, with Clementine's willing aid, in the last two letters that the lovers write to one another (136–39, 143–44). Clementine, in fact, transcends the usual limits of wifely consideration by insisting that even if her husband were to die, she would not remarry: women, she says, are not possessions that can be passed from one man to another. She was "ganz, ungetheilt, frei und frisch an Geist und Leib" only once (136) —and Robert failed to claim her then.

Harriet Margolis points to the autobiographical nature of this novel and to the manner in which Lewald resolved the pain of rejection by her cousin, Heinrich Simon, by making his literary double suffer (124). While this connection seems more than plausible—and it is indeed interesting to watch Clementine and Robert himself thrash the fickle suitor so soundly— Lewald's novel also undermines the marriages for which Clementine promises to perform metaphorical suttee. Margaret Ward argues that Lewald reads her character's life and choices negatively. Clementine, for instance, reappears in Lewald's second novel, *Jenny* (1843), as Jenny's confidante. At this point, the character "suffers from 'große Reizbarkeit der Nerven' and 'Schlaflosigkeit'" (Ward 72). Clementine's illness and the self-denial that engenders it contribute to Lewald's argument against marriages of convenience. Although she constructs her character as susceptible to the notion that "duty" is worthwhile in itself and that duty to others takes precedence over her own interests, self-sacrifice alone cannot make even the worthy Clementine happy. "Bestimmung," too, fails to satisfy her. Life as a spouse and a housekeeper falls short of its alleged promise, and the conditions of her marriage perversely preclude motherhood. Only the suitor for whom she feels affection promotes her maternal interests, yet the text suggests that her affection is misplaced. An intelligent woman cannot be "Gattin, Mutter und Hausfrau" with a man she does not love—nor, apparently, with a man whom she does.

III

Lewald's *Schloß Tannenburg* (1859) examines "ideal families," the secrets that undermine them, and the misjudgments and deviance familial love may engender. The author returns in this vaguely Gothic novel to the subject of incest, unwitting and otherwise, which she had treated with more melodrama—the guilty lovers take their own lives when they discover their connection—in 1846 in the novella "Ein armes Mädchen." Incestuous love, identified in *Schloß Tannenburg* by one of the observers as the logical outcome of an affectionate family life that is too comfortable, challenges none too subtly the contemporary conception of family as a laudable device for "improving" its members.[12] Hugo's family may be appalled by what the reader knows is an erroneous assumption that he is in love with his own sister, but they are strangely unsurprised by their own "discovery." As though it were a door in an interior wall leading to a hidden chamber, Lewald papers over this lack of surprise with a plot development that absolves the brother, while leaving the dumbfounded reader to stare at the outline beneath the floral pattern. The secret concealed in this narrative space appears to be the author's own ambivalence toward the benefits of domestic life and traditional family hierarchy.

While Lewald's fiction tends to be too level-headed to generate real horror, this novel avails itself of several Gothic conventions to underscore the plot's suggestion that family life may not be as uncomplicated as it seems. Gothic novels were popular in the late eighteenth and early nineteenth century; these are the ancestors of the modern Gothics that are still being produced in the twentieth. The earlier novels featured "medieval castles complete with secret passageways, mysterious dungeons, peripatetic ghosts, and much gloom and supernatural paraphernalia" (Beckson and Ganz 101). While Lewald's narrative avoids the more lurid architectural features of the original genre, it makes much of the secret hidden within the home of this aristocratic family. David Sonnenschein remarks on the "feeling of uneasiness underlying" the plots of the modern Gothics and the way in which these stories offer a "sense of some of the risks that simply being a woman can entail." In these novels, "[r]elationships are volatile, hostile, and even dangerous; in contrast to male-oriented erotica, it is trauma, rather than sex, which is 'just around the corner'" (qtd. in Russ 34). Sonnenschein's analysis suggests that the family lives of women are fraught with mysterious peril. Joanna Russ cites a publisher who claims that the readers of Gothics are women who "marry guys and then begin to discover that their husbands are strangers" (32). Lewald's novel, too, intimates that love and domesticity can have an unexpectedly sordid and perilous aspect.

This aspect, however, must first be uncovered. The novel's introduction suggests that life in East Prussia is a metaphor for life within the enlightened domestic circle: isolated from the hectic pace of the metropolis, one attends quietly to education, letter writing, and the vicarious joys of the travelogue. The insular character of Prussian life apparently promotes family values: nowhere, in fact, can one find "ein edleres Familienleben" (8). Somewhat ominously, the narrator notes as well that the isolation is conducive to the development of "ein mystisches oder ein überspanntes Gefühlsleben" (9), but Lewald spares the first generation of her family protagonists the more criminal of such manifestations.

Baron Heinrich von Wachstetten has returned to the restorative seclusion of Schloß Tannenburg after being betrayed by his fiancée, Selma, and the prince he had served. After two years of solitary hard work on the estate, which had fallen into disrepair in his absence, he attends a party at a nearby estate. There he meets a woman everyone refers to as "the cousin," a neighboring property owner of androgynous appearance, whose straightforward manner at first dismays him. As the regional busybody, she has already learned of the baron's romantic imbroglio, and she censures him for his failure to help Selma after the prince had abandoned her. Selma is, after all, the woman he had had educated according to his tastes in order to reap the admiration of others for his handiwork (67). The cousin argues that it is her duty,

> die Männer daran zu erinnern, wenn sie mit einem Frauenschicksal wie mit einem Spielwerk umgehen. Die Stellung der Frau ist durch die Erziehung, die man ihnen giebt, und welche sie unfähig macht, sich selbst zu helfen, oder auch nur zu begreifen, was sie eigentlich wollen und sollen, so beklagenswerth, daß [sie] immer Mitleid mit ihnen [hat], und [denkt], [sie] müsse sie beschützen. (81)

The cousin is herself in the process of "raising" her beautiful young companion, Malwine, although in a rather unorthodox manner: she believes that the customary feminine accomplishments make women impractical and unhappy (53). Malwine prefers music, but she accedes to the vigorous physical regimen the cousin has instituted.

The cousin carries her point with the baron: although he knows that public opinion would absolve him of any guilt toward a woman who had betrayed him (67), he feels a new sense of responsibility for Selma. He attempts to find and help her, but fails. Once recovered from this reminder of his lost love, he visits the cousin and proposes to the beautiful Malwine, whose dependent plight moves him. The cousin has said that women should be raised for obedience and humility in marriage and for independence should they remain single (85), and Malwine appears to fulfill everyone's expectations in her marriage to the baron. Because they were barely acquainted at the point of his proposal, the baron had wondered nervously, "Welch ein Loos werde ich für mein Leben gezogen haben, wenn Malwine sich für mich erklärt?" (94–95), but a reader looking for an object lesson in the advantages of caution will be disappointed.

Malwine knows about the baron's unhappy previous engagement. She determines to restore his faith in love, fidelity, and the "nie endende Dankbarkeit des Frauenherzens."

> Hatte Selma sein Ehrgefühl beleidigt, so wollte sie wachen über die ihr anvertraute Ehre seines Namens, wie über ein Heiligthum; sein Haus sollte ihm ein Tempel alles Guten, Reinen und Schönen werden, und wie er ihr ein neues geistiges Leben erschloß, so wollte sie ihm das sichere, friedensvolle Ruhen in

seinem Hause und in seiner Familie bereiten. (104–05)

Her eager plans conform to contemporary expectations that wives make of their households a domestic shrine and of themselves a badge of their husbands' honor. Their subsequent happiness suggests their suitability to their respective roles: he becomes her eager teacher; she is his ecstatic student and "sorgsame Hausfrau" (106–07).

In 1806 the baron leaves home to fight against Napoleon. Malwine, now pregnant, responds with patriotic composure. At first her husband writes daily; then the letters stop. After a long interval, she receives a note that closes with a cryptic message: "Ich habe Selma wiedergesehen, mehrmals wiedergesehen! Frage mich aber nichts weiter! niemals! und erinnere mich auch später nicht daran" (113). The reader hears no more of these mysterious encounters during the baron's lifetime and concludes that Malwine is indeed a model of wifely self-restraint.

Their newborn son, Hugo, effects a transformation of the androgynous cousin: she subordinates herself to Malwine's wishes; lowers her voice; nurses the baron, who returned from the war wounded; offers her help wherever needed; and makes the boy her heir (115, 117). Her relationship to the family becomes "ein ganz mütterliches" (118).

Three years later the king and queen of Prussia spend a night on the baron's estate. Queen Louise blesses their domestic idyll with her own motherly words of advice to Malwine: "Erhalten Sie Sich das Glück Ihrer Ehe und die Reinheit und den Frieden Ihrer Häuslichkeit, das ist das Höchste auf dem Throne wie in der Hütte" (123), and Malwine is moved. She vows to herself that she will continue to protect her home (124), although this oath is something of a narrative red herring. Hugo is the family member who later takes on the active task of protection, while Malwine never learns what he has done. Lewald actually highlights Malwine's impotence as a wife and mother with her character's pointless vow.

In 1812, after the birth of a daughter, Louise, the baron again leaves home to fight Napoleon. Before he goes, six-year-old Hugo promises that he will take care of his mother. When the baron dies in battle, Malwine, although devastated, rises nobly to the task of raising her fatherless children as the baron would have wished. In accordance with contemporary models, she hires a tutor for her son and educates her daughter herself. She also takes over the management of the estate and devotes herself to "duty" (130). The cousin leaves her own estate for theirs and contemplates with satisfaction the day that Hugo will inherit her land, making her dependent on him. She enjoys spoiling the boy and argues that one must raise girls for "Gehorchen und Dienen" and boys for "Herrschen und Befehlen" (131). Hugo never forgets his promise to his father. His mother, his tutor, and the cousin augment his sense of masculine destiny with serious study, healthy physical exertion, business trips with the cousin, estate management with his mother, poets, the history of the families of the province, hunting, swimming, and riding. However, the narrator tells us, he remains child enough to play with his sister and to shiver at the secrets hidden in Schloß Tannenburg, one of the castles of the Teutonic Order (133).

Hugo idealizes his own family: he imagines his father a man of flawless honor and worships his mother as an exemplary woman (134). Before he leaves home for the university he tells his mother that he recalls once seeing his father receive a letter that startled him and that he hid in a secret compartment of his desk, which now stands in Hugo's room. He has been unable to find the compartment himself. His mother asserts that she knows of no such letter and that she and her husband had no secrets from one another. Hugo rather tactlessly tells her one: not only does he know about Selma, he had heard the story from one of the baron's fellow officers, who also told him that the baron had seen Selma again in 1806 and that their love "damals nicht erloschen gewesen wäre" (140). His irritated mother tells him that he is mistaken and that he, like all young people, enjoys imagining that there are secrets in old houses; "[d]as aber ist der Zauber dieses Hauses, daß Alles in ihm klar und offen ist, und nichts darin, was sich zu scheuen hätte vor dem Tage" (140). There are, however, a number of real and apparent secrets in this allegedly ideal family, which suggests that it is the province of families in general to conceal and to misread their own signs.

Malwina, of course, has deluded herself about the letter as well. Hugo finds the secret compartment and its epistolary contents that night. The letter leads him to believe that the baron had fathered a child with Selma in 1806 and that Selma, begging him to care for the boy, had died shortly before his father had in 1812. "Also," he concludes for the reader, "dieses alte Schloß hatte doch auch seine Geheimnisse, auch das Leben seiner

Familie, sein eigenes Dasein waren nicht so klar, wie seine Mutter das stets gerühmt hatte!" His parents' marriage had not in fact been "so idealisch, so ungetrübt" (144). But what had happened to the mysterious child? Hugo resolves to find this "brother" and "im Sinne seines Vaters, als Haupt seiner Familie, für den jüngeren Bruder sorgen," an undertaking that he will conceal from his mother (145)—also, apparently, as his father would have wished.

Now a student at the university in Berlin, Hugo discovers that Selma had married and that her husband, a French painter, had been killed in a duel. After his death, she had moved to Switzerland. No one, however, has heard of a son. After subsequent fruitless inquiry, Hugo decides to wait for chance to solve his problem. He finishes his studies and returns home to his property, which his mother and the cousin have managed so well in his absence that they have doubled its value. His sister is now eighteen, yet no one but the cousin expresses an interest in marriage for either her or her brother. In response

> hatten die Baronin und ihre Kinder sich gefragt, wie es denn möglich sein werde, dieses gewohnte innigste Beieinandersein zu trennen, oder neue, fremde Persönlichkeiten in einen Kreis zu ziehen, der einander so vollständig genügte, daß man nirgend eine Lücke fühlte; und in der That konnte man kaum ein edleres Familienleben und trefflichere Frauen finden, als in der Tannenburg. (151)

The mid-nineteenth-century family values promoted by Riehl, who argues, for instance, that a house with windows looking onto the inner courtyard and away from the street reflects an ideal domestic environment (186), take on a pathological dimension in this vision of a domestic circle unwilling or unable to look outward.

The baron's absence also compels a renegotiation of roles: the cousin performs his active part, although in her own androgynous fashion. She takes over "das ganze Regiment des inneren Hauswesens und die Details der äußeren Wirthschaft." She "schaltete und waltete mit frischer Kraft," acting "überall wie ein Mann bestimmt und schnell," but sacrificing her own comfort for that of the children (152). The baroness, after a life of exemplary widowhood, enjoys the leisure that the cousin's activity permits her and "weilte...in der Zurückgezogenheit ihres Arbeitszimmers oder im stillen Schatten des Gartens, je nach der Jahreszeit" (152). Her son views her as "das Ideal der Weiblichkeit, der Inbegriff des Heiligen und

Schönen" (153), despite the abdication, otherwise unremarked, of her housewifely responsibilities. As a mother, however, her contributions appear unimpeachable. Although the cousin asserts that "zu viel Liebe...gefährlich überall [ist]," Malwine's children seem at first glance exemplary: Hugo is "ein tüchtiger praktischer Mann" and Louise is "der Liebling aller derer, welche sie kannten." Her admirers include Hugo himself, "der es oftmals liebevoll aussprach, daß sie nur den einen Fehler habe, seine Schwester zu sein, weil dies sie hindere, seine Frau zu werden" (155–56).

An outsider does eventually join the family circle at Hugo's request: Hugo meets the orphaned painter Selmar in Königsberg and, based on the latter's account of himself and his own attraction to him, concludes that Selmar is his half-brother. Selmar at first asserts that he is fortunate to have no family, since only those who have no ties are free to use their talents to the best of their ability (160). Once a guest on Hugo's estate, however, he yields to the joys of domesticity: "er empfand in diesem Hause zum ersten Male den Zauber des Familienlebens, der Familienliebe, und mit jedem neuen Tage, an welchem er desselben genoß, fühlte er deutlicher, was ihm bis dahin gefehlt hatte, was er fortan immer und überall vermissen werde" (187–88). Hugo, who, in order to spare his mother's feelings, has told neither his family nor Selmar of his suspicions, has invited him there to paint his mother and the cousin. Louise, too, becomes a part of the portrait, which Selmar envisions as a representation of the "drei großen Typen der weiblichen Natur, die Greisin, die Mutter und das Mädchen." He wants to link this conventional imagery to the historical epoch with which he associates each: "Ich finde in ihnen den Typus der barocken und doch tüchtigen Zopfzeit, den Typus der Gefühlsepoche, und endlich das Bild unserer frischen, gesunden Gegenwart" (184–85).

Selmar and the "fresh and healthy" Louise fall in love; Hugo rejects Selmar's suit out of hand. Unwilling to reveal his secret to the family, Hugo reminds himself rather desperately that because he is the head of the family, Louise must wait for his blessing (202–03). Because he had earlier effusively invited Selmar to spend his life with the family and had promised to free him from want, his family and Selmar are baffled by his refusal to consider the marriage. Thanks to an outburst by the cousin ("Diese leidenschaftliche Geschwisterliebe ist ja krankhaft, ist ja unnatürlich, es ist ja Alles Überspannung! Alles die Folge der Erziehung durch die Liebe!" [212]), to several dark hints Hugo makes to Selmar ("Ein unseeliges Geheimnis…trennt Euch für immer. Verlange es nicht zu wissen, genug, daß es mein Fluch geworden ist" [217]), and to Hugo's suddenly erratic and yet devoted behavior towards his sister ("Wer ihn nicht kannte, hätte ihn nicht für den Bruder, sondern für einen Bewerber um Louisens Gunst ansehen müssen" [205–06]), the painter begins to fear that his good friend has succumbed to a "Herzensverirrung" (221). He communicates his suspicions to the mother and cousin, and the three of them seek a means to free Hugo from the grip of his criminal passion.

Hugo, meanwhile, attempts to save Louise and Selmar from what he believes is *their* criminal passion. The encounters between the painter and the brother, in which Selmar tries to confess his love and Hugo interrupts him in order to prevent his speaking the unspeakable, have what are presumably unintentionally comic overtones. Finally, however, Hugo has no recourse but to show his friend Selma's letter to the baron, which catapults Selmar into the position of incestuous lover. This story compels him to reimagine his own family as the antithesis of the "ideal" domesticity he had found at Schloß Tannenburg:

> Seine blasse, arbeitsame Mutter, deren er immer mit Rührung gedacht, die ihm die einzige liebe Erinnerung seiner frühen Jugend gewesen war, wurde ihm in eine Buhlerin verwandelt, es wurde ihm ein Vater aufgedrängt, der ihn im Ehebruch erzeugt, der ihn allen Zufällen des Lebens sorglos überlassen hatte…. Ein Bruder stand vor ihm, der in falscher Selbstüberhebung sich vermessen zum Leiter seines Schicksals gemacht; er hatte eine Schwester gefunden, und diese Schwester liebte er, daß er nicht wußte, wie er ihr entsagen sollte! (234–35)

The "ideale Familienliebe" he has witnessed in Hugo's home serves both as a cultural reproach and as the source of his own flawed family ties, suggesting the sordid variety comprehended in the concept of the "family" and the pernicious effects of the mythologizing of the ideal.

The two men eventually turn to the cousin for information. She, as it turns out, had known about the letter, but had been unable to find Selma's son after the baron's death. Selmar is in fact the son of the French painter whom Selma had married. The baron had attempted to help her in 1806, after she had lost her husband, but had had no sexual contact with her. The reader learns with surprise that had Malwine not been "foolishly jealous" of the baron's first love, he would have told her about Selma's letter and located the errant former girlfriend earlier. Their "ideal" marriage receives another subtle drubbing from the plot in the shape of Malwine's hitherto unsuspected jealousy. Hugo and Selmar are jubilant, Selmar and Louise marry and leave, and Hugo, too, finds a wife. The baroness never learns about Hugo's mistaken assumptions and his subsequent dilemma, for which Hugo congratulates himself: he had kept his promise to his father to care for his mother in the baron's own spirit.

Once again, an apparently happy ending raises more questions than it answers. What is the ideal family? Can it ever be what it seems? Is the pursuit of the ideal not an inherently futile and even dangerous endeavor? Lewald explicitly frames this domestic circle as a transcendent example of familial perfection and then systematically undermines the domestic role and behavior of virtually all of its members. Hugo succumbs to the "authority" of his position, frequently and joyfully confirmed even by the family's most "masculine" woman, and presumes to conceal information from a "brother," as well as from all the women in the family, in order to redress a wrong he did not commit. With this character, Lewald indicts the patriarchal tradition also embodied by the origins of Schloß Tannenburg itself, which had so fascinated the young aristocrat. Malwine becomes a ghostly inhabitant of the home in which she once vowed to be a champion of family happiness. The cousin sows disorder from the beginning, attempting to mold first Malwine and then Hugo in accordance with her own gender paradigms. She eventually usurps both Malwine's place and then—by knowing more than he does—Hugo's. Louise becomes the apparent object of desire for both of her "brothers." In the end, Lewald indicates, one honors the idea of "family" best by embracing (bourgeois) outsiders and then by leaving home, returning only for occasional visits after having extricated oneself from the "überspanntes Gefühlsleben" of the domestic circle.

### IV

Almost forty years after the publication of *Clementine*, Lewald allows the protagonist of "Der Magnetberg" (1880) to rebel briefly against the domestic imperative. The outcome, however, appears at first glance to make the conservative point that women ignore their "Bestimmung" at their peril. Lewald had certainly argued elsewhere that women prefer a happy marriage to employment (*Für und wider* 171), but here her text seems to acknowledge that they may in fact require some heavy-handed prompting to recognize their preference. The narrator begins her story with a reference to the "Magnetberg" of the fairy tale, which had lured so many sailors to their doom. As a child, the narrator claims, she had been particularly moved by the plight of the captains' wives and children she saw on the Dutch ships in the harbor of her hometown. They would perish with the husband and father who had set his course for the alluring, though fatal, floating mountain of gold and precious stones. Only a last-minute change of course or the intervention of another can save such a sailor. The small-town protagonist, Frieda, feels drawn to the glamour and the possibilities of Berlin as surely as the seafarers had been to the "Magnetberg." She learns after years of struggle in the city that an honorable proposal from the boy next door is far preferable to the promise of adventure or more mysterious romance elsewhere.

At home in her provincial town Frieda had been considered the prettiest, the worthiest, and one of the best educated of her circle (181). Unfortunately, however, thanks to her mother's imprudent marriage to an officer who had invested her fortune unwisely and then died, her charms are purely personal and thus not substantial enough to persuade the men of her class to consider her as a potential wife. Her education has enabled her to teach young children, which contributes to the family income, but Frieda begins to long for Berlin as the place where she might really make her fortune. The narrative does not specify just how she might achieve this goal beyond an offer on the part of an old friend to help her make a career on the stage and the suggestion that "manche, die weniger schön gewesen war,…eine reiche Heirat geschlossen [hatte]" (182), but the nebulous possibilities of large cities attract one young woman from the provinces after another (217).

The real source of Frieda's discontent, however, is not the lack of suitors or the limited family funds, but the constriction and familiarity of her surroundings: "Sie hätte etwas Andres, hätte viel, viel mehr thun, sich müder machen mögen, nur um nicht alle Tage den gleichen Weg zu gehen, die gleiche Beschäftigung üben zu müssen fort und fort, Jahr für Jahr! vielleicht ihr Leben lang" (184). When her mother dies, she decides to leave home, ignoring the advice and the warnings of her friends. The narrative underscores Frieda's determination with an unexpected proposal

from Gottlieb, the son of her landlady, who owns a textile shop. He makes
his case to the reader by telling Frieda that he would have studied had his
family been able to afford it, but that he nevertheless intends to make a
name for himself. He offers Frieda a middle-class existence, telling her that
she will not have to work in the family business as his mother had, but that
she can "sing, read, do whatever she likes." Whatever she does will make
him happy when he comes home from work (191). She hesitates, knowing
that he would be a good husband, but then insists, "ich muß wirklich fort,
es leidet mich nicht länger in der Enge" (192).

Although the narrator suggests that life in this town is truly quite
circumscribed, her tale will not permit Frieda to succeed outside it. The
narrator is an author to whom Frieda had appealed for advice while still
living at home. She had counseled Frieda, she says, the way she does all
such correspondents, telling her to learn from the example of the many
men who work dutifully as lawyers, doctors, clerics, and teachers in the
most isolated areas. Their education entitles them to more than any young
woman can demand, and they are in more of a position to expect a change
in fortune (195). Almost two years after Frieda has ignored that
disappointing advice by going to Berlin, she visits the narrator and relates
the story of her difficulties to her. There was great competition for the
teaching positions she had anticipated finding, she explains, and she had
had no money for additional schooling to improve her own abilities.
Eventually she had turned to her mother's relatives, who either had too
many daughters of their own to be able to help her or were simply
unwilling to aid the vast army of provincial distant relatives who hoped to
make an advantageous marriage in the city. She then had no choice but to
approach the son and daughter-in-law of a wealthy merchant she had
known in her hometown. She had once hoped that the son, Leo, might
propose to her. Leo remembered her fondly, even too fondly. His wealthy,
kind, but rather plain wife had offered her assistance immediately, and Leo
had suggested that she would be suited for a career on the stage. Later,
however, he had revealed his plan to keep her in a nearby apartment while
his wife financed her singing lessons and he "secretly" arranged the
beginning of her theatrical career. Frieda had rejected this insult to both
herself and Leo's worthy wife and found herself with no recourse but to
visit the narrator. The narrator then tries but fails to help her to find
employment. Despairing, Frieda considers throwing herself into the Spree,

but her courage fails her.

One of the narrator's letters of introduction, however, later leads to an offer of work as a "Probirmamsell" at a kind of dressmaker's shop. These women must "auf Befehl in jede beliebige Kleidung hineinschlüpfen" and "vor den Augen der kaufenden Männer und Frauen durch ihre Wohlgestalt den begehrten Anzug zu einer Geltung...bringen, welchen die oft unschönen Käuferinnen ihm nicht zu geben vermögen" (223). Although the owner tells Frieda that he values her respectability, this nineteenth-century equivalent to runway modeling functions here as an occupation just a step or two above prostitution: her relatives will now be unable to see her socially (225) and the women are subjected to the "langsame Geflissenheit, mit welcher die Männer [sie] betrachten, wenn sie für die Ihren ein Kleidungsstück zu wählen kommen" (226). Mortified but destitute, she accepts the offer, reflecting in the months that follow that she had driven herself out of the "paradise" of her youth (227).

In the preceding years Frieda had heard that Gottlieb was building a factory and a new house and that he had been elected to the city council. After eight months of practicing her shameful trade, she actually encounters Gottlieb in the store. He wants to see the mantilla he plans to buy, and her employer calls on her to model it. Frieda faints when she sees him; her employer sends her home to recover. Gottlieb visits her in her lowly lodgings, where he tells her that he is traveling on business to England, Belgium, and the Rhineland, that he is busy moving into his new house, and that they will write to his mother to let her know that Frieda is coming home. Frieda understands this statement as the marriage proposal that it is and responds with gratitude, a fortunate response, since Gottlieb has already told her employer that she will be leaving. They then drive out into the countryside. Frieda sits at Gottlieb's side, "ein von sich und alle seinem eigenen falschen Wahn und Streben zu seinem Heil, durch des treuen Mannes erlösende Liebe, befreites Geschöpf" (234). Frieda's story ends with the birth of a son and Gottlieb's joke that if she had followed the narrator's original advice and had stayed with him "wo [sie] hingehört[e]," they might have a daughter by now, too (236). Knowing one's place, the narrative intimates, promotes the growth of families. The narrator adds her own fear that perhaps she should not have suggested that a story like Frieda's can have a happy ending. After all, "nicht Jede findet das treue Herz und die feste Hand, sie noch zur rechten Zeit zurück

zu reißen aus des verlockenden Magnetberges verhängnißvollem Strudel."
Still, she concludes, she enjoys speaking of people like Gottlieb und telling
tales in which happiness succeeds suffering (237).

What kind of happiness has Frieda achieved? After having
"overestimated" herself and her abilities (222), thanks to those who,
according to Gottlieb, "[ihr] den Kopf verdreht [hatten] von Kindheit an"
(233), she can appreciate the narrator's early advice to stay where "gute
Menschen von [ihr] wüßten, und das Nächstliegende…thun" (236). Her
story ends with marriage, one baby and the promise of more, and a
provincial paradise regained. The tale, as well as the narrator's complacent
asides, indicates that a woman's special destiny cannot be eluded and that
the task of the "Familienvater" is to guide grateful women back to the
hearth.

Oddly, however, Frieda appreciates this hearth only after the narrative
has soundly humiliated her, exposing her not only to the ogling of male
customers, but to Gottlieb's instant recognition of how completely she has
failed to make her mark in Berlin. Does the author shame her character as
punishment for her inappropriate desires or in order to compel her
appreciation of domesticity? Telling her story, Frieda asserts that she is
now so happy that she would not wish to eliminate the "Dornenpfade und
das Dunkel, durch die [sie] gegangen [war]" (218). Without this litany of
punishments, the story suggests, she might have failed to recognize her
own "happiness." Most readers will be satisfied at this point that only
marriage can save Frieda from starvation or suicide. Once she ages, she
will no longer be able to work as a "Probirmamsell," and her qualifications
have proven insufficient to secure her any other employment. The author,
however, takes no risks. Even Gottlieb, already "groß und kräftig" (189),
must undergo a makeover in order to drive home the desirability of this
match. Within three years, by the time he is about thirty, this
undereducated salesclerk in a family fabric store has become a city
councillor and built a factory and a business that necessitates far-flung
travel. Marriage, even in the provinces, must be palatable to Frieda now.

What recourse, however, do women without a heroic suitor have? The
narrator asks this question indirectly by concluding her tale as though it
were about "good people like Gottlieb" and by saying that not everyone
will find such a savior. She has already told us that the death of Frieda's
mother meant that a large part of the family income disappeared as well.

Frieda had failed to find another suitor in her hometown and was inadequately educated to meet the standards expected of teachers in the metropolis. On second glance, it does not surprise us that Gottlieb permits himself the presumption of announcing Frieda's engagement to her and that the author dedicates her story to him: without him, Frieda might well have drowned herself. The stacked deck of cards that life and the author have handed the female protagonist may, in fact, be Lewald's point. While Frieda may be satisfied with marriage and motherhood in East Prussia by the end of the story, what other options does she have?

## V

All of the families represented in these texts confront in some sense the domestic norms and limitations operative in Lewald's own culture. The female protagonists assent to these norms, albeit reluctantly in two instances. Reluctance postpones the moment of domestic definition for these characters, while suggesting to the reader that their eventual submission should be read as a "choice." Malwine's unquestioning acquiescence, on the other hand, leads immediately and more obviously to her marginalization even within her own home. The problematic outcome of even the most obedient character calls domestic ideology as a whole into question, as one woman after another—in direct contradiction of the promises of contemporary theorists—finds the exercise of "Bestimmung" unsatisfying, conducive to both marginalization and pathological attachment, and appealing only as an alternative to indigence.

## CONCLUSION

# Re-reading Sophie

Fanny Lewald's authorial ambivalence toward the joys of women's alleged vocation suggests a corollary skepticism of the discourses that contributed to marking its parameters: the ideal "spouse, mother, and housewife" was a gendered reproductive body, a legal entity, and an educational project. As we have seen, this bourgeois paragon owed her existence to domestic ideology; she, in turn, was the fundamental principle upon which its tenets were based. The myriad attempts made over the course of the nineteenth century to define "Woman" focused on the elucidation of the characteristics that made her so ideally suited to family life and, increasingly, on determining how best to keep her within the domestic circle. These attempts derived support from various discursive realms. Medical, legal, and educational theorists contributed their disciplinary evidence and arrived at the same conclusion: for the sake of the state, the culture, and women themselves, "Bestimmung" will and must prevail. Their bodies demand it, the law acknowledges it, and education ensures it. Lewald's texts probe the boundaries and the determinants of this vocation in the construction of female characters and gendered dilemmas.

In recent decades critics have lauded Lewald's perceptive and critical essays on the subject of the position of women, particularly with respect to education and employment. These critics have argued that her fiction, on the other hand, uncritically reproduced cultural norms of feminine behavior and "nature." As I have demonstrated, however, these texts also exhibit an awareness of the exigencies of nineteenth-century femininity and of the way in which contemporary discourses determined these. Her work both presents and confronts the issues under discussion in her era, which included the medical, the legal, the educational, and the familial aspects of the construction of "woman."

Countless commentators have noted that women's childbearing capacity was the defining feature of female physiology in the nineteenth century and that theorists extrapolated a proclivity for domestic life from this feature. These thinkers sought support for that view from the rest of the body as well. Johann Ludwig Ewald claimed in 1807, for instance, that women can breathe more deeply than men, which enables them to live indoors without injury to themselves (41). Their physical form also destines them for marriage: "delicate, fine, and round," women are clearly designed to appeal to men, their complements (74). Somewhat more soberly, Jakob Ackermann had argued in 1788 that not only did women's reproductive organs differ from those of men, so did every part of their bodies (Frevert 54). While Ackermann did not explore the "social" and "moral" implications of his physiological research, subsequent writers, physicians, and philosophers did (Frevert 55). Wilhelm Heinrich Riehl, for example, argued, "Es gibt nur *einen* menschlichen *Geist*, aber es gibt eine männliche und weibliche *Seele*, die mitbedingt ist durch die höchst verschiedenartige Nerven-, Knochen-, Blut- und Muskelbildung von Mann und Frau. Es entspringt daraus ein gesonderter und weiblicher Beruf" (93). Proponents thus insisted that the doctrine of separate spheres originated not in a politics of difference, but in the "natural" body. In three of the texts I have discussed, "Doktor Melchior," *Liebesbriefe. Aus dem Leben eines Gefangenen*, and *Treue Liebe*, Lewald does not dispute the concept of gendered physiological difference. These narratives, however, rewrite the female body as an advocate for better working conditions for wives and mothers.

As several of Lewald's stories and novels make clear, the "natural" inferiority identified by medical writers translated readily, though less obviously, to the legal realm as well. Here, too, "Woman" could be constructed as subordinate because in need of "protection." This protection, however, was proffered in a manner that demanded her continued legal subordination. The legal code gave authority to husbands and left it to them—and their persuasive wives—to determine a personal degree of magnanimity. The subtext of this argument was the state's reliance on the domestic hierarchy: families were the state in miniature. Those that honored the father as an absolute ruler produced good citizens. "Ruler" was the operative word: the law invested husbands with complete control of their wives' lives, a control exemplified by the financial relationship. Control of a wife's fortune made manifest both masculine superiority and feminine distance from the world of work and commerce. Lewald's *Eine Lebensfrage*, "Das große Loos," and "Kein Haus. Eine Dorfgeschichte" take issue with the consequences of women's exclusion from the legislative process that, among other things, deemed them their own husbands' "wards."

Most often, however, Lewald promoted improvements in girls' education as a means to improve women's lives. Nineteenth-century education in general participated in the constitution of women who understood the boundaries of their "nature" and were unprepared to go beyond them. Late eighteenth-century thinkers had begun to advocate the reform of girls' education, arguing that education should make girls better mothers and teachers of their young children and more interesting companions to their husbands. Throughout much of the subsequent century, the curriculum supported this goal with needlework and lessons that emphasized literature and ignored the natural sciences. Anxiety that girls might be stimulated into unsuitability for their "natural" vocation precluded more thoroughgoing instruction. Few were satisfied with the results, however. According to critics, girls were neither adequately trained in domestic skills nor adequately educated in the disciplines permitted them. Riehl complained that women were feminizing masculine science and art by virtue of their misguided education; meanwhile, they neglected the "Mysterien des deutschen Hauses" (26). Davidis also bemoaned the neglect of housekeeping skills in favor of French and dilettantish knowledge (4), but her complaints focused on the attempt of the schools to cover too many subjects, which resulted in deplorable gaps (13). Predictably, women did not become the enlightened companions to their husbands that the early theorists had promised (Rosenbaum 346). Lewald's essays, "Einige Gedanken über Mädchenerziehung" and the open letters in *Für und wider die Frauen*, argue that educational options should in fact be expanded. Her *Nella. Eine Weihnachtsgeschichte* and "In Ragaz" take a carrot-and-stick approach to the issue in fictional form: the former makes a gift of a demure but educated woman to a happy husband, while the latter warns of the dangers to which an empty-headed wife is prey.

Medicine, law, and education cooperated in the endeavor to identify the characteristics of a model femininity and to cultivate these in the production of ideal spouses, mothers, and housewives. The energy expended on this endeavor, however, suggests that the ideal was contested. Despite Lewald's nominal adherence to a gendered code of behavior for her female characters, her work can be read as voicing dissent, proposing modifications to the prevailing representations, and advocating recognition of the very real disadvantages attendant upon a feminine vocation and destiny that mandated passivity, self-denial, chastity, ignorance, and modest contentment. Her narratives suggest the difficulty of achieving this profile and the probability that those who succeed will find it difficult to live with the consequences. Her work suggests further that such excellence in fact benefits no one except the scoundrels her tales are at pains to discredit. Hence, her heroines discover that illness may be their only recourse in untenable situations, that worthy femininity is no defense before the law, which excludes them by definition, that only the education decried as "unfeminine" can gain them the domesticity for which they are destined, and that a life focused inward may prove monotonous, even diseased.

Writers such as Ewald, Davidis, and Riehl preach patience to the hapless wives trapped in their own "Bestimmung," but Lewald offers narrative solutions: divorce, rival suitors who shame failed husbands and lovers, deaths that point an accusing finger, illness that liberates, education that attracts, domesticity that visibly fails to satisfy. She became a best-selling author, which suggests that her solutions resonated with her (presumably largely female) readership. As Linda Alcoff has suggested, women may "utilize" their position for "the construction of meaning, [as] a place from where meaning is constructed, rather than simply the place where a meaning can be *discovered* (the meaning of femaleness)" (434). Lewald's texts identify the prevailing "truths" about femininity and its significance and challenge these by spotlighting the contradictions and inadequacy of contemporary paradigms. By imagining both the constraints and the possibilities of the lives of her female characters,[1] by choosing to laud some aspects of acceptable femininity and discarding others, Lewald's work demands a revision and an expansion of the "meanings" and the practical options available to her female readers.

In the scene I described in my introduction, *Eine Lebensfrage*'s Sophie Harkourt does not, at first, change her clothes and "become" a woman who conforms to Julian Brand's notions of gendered behavior. Rather, she takes off her jacket and, in her tight-fitting gold brocade men's vest, arouses

Julian's lust. In other words, she captivates him with a self-conscious awareness of the contradictions of her feminine form and her masculine costume, and he succumbs to her transgression and mockery of the very norms he claims to support. When he finally does end their relationship— because of her lack of decorum—she becomes a "barmherzige Schwester" in a French paupers' hospital. Julian learns about her decision once he recovers from a life-threatening illness, and the last words of the novel are his: "Arme Sophie!"

Lewald writes two stereotypical female roles for Sophie: mistress and nurse. The latter redeems the former for Julian's sister and friend and, presumably, for Lewald's readers. Sophie turns to her life of penance with the ailing poor, however, in apparent opposition to Julian's wishes: he had assumed she would continue acting. While this choice may not appear to constitute much of a rebellion, Sophie fixes upon what, for the former actress, is the least predictable of the few options available to her. She thereby compels Julian's pity and, perhaps, remorse. Nineteenth-century readers who read Sophie's sacrifice as sententious proof that illicit relationships must be punished were compelled also to recognize with Sophie in the earlier scene that gender is a matter of performance. Like her fictional sisters, Sophie indeed "becomes" a woman, but she determines what form her femininity will take—"ministering angel" as opposed to "sexually available actress"—and she highlights some rather disturbing messages about the lack of appeal of pure "femininity" along the way.

# NOTES

## INTRODUCTION

1   This is of course a generalization. Gabriele Schneider's *Vom Zeitroman zum "stylisierten" Roman*, for instance, represents an exception. Her study of the influences on and development of Lewald's literary technique examines texts written over the course of Lewald's entire career, including many of the texts I discuss here. Schneider also notes that the reception of Lewald's work has in general been limited to her early novels and her autobiography (1). She takes issue with the critical tendency to treat Lewald's "erzählerisches Werk als Beiwerk, Illustration und Ornamentik der emanzipatorischen Thesen und Ausführungen" of the author, arguing that the work itself thus "zu sehr ins Abseits [gerät]" (1). Although I agree that Lewald's later fiction has been ignored because of its alleged lack of emancipatory models, I cannot fully concur with Schneider's criticism, since it is my own thesis that an emancipatory tendency can and should be read more generously in Lewald's fiction than has previously been done, including by Schneider herself. She argues, for instance, that neither the fiction nor the essays demonstrate much in the way of emancipation (120). Schneider examines Lewald's fiction for general social criticism, finding, among other things, positions on socialism, Jewish emancipation, the nobility, the Catholic church, marital property law, and divorce law. With the latter two issues Schneider's interests overlap with mine in this study, but gender *per se* is not the focus of her investigation. When she comments on Lewald's conception of women as the family's moral instance, for example, she cites "[j]üdisches Denken und jüdische Tradition" as formative influences (73), rather than the nineteenth-century constructions of femininity I discuss.

## CHAPTER ONE

1   Julie Burow (1806–1868), whose married name was Pfannenschmidt, began writing novels after her children were grown. She "[s]childert hauptsächlich das Leben in den kleinen Städten unter besonderer Berücksichtigung der Stellung der Frau in der kleinbürgerlichen Familie" (Brinker-Gabler, Ludwig, and Wöffen 50).

2    See, for instance, Carl Niekerk's study of Goethe's use in *Faust II* of competing
     scientific models of the body.

3    Londa Schiebinger notes that "[a] number of manuals on the illnesses of women
     appeared in the late eighteenth and early nineteenth centuries" and cites several of
     these, three of which are German sources (80, note 101). According to Barbara
     Duden, a "wealth of health manuals" from the late eighteenth century gave
     general instructions to the layperson on the maintenance of health (15). My own
     online search under the rubric "Diseases of Women" turned up 103 variations on
     this theme, the vast majority of which were published between 1740 and 1903.

4    *Dorland's Illustrated Medical Dictionary*, on the other hand, appears to link chlorosis
     to the nineteenth century itself: it is "a disorder, especially common during the
     nineteenth century and disappearing abruptly soon thereafter, generally affecting
     adolescent females, believed to be associated with iron deficiency anemia, and
     characterized by greenish yellow discoloration of the skin and by hypochromic
     erythrocytes" (257).

5    Twentieth-century researchers also cite an average red blood cell count that is
     somewhat higher in men than in women, although they tend to draw different
     conclusions from this finding. As one textbook puts it, women thus "usually" have
     a lower concentration of hemoglobin. Because of this lower concentration and a
     "smaller blood volume, they have a smaller maximal oxygen-carrying capacity
     than men," which probably explains differences in "maximal aerobic power"
     between adult men and women (O'Toole and Douglas 15–16). For the purposes
     of my discussion, the ideological significance of gendered erythrocyte counts is the
     nineteenth-century intimation that "health" accrues only to men, the richly
     globuled.

6    This general assumption is still apparent even in late twentieth-century physiology
     texts. W.F. Ganong, for instance, gives the "average normal red blood cell count"
     for both men and women and then, with this count, computes the amount of
     hemoglobin in the "circulating blood of the adult man" (429). Anyone interested
     in the hemoglobin values of the adult woman will have to compute it herself. The
     organization of the sections on male and female reproductive physiology in Arthur
     J. Vander, James H. Sherman, and Dorothy S. Luciano's textbook, published in
     1994, suggests that infertility is solely a female physiological issue, although the
     authors acknowledge that "the number of infertile men and women [is]
     approximately equal" (690). Conception and contraception are also discussed in
     this textbook under the rubric of female physiology, making vasectomies and
     condoms (688) women's issues.

7    Chapter 2 of Thomas Laqueur's book, for instance, is titled "Destiny is Anatomy,"
     but the entire book makes this point.

8    Laqueur mentions an exception and comments on its similarity to nineteenth-
     century medical imagery: W.F. Ganong's *Review of Medical Physiology*'s single
     "moment of fancy" is in the section on the menstrual cycle; it is "the only lyrical

moment linking the reductionism of modern science to the experiences of humanity in 599 pages of compact, emotionally subdued prose: 'Thus, to quote an old saying, "Menstruation is the uterus crying for lack of a baby"''' (225). Laqueur refers to the 1977 edition of Ganong's text. By 1985, Ganong had distanced himself—but only somewhat—from the earlier statement, which became "This is why it used to be taught that 'menstruation is the uterus crying for lack of a baby'" (363).

9   Although midwives remained active in Germany throughout the nineteenth century and into the twentieth, they were increasingly the object of regulation by the state. It was also expected that they would "bei regelwidrigen Geburtsfällen... rechtzeitig und unbedingt die Hinzuziehung eines Geburtshelfers [anordnen]" ("Hebammen," *Brockhaus* 8: 922–23). The era of Justine Siegemund, the famed German midwife of the late seventeenth century who had written a book on midwifery, was at an end. Siegemund is the only female practitioner cited in the German section of Irving S. Cutter's history of midwifery. For Cutter, the history of German midwifery begins again in 1751 with the first of a long series of achievements and publications by male obstetricians (95–98). While some midwives may have remained "experts" in the eyes of their loyal female clients— and Shorter insists that there were increasingly fewer of these, as "middle-class [German] women began in the nineteenth century to engage man midwives and doctors for normal deliveries"; in fact, doing so became a veritable "fashion" (*Bodies* 142)—they apparently no longer enjoyed the independence and the prestige necessary to publish. They were thus presumably not legitimate sources of privileged "scientific" theory and discourse.

10  Kisch's text suggests that doctors know less about male bodies. For instance, repeated microscopic examination of the semen may be necessary to diagnose azoospermia (115), and men are apparently more able to resist being examined at all (147–48). Mantegazza finds men physically more diverse and individual than women, "aus demselben Grunde, warum die civilisierten Menschen sich mehr von einander unterscheiden als die Wilden, die Erwachsenen mehr als die Kinder" (75), and hence presumably less knowable. Their bodies also did not offer the opportunity for manual and surgical penetration available to late nineteenth-century gynecologists (Tatlock 306).

11  The armamentarium available to the gynecologist for visualizing the invisible was vast: Kisch gives instructions on the "genaue Weise" in which the female genitals should be examined to determine the causes of infertility and recommends the fingers, the speculum, bimanual palpation, the "Uterussonde," chemical tests, and a microscope to examine the various structures and their secretions (*Sterilität* 146– 47).

12  Other physicians displayed the same confidence. According to S. Weir Mitchell (originator of the infamous "rest cure" that so depressed Charlotte Perkins Gilman), "No group of men...so truly interprets, comprehends, and sympathizes

with woman as do physicians, who know how near to disorder and how close to misfortune she is brought by the very peculiarities of her nature" (qtd. in Shorter, *Doctors* 112). Perhaps Mondot's lack of such confidence explains his exclusion from the various biographical encyclopedias I located. Almost all of the other physicians I discuss are to be found in one or several of them.

13   Edward Shorter also includes a number of historical and contemporary sources on the physician's insistence on maintaining an impression of infallibility. See, for example, the autobiography of a doctor who recalled an ear, nose, and throat specialist who told a patient that he had taken out only the "male tonsils" and that the "female tonsils had grown again," rather than admit that he had done an inadequate tonsillectomy the first time (*Doctors* 172). See also the respect allegedly accorded by other physicians to those who were able to make instant diagnoses. One that Shorter cites, for instance, had written in a medical journal article on the "practioner of the future": "Ignoring my carefully written history, he pulled down the bed clothes, gave two or three prods in the right iliac region [right lower part of abdomen] and curtly announced 'osteosarcoma of the ilium; inoperable' and walked away" (*Doctors* 86).

14   Miriam Bailin also discusses the paid nurse exemplified by Dickens's Sairy Gamp, who stood in contrast to the idealized sort envisioned by Nightingale and also propagated in fiction. Sairy Gamp, "with her mercenary pieties and comic violence against the ill, for most of the century epitomized the popular view." However, "opposites that are embodied in the same figure have a way of merging with or invading each other with unintended or ironic effects. The attributes and tendencies of the hired nurse both qualify nursing as redemptive act and make manifest the reductive terms upon which such redemption is achieved" (38).

15   The female protagonist of Marie von Ebner-Eschenbach's *Unsühnbar*, for instance, suffers a "Herzruptur" and dies after re-encountering the seducer who had destroyed her happiness (140), suggesting that this connection was still quite plausible in the late nineteenth century.

16   Barbara Duden, for instance, mentions Norbert Elias's examination of "how the external disciplining of the body of the upper classes, which at the beginning of the [seventeenth] century still was accomplished primarily by strict ceremonial rules of etiquette, shifted toward an inner disciplining. It included mental control, *moderation of the passions*, but also restraint of movement and a calculated awareness of environmental influences as they affected 'health'" [my emphasis] (14).

17   In her article on "discipline and daydreaming" in Lewald's work, Regula Venske details Lewald's own suspicion of "'irrational' imagination" (189) and her focus on "self-control, self-discipline, and self-denial" (188).

18   The "Sturzbad" in question is perhaps a reference to James Currie's "cold water affusion" treatment for fever, which apparently consisted of pouring buckets of cold water over patients whose temperatures are and have been elevated for quite a while, and whose extremities are also hot, and who are not generally or

profusely perspiring. Currie and other proponents wrote that the method was not as well-accepted as it should have been, because when it was "resorted to improperly, the consequences...brought it into disrepute" (Currie v). This "disrepute" perhaps explains Lewald's intimation of the drastic nature of Konrad's methods. The *Brockhaus* of 1892–95 states that the "Kaltwasserkur" had been used in antiquity and then abandoned until Currie in England "mit Erfolg die fieberhaften Krankheiten mit kalten Bädern behandelt hatte" (10: 62). In Germany, Sebastian Kneipp used water in 1848 to treat an illness of his own and then expanded his method into a systematic treatment (10: 438). A few years before Lewald wrote her novel, Heinrich Heine allegedly saved the life of Karl Marx's infant daughter, who was suffering convulsions, by putting her into a bath (Sammons 261). Although, as Jeffrey Sammons notes, this anecdote is unsubstantiated, its existence suggests a popular willingness to believe that being immersed in water might be an appropriate last resort for a patient in dire straits. As far as the "gewaltsame" treatment of cutting off Mathilde's hair is concerned, it seems unlikely that Lewald would simply have invented this "cure," but I can find no mention of it in any of the contemporary texts I have read on the treatment of fever. Perhaps one can (and did) extrapolate from remarks like this one found in Chitty's text: "very thick hair" can sometimes cause weakness, thanks to "undue warmth and perspiration" (434). Additional literary support may be found in Laura Ingalls Wilder's *By the Shores of Silver Lake*. In this book, part of a series in which the author fictionalizes her "pioneer girlhood" in the American Midwest of the 1870s and 1880s, a character contracts scarlet fever and nearly dies, losing her sight in the process. Because of the fever, her father cuts off her long hair.

19    Mathilde's insistence on retaining her own religious beliefs echoes a similar development in Lewald's *Jenny*. The eponymous heroine converts to Christianity but then tells her fiancé, Reinhard, that she cannot really accept its tenets. Reinhard, in contrast to Edmund, ends the engagement.

20    Beck's text indicates that this assertion is incorrect (501–08), but accuracy was not the point. What was interesting to Chitty and his audience was the possibility of establishing a mother's guilt or innocence. This motivation presumably explains the tests that Beck details—and "detail" is the operative word here—in which fifteen infant cadavers were used as forensic crash dummies to determine exactly what sort of injury (i.e., accidental or otherwise) would cause particular head wounds (553–54).

21    Underdeveloped or malformed sexual organs not attributable to masturbation also appear regularly in Kisch's account. The litany of deformations and the female reproductive monsters that haunt his pages and Beck's give additional credence to the theory that "female" was synonymous with "pathology."

22    One aspect of the modern body that Laqueur describes was the rising assumption of the inferiority of female sexual sensation and a corollary decrease in the presumed importance of the female orgasm to reproduction (see, for example, 1–

4, 150, and 161). Acton's views exemplify this tendency. He maintains that (otherwise unidentified) "competent witnesses" confirm that the "majority of women (happily for them) are not very much troubled with sexual feeling of any kind. What men are habitually, women are only exceptionally" (133). Lack of sexual desire becomes a mark of excellence: "The best mothers, wives, and managers of households know little or nothing of sexual indulgences. Love of home, children, and domestic duties are the only passions they feel" (134). Female desire as comparable to male desire and female orgasm as a necessary constituent of intercourse resulting in conception, however, were still contested issues in the late nineteenth century and, as Kisch's anecdote illustrates, found both popular and medical support.

23  Acton, for instance, praises wifely duty and self-sacrifice in the context of women who overcome their "natural repugnance" toward sex (136) for the sake of their husbands: "I believe this lady is a perfect picture of an English wife and mother, kind, considerate, self-sacrificing, and sensible, so pure-hearted as to be utterly ignorant of and averse to any sensual indulgence, but so unselfishly attached to the man she loves, as to be willing to give up her own wishes and feelings for his sake" (135).

24  Lewald's *Eine Lebensfrage* (1845) provides excellent examples of acceptable and unacceptable male illness. Literally overnight, the worldly and powerful Julian becomes acutely ill with a raging fever after an incautious late-night flower delivery to his former mistress. His sickness is the catalyst for several epiphanic moments that change the lives of a number of his friends and relatives, several of whom attend him in his brief but dangerous illness. The young and delicate Theophil, on the other hand, suffers for months from headaches and a persistent melancholy with which most of his friends eventually lose patience.

25  Theodor Fontane's *Effi Briest*, on the other hand, does seek treatment for infertility at Ems, but the narrative brings her adultery to light before she can achieve a cure.

## CHAPTER TWO

1  Hereafter referred to as the *ALR*. Further, all laws referred to by paragraph are from the *ALR*.

2  Someone with the "Fähigkeit, Träger von Rechten und Pflichten zu sein."

3  Gerhard quotes this definition of "Sonderrecht": "Das Wesen des Sonderrechts besteht darin, daß es...bestimmte Klassen aus dem Herrschaftsgebiet einer allgemeinen, an sich also auch für sie geltenden Regel herausnimmt und einer besonderen Vorschrift unterstellt, mithin ein besonderes Recht, ein jus proprium für diese Klasse bildet, das von dem für die übrigen geltenden jus commune abweicht" (213, note 1).

4  Rudolf Huebner, for instance, writing in 1908, suggests that the revival of "sex-guardianship" in the German states beginning in the 1500s "was aided by the

reception of the Roman law" (67). Johann Kaspar Bluntschli would disagree that this relationship constituted a disadvantage for nineteenth-century women. While he acknowledges that the "Vormundschaft" of the husband and father resembles that of the Roman "potestas," he argues "[w]ar die *potestas* vorzugsweise eine *Herrschaft* des Gewalthabers, so ist der Charakter der Vormundschaft mehr Sorge, *Schutz* und *Vertretung* des Hülfsbedürftigen, und daher wesentlich *Pflicht* der Familie und des Vormundes" (562–63). Law and gendered social codes cooperate to support the continued existence of the dominant family father.

5   A "hoher preußischer Richter" whose name was never mentioned and who was called in 1830 to draft revisions of the *ALR*'s family law (Blasius 31; Gerhard 213, note 13). Gerhard argues that his work gives us insight into the "Rechtsmeinung und -praxis zum ALR" for the first few decades of its existence (156).

6   Christian Friedrich Koch calls on I Corinthians 7: 4–5, which states that the "wife hath not power of her own body, but the husband: and likewise also the wife unto the husband" and which supports the idea that the issue is gender neutral, as one of his sources in his commentary to this paragraph, but the opening sentences of his note belie that neutrality: "Was heißt das? Wie mag einer sittsamen Frau zugemuthet werden, diesen Punkt vor ihr völlig fremden Mannspersonen zu verhandeln!" (72, note 4).

7   Gerlach's religious fervor and his indignation at the concept of marriage as contract are evident in his plea to the king for resistance to the foes of divorce reform: "Aus den frivolsten Gründen, in den unwürdigsten Prozedurformen, werden die Ehen von den Untergerichten zerrissen; Ehebruch und andere Frevel gegen die Ehen werden ohne Rüge, wie erlaubte Rechtsgeschäfte, vor den Gerichten verlautbart, zum Teil belohnt; ganze Generationen werden durch diese in christlichen Staaten unerhörten Zustände vergiftet" (qtd. in Liermann and Schoeps 526).

8   Gabriele Schneider would not agree with this conclusion. She reads *Eine Lebensfrage* as evidence that "auch in der Ehe das Individuum im Zentrum des Interesses Fanny Lewalds [steht]" and argues that Lewald concerns herself in this novel with two issues. First, using the example of Caroline and Alfred's marriage, the author demonstrates that women are not the only victims of their poor education, and second, she contradicts the reformers' assertions that the desire for divorce is the result of "Leichtfertigkeit" (*Zeitroman* 155). Schneider argues, though, that there was a tendency from the mid-1830s on toward institutionalizing marriage and "reducing" it to a civil law contract, and that this "widerspricht aufs Äußerste den liberalen Vorstellungen Lewalds" (*Zeitroman* 155). However, these were two opposing viewpoints, the latter of which had been the operative form since 1794, a form that the character Julian, whose views relating to legal matters are always privileged, supports in his evocation of the French *Code civil* as the worthier model in its conception of marriage as a matter of civil law, which can be followed with the blessings of a priest (II: 136). The "institutionalization" of

marriage is also not a phenomenon that contradicts Lewald's views. She describes marriage in terms similar to those of the divorce reformers, but she does not believe that this "vollste, edelste Entwicklung der menschlichen Natur" (I: 81) should be a legal prison.

9    Renate Möhrmann identifies the male "sufferer" (140) as one of two new elements in Lewald's third novel. (The other new element is the choice of subject matter not based on her own experience [138]). She points out that Lewald's choice of a suffering male protagonist enables her to argue that "die Befreiung der Frau nicht bloß ein feministisches Problem ist" (140).

10   Although the population growth Friedrich II wanted to encourage was no longer a goal for mid-nineteenth-century Prussia, Koch includes the king's decree in his discussion of situations in which the ALR permits the dissolution of childless marriages and does not comment on the current irrelevance of Friedrich II's population policies (186, note 53).

11   At this point Lewald's reader may recall that the ALR forbids parents to force their children into marriage (II 2 §119). Koch, in his commentary to this paragraph, snorts that it is entirely superfluous, "da keine Ehe zustande kommen kann, ohne freie Einwilligung der Brautleute selbst" (263, note 23). Historical and literary evidence from the period indicates, however, that the definition of "voluntary" is a matter of debate. A daughter's dependent position, a social inequality that predated the legal code, often proved to be a more decisive factor than the law itself. Lewald's male protagonist, Alfred, calling on Rahel Varnhagen, makes a virtual comparison of such loveless marriages with prostitution (II: 141–42), which is a view Lewald had given to the heroine of her first novel as well: "Die Ehen, die ich täglich vor meinen Augen schließen sehe, sind schlimmer als Prostitution....Der Kaufpreis ändert die Sache nicht" (Clementine 16).

12   See Gayle Rubin's essay on this subject. She argues that the "sex/gender system" that organizes sexuality in the service of society is predicated on the definition of women as "goods" to be traded in the creation of male relationships. The "commodity" has no right to do any trafficking of her own.

13   In fact, an amendment to the law in 1803 allowed fathers to determine the religious instruction of children of both sexes, because the provision allowing mothers to educate daughters in their own religion served only to perpetuate religious differences in the family (Koch 256–57). There should be only one religion and the mother's faith will be the one effaced.

14   In her England und Schottland: Reisetagebuch, she states, "Am Auffallendsten jedoch erscheint dem Engländer unser Bevormundungssystem, wo es sich in die ganz persönlichen Angelegenheiten des Einzelnen hinein mischt" (II: 74), a system she finds incompatible with the "Selbstregierung" that alone "gute Bürger und Zufriedenheit mit den Institutionen des Staates erzeugen [kann]." If the continental princes could only grasp the potential advantage to themselves, they would certainly eliminate the invasive "Bevormundungssystem" (II: 76). Gerhard

also comments on this system: she asserts that the *ALR*'s alleged attempt to promote the well-being of every inhabitant (stated in the "Patent wegen Publication des neuen allgemeinen Landrechts für die Preussischen Staaten") served to legitimate a "bis in groteske Einzelheiten reichende Bevormundung" (88).

15  Lewald and Stahr's prenuptial agreement, incidentally, specifically includes "Erbschaft, Geschenke oder Glücksfälle" as potential sources of income that would then belong entirely to Lewald (Schneider, *Zeitroman* 369).

16  Schneider describes this story as an example of Lewald's social criticism, arguing that it demonstrates that marriage itself can be an "Ort sozialer Diskriminierung" (*Zeitroman* 103), a conclusion with which I agree, although Schneider's reading otherwise differs from mine. She, for instance, notes that the *ALR* itself would have given Christel more legal possibilities than were available by the 1860s (*Zeitroman* 105–06), while my argument is that even the *ALR*'s provisions were inadequate to a woman in Christel's situation. She also claims that Christel was reluctant to protect herself from Ferdinand "aus familiären Rücksichten, Dankbarkeit gegen den Ziehvater, aber auch aus Achtung vor der Ehe" (*Zeitroman* 104). My point, however, is that Christel's socially mandated character made it impossible for her to avail herself of the limited legal means at her disposal, which constitutes Lewald's criticism of those limited legal means.

17  Koch calls this provision mandating the responsibility of the father's parents "eine enorme Gesetzgebung" in which the *ALR* "zu gunsten der Weibspersonen alles billige Maß überschreitet." However, he concludes that such provisions were probably intended to prevent the murder of illegitimate infants, rather than to protect the women involved (qtd. in Weber 340–41).

18  Marianne Weber notes that a mother would receive "Alimente" "sobald [sie] unter Eid einen Mann, mit dem sie verkehrt hatte, als Vater bezeichnete" (340). The new law left it to the judge's discretion to accept such an oath as evidence (Koch 228, note 1), which meant that, once again, women were effectively silenced in the courtroom.

19  The Prussian nobleman F.A. von der Marwitz, nostalgic for the feudal relationship, makes a similar connection in 1836 between laws that mandate support of the women one impregnates and women's immoral behavior: the "Erziehung, Zucht und Ordnung" effected by the "Zwangsdienst" is no more, and "keine Mutter [macht] der Tochter mehr Vorwürfe…, wenn sie schwanger wird, denn es ist für sie die sicherste Art des Erwerbs: entweder bekommt sie einen Mann oder Alimente oder, wenn beides fehlschlägt, so zieht sie in die Stadt als Amme" (qtd. in Gerhard 53). Koch agrees: the law "war zum Reizmittel zur Unsittlichkeit umgeschlagen und hatte die Unsittlichkeit zum Erwerbszweige gemacht" (227, note 1). Weber, however, points out that the life of a woman supported by "Alimente" was not as luxurious as these accounts intimate: the amount was tied to that required by those of the "Bauern- und gemeinen Bürgerstandes." In rural areas at the end of the eighteenth century, only 8–12

Thaler per year were awarded, "'wofür kein junger Hund aufzuziehen ist' und 'auch diese sind in den allermeisten Fällen nicht von dem Vater zu erlangen.'" Furthermore, the father could opt to take the child after its fourth year; keeping her child would then require the mother's renouncing her claim to support (341).

20   Klaus-Jürgen Matz, in his *Pauperismus und Bevölkerung: Die gesetzlichen Ehebeschränkungen in den süddeutschen Staaten während des 19. Jahrhunderts* (1980), notes that these restrictions affected tens of thousands of couples in south Germany who wished to marry (qtd. in Schneider, *Zeitroman* 99).

21   Schneider describes the deterrent function of the workhouse, which was to serve as a kind of "Präventivjustiz gegen Landstreicher, Bettler und Zigeuner." In order to reduce the costs to the community of supporting the poor, aid was given only to those who submitted themselves to forced labor there. The habituation to work was also offered as a rationale for the workhouses, but Anne clearly is not a recalcitrant worker (*Zeitroman* 99–100).

## CHAPTER THREE

1   Lewald, *Für und wider* 146. Ulrike Helmer has collected both Lewald's *Osterbriefe für die Frauen* (1863) and her *Für und wider die Frauen* (1870) in one volume entitled *Politische Schriften für und wider die Frauen*, from which I take my citations.

2   "Education" in these texts can be interpreted narrowly as formal schooling, or it can be extrapolated to the kind of "Erziehungsarbeit" performed by husbands in shaping the characters of their wives. Lewald herself had experienced both types of pedagogy and found each useful to female development.

3   I will use the terms "women's education" and "girls' education" more or less interchangeably, since the education that women received generally did not extend past girlhood and adolescence. In other words, there was no real opportunity for higher education until the second half of the nineteenth century and even that was only available abroad. "Women's education," as I use it, was the schooling of girls, which usually included preparation for "womanhood" and its attendant role expectations and tasks.

4   Written 1845–46 in Rome, it was published in serial form for the first time in 1879 and then posthumously in 1927 (Schneider, *FL* 147).

5   Lewald states in her autobiography: "War es mir nicht vergönnt, wie die Männer in meiner Nähe und wie die Mitarbeiter der [Halleschen] Jahrbücher, im offenen und entscheidenden Kampfe mitzufechten, so wollte ich ihnen wenigstens unter der Schutzwehr der Dichtung so gut ich es vermochte, die Kugeln zutragen helfen" (*ML* III: 27). She also compares her work to Heinrich Simon's: her novel is "ein Gleiches" to the book he had produced, and she had taken as the printed "Motto" for her novel his statement that "ein Stamm" that had produced both Christ and the Virgin Mary, in addition to having maintained itself in the face of so much resistance, must be equal to any other (*ML* III: 68–69).

6   In 1870, in the thirteenth open letter of "Für und wider die Frauen," Lewald does

argue that women's opinions should be consulted on legislation that affects them, such as divorce law, the establishment of homes for foundlings, and on crimes such as infanticide. She also complains about the injustice of the laws governing the property and wages of married women (191). This subject, however, takes up exactly one page of the 105 pages of essays.

7    Dorothea Leporin Erxleben published her *Gründliche Untersuchung der Ursachen, die das weibliche Geschlecht vom Studieren abhalten* in 1742. Mary Wollstonecraft's *Vindication of the Rights of Women* appeared in 1792; a two-volume German translation, *Rettung der Rechte des Weibes mit Bemerkungen über politische und moralische Gegenstände*, was published in 1793 and 1794.

8    The regulations, however, did not necessarily reflect reality. Rolf Engelsing cites statistics that show that as late as 1871 in Prussia, for instance, 10% of males and 15% of females older than ten were illiterate (98). These statistics support those that show that relatively high percentages of recruits in the Prussian army had had no formal schooling. Engelsing cites figures on this from 1836 to 1868 (the worst case being those from the province of Posen in 1836–37 with 46%); over this period of time, of course, the numbers improved (96–97).

9    This was a view not necessarily shared by the state. Parents often had to offer city governments financial guarantees in order to persuade them to support higher public schools for girls, since cities tended to regard such education as a "luxury" (Albisetti 36–37). Even in the second half of the century, public secondary schools were surprisingly rare in some of Germany's largest cities (Albisetti 38–39).

10   Elisabeth Blochmann notes that this book appeared in 10 editions until 1832, and that it was cited repeatedly in subsequent works. She asserts that it is the most important text of the period on the subject of girls' education and the most representative (35).

11   Here it must be noted that the teacher of the class Gleim observed was male. Rudolphi believed that the girls should receive "wissenschaftlichen Unterricht" from men, "denn alle Verstandeskultur soll vom Mann ausgehen" (qtd. in E. Blochmann 70).

12   This was described as "Lehre von der Luft, vom Wasser, vom Licht, vom Feuer, von der Elektricität, vom Magnetismus. Meteorologie, 2 St." (22).

13   One writer (probably J.H. Campe) on girls' education, for instance, gave vent to his indignation that "ein Vater aus der Klasse der deutschen Regenten seine Tochter in der Kunst, auf der Geige zu spielen, unterrichten ließ!" (qtd. in E. Blochmann 119).

14   Brigitta van Rheinberg, for instance, maintains that no other woman of her time had passed judgment on women in so "scharf und teilweise gnadenlos" a manner. She lists several of Lewald's critical comments on her female contemporaries: "'In der Masse'...seien die 'Weiber wirklich noch nicht über den Standpunkt des Harems hinaus'"; "'[Frauen] sind meist wie brei! Hat eine Erfahrung sie

zerdrückt, so bleiben sie liegen,' bis jemand kommt und etwas aus ihnen macht";
"in ihrem ganzen Bekanntenkreis könne sie nicht 'sechs wirklich bedeutende
Frauen zusammenbringen'" (205–06).

15 Of the Lewald novels I know, the title character of her *Jenny* may be an exception
to this norm. The (in many respects) autobiographical nature of this novel
perhaps explains this difference.

16 Lewald's opinion of George Sand "bleibt nach anfänglicher Bewunderung
zeitlebens zwiespältig" (Schneider, *FL* 72–73). She mocks Sand's
"Frauengestalten," whose "große Herzen die Männer nicht zu schätzen
vermochten und die zu keinem Frieden und zu keinem Glück gelangen konnten,
weil sich nie ein Mann vorfand, der solch ein Herz zu würdigen und zu verdienen
imstande gewesen wäre," and her own youthful identification with such figures.
Because of the "Unwürdigkeit und Unwahrheit" of these female characters, she
writes, she had at first overlooked or underestimated "das wirklich Große und
Bewundernswerte" that Sand demonstrates when she "sich auf dem Boden der
Wahrheit und der Wirklichkeit befindet" (*ML* III: 218–19). As to socialism,
Schneider maintains that "[a]uch wenn sich Fanny Lewald in diesen Jahren
[around the period of the revolution in 1848] zum Sozialismus bekennt, so meint
sie damit lediglich assoziative Zusammenschlüsse, Vereine, Genossenschaften und
Selbsthilfeorganisationen, die der politische Liberalismus als Lösung der
Arbeiterfrage ansieht, eine für den Mittelstand auch durchaus erfolgreiche
Konzeption." Factory workers, however, lacked the prerequisites for such
independence without outside help, which "Arbeiterführer wie Ferdinand Lassalle
später klar erkennen" (*FL* 73). In her study of Lewald's literary technique,
Schneider argues that Lewald's *Nella* demonstrates that Lewald "auch zur Zeit
des theoretisch/wissenschaftlichen Sozialismus an den vormärzlichen/frühso-
zialistischen Assoziationsideen festhält": in this novel, the teacher "[lobt] die
sozialen, nach 'den Prinzipien der Association'…organisierten Einrichtungen des
Unternehmers als vorbildlich" (*Zeitroman* 61, note 17). Schneider also notes that
Ferdinand Lassalle had been a regular guest at the Lewald salon in the late 1850s.
By 1864, Stahr would write to him that "he and his wife" could not invite him
again, because his views were too great a subject of contention. And a decade
after writing *Nella*, Lewald had no interest "an einer anderen als einer sozialen,
einer politischen Lösung der Arbeiterfrage." "[I]hre Jugendbegeisterung für den
Sozialismus ist der Angst vor einer nicht zu berechnenden Gefahr gewichen, vor
zerstörerischer Gewalt und Barbarei, die für sie vom Sozialismus und
Kommunismus ausgeht" (*FL* 113).

17 Helmer, "Anmerkungen" to *Meine Lebensgeschichte* 291, note 26.

## CHAPTER FOUR

1 From the dedication of Henriette Davidis's *Die Hausfrau: Eine Mitgabe für angehende
Hausfrauen* (iv).

2    Alissa Walser is the daughter of Martin Walser; the review appeared in the *Neue Zürcher Zeitung*. The actual quotation was a reference to "a *father's* love." Irmela Marei Krüger-Fürhoff opens her article on "father-daughter incest" in *Die Marquise von O...* with the story of the critical response to Walser's text (71).

3    Karen Pawluk Danford's study, *The Family in Adalbert Stifter's Moral and Aesthetic Universe*, demonstrates, by the way, that an author (in this case Stifter, whose support of the contemporary familial ideal has been generally considered unequivocal) can express a degree of unease about the "negative potential" (15) of the family even without calling into question the socially mandated role of women within it.

4    Is it parents, children, and "sonstige Hausgenossen" (all those subsumed under the "ganze Haus")? Just parents and children? Or all those who are descendents of a common ancestor?

5    This consignment was not, of course, effective in all cases. Gerhard argues that these definitions were also imposed on poorer families who had no way of conforming to the cultural ideal to which they, nevertheless, were supposed to aspire (see, for instance, 140–43).

6    Riehl argues that the family is determined by the "Idee der Sitte," while the state is built upon the "Idee des Rechtes" (127). The twain do meet, however, in the moral influence that the family exercises on bourgeois society and, from there, on the state (131).

7    I use the thirteenth edition, which was published in 1925, 28 years after Riehl's death in 1897. This edition contains the preface to the first edition and the preface to the ninth, published in 1881. In the latter he notes that he has made changes to his text in large part by adding examples that illustrate his central points, which he has not revised (xiv).

8    Riehl notes at one point that the glorification of women's emancipation had up to the present (1854) taken place primarily in fiction (7). One wonders what he was reading. He also makes the baffling point that women do not really understand the theory of emancipation and that those who do, have understood it incorrectly (19).

9    Compare the dilemma of the character Christel in Lewald's "Das große Loos": here, too, a wife hesitates to suggest to the outside world that her husband has failed, yet Christel's husband is not so "negligent" that he will allow her to take control of the family finances.

10   Karin Hausen cites the *Frauen-Spiegel* (1840) as a source on this topic (116, note 14), although it is not clear whether she is referring to the literary portrayals she mentions or the claims by "radikale Kritikerinnen" of the same period that forcing women into a "Versorgungsehe" by denying them other employment was tantamount to forcing them into prostitution (93).

11   *Wigand's Conversations-Lexikon* (1847) entry on "Frauen": "mit dem Aufkommen des Bürgerthums trat das Weib von der Prunkbühne des Ritterthums in die engbeschränkte Sphäre der bürgerlichen Häuslichkeit zurück" (qtd. in Gerhard 93).

12   Lewald was not alone in her representation of this sort of pathological closeness within the family. Danford's discussion of Stifter's "Der Hochwald" identifies "familial bonds so intimate and intense that they are unnatural and lead to a confusion beween familial and sexual love and finally to infertility and destruction" (69), although the topic of incestuous love as such is not raised by the characters themselves, as it is in Lewald's novel. Danford also notes, citing Christine Sjögren in her comments, that Stifter's *Nachsommer*, in its characterization of a sister who insists that she will never marry, because she loves only her family and could never love someone who wanted to take her away from it, "may be warning against 'einer allzugroßen Umhegen und Abgeschlossenheit' in the family, much as [Stifter] did by negative example in 'Hochwald'" (124–25), although the novel is otherwise a veritable hymn to family life.

## CONCLUSION

1   I also include here the women who appear in Lewald's essays and whose "real" lives have been narrativized in the selective re-telling of their stories.

# WORKS CITED

Acton, William. *The Functions and Disorders of the Reproductive Organs in Childhood, Youth, Adult Age, and Advanced Life, Considered in Their Physiological, Social, and Moral Relations*. From the last London ed. Philadelphia: Lindsay & Blakiston, 1865.

Albisetti, James. *Schooling German Girls and Women: Secondary and Higher Education in the Nineteenth Century*. Princeton: Princeton UP, 1988.

Alcoff, Linda. "Cultural Feminism Versus Post-Structuralism: The Identity Crisis in Feminist Theory." *Signs* 13 (1988): 405–36.

*Allgemeines Landrecht für die Preußischen Staaten von 1794*. Ed. Hans Hattenhauer. 2nd, rev. ed. Neuwied: Luchterhand, 1994.

Armstrong, John. *Practical Illustrations of Typhus Fever, of the Common Continued Fever, and of Inflammatory Diseases*. From the last London ed. New York, 1824.

Bailin, Miriam. *The Sickroom in Victorian Fiction: The Art of Being Ill*. Cambridge: Cambridge UP, 1994.

Beck, Theodric Romeyn, and John B. Beck. *Elements of Medical Jurisprudence*. Rev. by C.R. Gilman. 12th ed. Vol. 1. Philadelphia: Lippincott, 1863. 2 vols.

Beckson, Karl and Arthur Ganz. *Literary Terms: A Dictionary*. 3rd ed. New York: Noonday P, 1989.

Bischoff, Ignaz Rudolf. *Grundsätze zur Erkenntniss und Behandlung der Fieber und Entzündungen*. 2nd, rev. ed. Vienna: Strauss, 1830.

Blasius, Dirk. *Ehescheidung in Deutschland im 19. und 20. Jahrhundert.* Frankfurt: Fischer, 1992.

Blochmann, Elisabeth. *Das "Frauenzimmer" und die "Gelehrsamkeit": Eine Studie über die Anfänge des Mädchenschulwesens in Deutschland.* Heidelberg: Quelle & Meyer, 1966.

Blochmann, Maria. *"Laß dich gelüsten nach der Männer Weisheit und Bildung": Frauenbildung als Emanzipationsgelüste, 1800–1918.* Pfaffenweiler: Centaurus, 1990.

Bluntschli, Johann Kaspar. *Deutsches Privatrecht.* 3rd ed. Munich: Cotta, 1864.

Brinker-Gabler, Gisela, Karola Ludwig, and Angela Wöffen. *Lexikon deutschsprachiger Schriftstellerinnen 1800–1945.* Munich: dtv, 1986.

*Brockhaus Konversations-Lexikon.* 14th ed. 16 vols. Leipzig: Brockhaus, 1892–95.

Campe, Joachim Heinrich. *Väterlicher Rat für meine Tochter.* 1789. Excerpted in Ute Gerhard. 369–81.

Chitty, Joseph. *A Practical Treatise on Medical Jurisprudence. With So Much of Anatomy, Physiology, Pathology, and the Practice of Medicine and Surgery, As Are Essential To Be Known by Members of Parliament, Lawyers, Coroners, Magistrates, Officers in the Navy, and Private Gentlemen; and All the Laws Relating to Medical Practitioners; with Explanatory Plates.* 2nd American ed. Philadelphia: Carey, Lea & Blanchard, 1836.

Cornelius, Steffi. "'...Ihr werdet nicht nur gute Hausfrauen, sondern auch edle Bürgerinnen erziehen': Schulbildung und Mädchenerziehung in Württemberg." *Schimpfende Weiber und patriotische Jungfrauen: Frauen im Vormärz und in der Revolution 1848/49.* Ed. Carola Lipp. Moos, Baden-Baden: Elster, 1986. 189–204.

Cox, Kathryn Schrotenboer. "Infertility." *EveryWoman's Health: The Complete Guide to Body and Mind by 15 Women Doctors.* Ed. D.S. Thompson. 4th ed. New York: Prentice Hall, 1985. 247–65.

Craig, Gordon. *Germany 1866–1945.* Oxford: Clarendon P, 1978.

Currie, James. *Medical Reports, on the Effects of Water, Cold and Warm, As a Remedy in Fever and Other Diseases.* Philadelphia, 1808.

Cutter, Irving S., and Henry R. Viets. *A Short History of Midwifery.* Philadelphia: W.B. Saunders, 1964.

Danford, Karen Pawluk. *The Family in Adalbert Stifter's Moral and Aesthetic Universe: A Rarefied Vision.* New York: Lang, 1991.

Davidis, Henriette. *Die Hausfrau: Eine Mitgabe für angehende Hausfrauen.* Leipzig, 1897.

Di Maio, Irene Stocksieker. "Jewish Emancipation and Integration: Fanny Lewald's Narrative Strategies." *Autoren damals und heute: Literaturgeschichtliche Beispiele veränderter Wirkungshorizonte.* Ed. Gerhard P. Knapp. Amsterdam: Rodopi, 1991. 273–301.

*Dorland's Illustrated Medical Dictionary.* 26th ed. Philadelphia: W.B. Saunders, 1981.

Duden, Barbara. *The Woman beneath the Skin: A Doctor's Patients in Eighteenth-Century Germany.* Trans. Thomas Dunlap. Cambridge: Harvard UP, 1991.

Ebner-Eschenbach, Marie von. *Unsühnbar.* 1889. Ed. Burkhard Bittrich. Bonn: Bouvier, 1978.

Engelsing, Rolf. *Analphabetentum und Lektüre: Zur Sozialgeschichte des Lesens in Deutschland zwischen feudaler und industrieller Gesellschaft.* Stuttgart: Metzler, 1973.

Erhart, Walter. "'Your Uterus is the Loneliness in My Soul': Male Voices in Medical Body-Discourse (1860–1900)." Paper given at 1995 MLA Convention.

Ewald, Johann Ludwig. *Die Kunst ein gutes Mädchen, eine gute Gattin, Mutter und Hausfrau zu werden.* Frankfurt, 1807.

Foster, Nigel. *German Law and Legal System.* London: Blackstone P, 1993.

Frederiksen, Elke, ed. *Die Frauenfrage in Deutschland 1865–1915: Texte und Dokumente.* Stuttgart: Reclam, 1981.

Frevert, Ute. *"Mann und Weib, und Weib und Mann": Geschlechter-Differenzen in der Moderne.* Munich: Beck, 1995.

Ganong, W.F. *Review of Medical Physiology.* 12th ed. Los Altos, CA: Lange Medical Publications, 1985.

Gerhard, Ute. *Verhältnisse und Verhinderungen: Frauenarbeit, Familie und Rechte der Frauen im 19. Jahrhundert. Mit Dokumenten.* Frankfurt: Suhrkamp, 1978.

Gilman, Charlotte Perkins. *The Yellow Wallpaper.* 1892. New York: Feminist P, 1973.

Gottschall, Rudolf von. *Die deutsche Nationalliteratur des neunzehnten Jahrhunderts.* 7th ed. Vol. 4. Breslau: Trewendt, 1902.

Grimm, Jacob. *Deutsches Wörterbuch.* Leipzig: Hirzel, 1854–1915.

Gunn, John C. *Gunn's Domestic Medicine: or Poor Man's Friend, in the Hours of Affliction, Pain and Sickness.* 8th ed. Pumpkintown, TN: S.M. Johnston, 1839.

Hattenhauer, Hans. Foreword and Introduction. *Allgemeines Landrecht für die Preußischen Staaten von 1794.* 2nd, rev. ed. Neuwied: Luchterhand, 1994. V–VI; 1–29.

Hausen, Karin. "'…eine Ulme für das schwanke Efeu': Ehepaare im deutschen Bildungsbürgertum." *Bürgerinnen und Bürger: Geschlechterverhältnisse im 19. Jahrhundert.* Ed. Ute Frevert. Göttingen: Vandenhoeck & Ruprecht, 1988.

Heidenstam, David, et al. *The Human Body.* New York: Facts on File, 1980.

Heinzelman, Susan Sage and Zipporah Batshaw Wiseman. "Revising Ancient Tales." *Representing Women: Law, Literature, and Feminism.* Ed. Susan Sage Heinzelman and Zipporah Batshaw Wiseman. Durham: Duke UP, 1994. 247–52.

Helmer, Ulrike. "Einleitung." *Politische Schriften für und wider die Frauen.* By Fanny Lewald. Frankfurt: Helmer, 1989.

———. "Nachwort." *Meine Lebensgeschichte.* By Fanny Lewald. Vol. 1. Frankfurt: Helmer, 1988.

Hudson, Alfred. *Lectures on the Study of Fever.* Philadelphia: Lea, 1869.

Huebner, Rudolf. *A History of Germanic Private Law.* Trans. Francis Philbrick. Boston: Little, Brown, and Company, 1918.

Kisch, E. Heinrich. *The Sexual Life of Woman in Its Physiological, Pathological and Hygienic Aspects.* Trans. M. Eden Paul. New York: Rebman, 1910.

———. *Die Sterilität des Weibes: Ihre Ursachen und ihre Behandlung.* Vienna: Urban & Schwarzenberg, 1886.

Koch, Christian Friedrich. *Allgemeines Landrecht für die Preußischen Staaten: Kommentar in Anmerkungen.* 4th, rev. ed. Vol. 3. Berlin: Guttentag, 1871.

Krueger, Christine L. "Witnessing Women: Trial Testimony in Novels by Tonna, Gaskell, and Eliot." *Representing Women: Law, Literature, and Feminism.* Ed. Susan Sage Heinzelman and Zipporah Batshaw Wiseman. Durham: Duke UP, 1994. 337–55.

Krüger-Fürhoff, Irmela Marei. "Epistemological Asymmetries and Erotic Stagings: Father-Daughter Incest in Heinrich von Kleist's *Die Marquise von O...*" *Women in German Yearbook* 12 (1996): 71–86.

Laqueur, Thomas. *Making Sex: Body and Gender from the Greeks to Freud.* Cambridge: Harvard UP, 1990.

Lewald, Fanny. *Clementine.* 1843. Berlin: Janke, 1872.

———. "Das große Loos." *Deutsche Lebensbilder.* 2nd ed. Berlin: Janke, 1865.

———. "Der Magnetberg." *Zu Weihnachten.* Berlin: Janke, 1880.

———. "Doktor Melchior. Eine Herzensgeschichte aus alter Zeit." *Zu Weihnachten.* Berlin: Janke, 1880.

———. *Eine Lebensfrage.* 2 vols. Leipzig: Brockhaus, 1845.

———. "Einige Gedanken über die Mädchenerziehung." *Archiv für vaterländische Interessen, oder Preussische Provinzialblätter.* May 1843. 380–95.

———. *Politische Schriften für und wider die Frauen.* 1863, 1870. Ed. Ulrike Helmer. Frankfurt: Helmer, 1989.

———. *Gefühltes und Gedachtes.* Ed. Ludwig Geiger. Dresden: Minden, 1900.

———. "In Ragaz." *Zu Weihnachten.* Berlin: Janke, 1880.

———. *Jenny.* 1843. Ed. Ulrike Helmer. Frankfurt: Helmer, 1988.

———. "Kein Haus. Eine Dorfgeschichte." *Deutsche Lebensbilder.* 2nd ed. Berlin: Janke, 1865.

———. *Liebesbriefe. Aus dem Leben eines Gefangenen.* Braunschweig: Vieweg, 1850.

———. *Meine Lebensgeschichte.* 1861–62. Ed. Ulrike Helmer. 3 vols. Frankfurt: Helmer, 1988–89.

———. *Nella. Eine Weihnachtsgeschichte.* Berlin: Janke, 1870.

———. *Schloß Tannenburg.* Berlin: Janke, 1859.

———. *Treue Liebe.* Dresden: Minden, 1883.

Liermann, Hans and Hans-Joachim Schoeps, eds. *Materialien zur preußischen Ehereform im Vormärz.* Göttinger Akademie der Wissenschaften, Nr. 14, 1961.

MacKinnon, Catharine A. *Toward a Feminist Theory of the State.* Cambridge: Harvard UP, 1989.

Mantegazza, Paolo. *Die Physiologie des Weibes.* Trans. R. Teuscher. Jena: Costenoble, 1893.

Margolis, Harriet. "The Ideal Marriage: Woman as Other in Three Lewald Novels." *Continental, Latin-American and Francophone Women Writers: Selected Papers from the Wichita State University Conference on Foreign Literature, 1984–85.* Ed. Eunice Myers and Ginette Adamson. Lanham, MD: UP of America, 1987. 107–17.

Mill, John Stuart. *The Later Letters of John Stuart Mill: 1849–1873.* Ed. Francis E. Mineka and Dwight N. Lindley. Toronto: U of Toronto P, 1972.

Möhrmann, Renate. *Die andere Frau: Emanzipationsansätze deutscher Schriftstellerinnen im Vorfeld der Achtundvierziger-Revolution.* Stuttgart: Metzler, 1977.

Moscucci, Ornella. *The Science of Woman: Gynaecology and Gender in England, 1800–1929.* Cambridge: Cambridge UP, 1990.

Mühlbach, Luise. "Briefe aus Ems an den New-York Herald." *Erinnerungsblätter aus dem Leben Luise Mühlbach's.* Gesammelt und herausgegeben von ihrer Tochter, Thea Ebersberger. Leipzig: Schmidt & Günther, 1902.

Niekerk, Carl. "Sexual Imagery in Goethe's *Faust II.*" *Seminar* 33 (1997):1–21.

Oppenheim, Janet. *"Shattered Nerves": Doctors, Patients, and Depression in Victorian England.* New York: Oxford UP, 1991.

O'Toole, Mary L., and Pamela S. Douglas. "Fitness: Definition and Development." *Women and Exercise: Physiology and Sports Medicine*. Ed. Mona Shangold and Gabe Mirkin. Philadelphia: F.A. Davis, 1988. 3–22.

Planck, Gottlieb. *Die rechtliche Stellung der Frau nach dem bürgerlichen Gesetzbuche*. Göttingen: Vandenhoeck und Ruprecht, 1899.

Rheinberg, Brigitta van. *Fanny Lewald: Geschichte einer Emanzipation*. Frankfurt, New York: Campus, 1990.

Riehl, Wilhelm Heinrich. *Die Familie*. Vol. 3 of *Die Naturgeschichte des Volkes als Grundlage einer deutschen Sozialpolitik*. 13th ed. Stuttgart: Cotta, 1925.

Rose, Phyllis. *Parallel Lives: Five Victorian Marriages*. New York: Random House, 1984.

Rosenbaum, Heidi. *Formen der Familie: Untersuchungen zum Zusammenhang von Familienverhältnissen, Sozialstruktur und sozialem Wandel in der deutschen Gesellschaft des 19. Jahrhunderts*. Frankfurt: Suhrkamp, 1982.

Rubin, Gayle. "The Traffic in Women." *Women, Class, and the Feminist Imagination: A Socialist Feminist Reader*. Ed. Karen Hansen and Ilene J. Philipson. Philadelphia: Temple UP, 1990. 74–113.

Russ, Joanna. "Somebody's Trying to Kill Me and I Think It's My Husband: The Modern Gothic." *The Female Gothic*. Ed. Juliann E. Fleenor. Montreal: Eden P, 1983. 31–56.

Sammons, Jeffrey L. *Heinrich Heine: A Modern Biography*. Princeton: Princeton UP, 1979.

Sappington, John. *The Theory and Treatment of Fevers*. Arrow Rock, MO, 1844.

Schiebinger, Londa. "Skeletons in the Closet: The First Illustrations of the Female Skeleton in Eighteenth-Century Anatomy." *The Making of the Modern Body: Sexuality and Society in the Nineteenth Century*. Ed. Catherine Gallagher and Thomas Laqueur. Berkeley: U of California P, 1987. 42–82.

Schneider, Gabriele. *Fanny Lewald*. Reinbek bei Hamburg: Rowohlt, 1996.

———. *Vom Zeitroman zum "stylisierten" Roman: Die Erzählerin Fanny Lewald*. Frankfurt: Lang, 1993.

Shorter, Edward. *Doctors and Their Patients: A Social History.* New York: Simon and Schuster, 1985. New Brunswick, NJ: Transaction, 1991.

———. *Women's Bodies: A Social History of Women's Encounter with Health, Ill-Health, and Medicine.* New York: Basic Books, 1982. New Brunswick, NJ: Transaction, 1991.

Spilleke, August. *Rede bei der Einweihung des neuen Schulgebäudes der Königlichen Töchterschule zu Berlin.* Berlin, 1827.

———. *Zu der öffentlichen Prüfung der Zöglinge des Königlichen Friedrich Wilhelms Gymnasiums, der Realschule und der damit verbundenen Töchterschule.* Berlin, 1827.

Tatlock, Lynne. "Theodor Storm's 'Ein Bekenntnis': Knowledge as 'Masculine' Credo." *Seminar* 31 (1995): 300–13.

Vander, Arthur J., James H. Sherman, and Dorothy S. Luciano. *Human Physiology: The Mechanisms of Body Function.* 6th ed. New York: McGraw-Hill, 1994.

Venske, Regula. "Discipline and Daydreaming in the Works of a Nineteenth-Century Woman Author: Fanny Lewald." *German Women in the Eighteenth and Nineteenth Centuries: A Social and Literary History.* Ed. Ruth-Ellen Boetcher-Joeres and Mary Jo Maynes. Bloomington: Indiana UP, 1986. 175–92.

Türk, Wilhelm von. *Beiträge zur Kenntnis einiger deutschen Elementar-Schulanstalten, namentlich der zu Dessau, Leipzig, Heidelberg, Frankfurt am Mayn und Berlin.* Leipzig, 1806.

Ward, Margaret E. "'Ehe' and 'Entsagung': Fanny Lewald's Early Novels and Goethe's Literary Paternity." *Women in German Yearbook* 2 (1986): 57–77.

Weber, Marianne. *Ehefrau und Mutter in der Rechtsentwicklung.* Tübingen: Mohr, 1907.

Zander, Sylvina. *"Zum Nähen wenig Lust, sonst ein gutes Kind": Mädchenerziehung und Frauenbildung in Lübeck.* Lübeck: Archiv der Hansestadt Lübeck, 1996.

# NORTH AMERICAN STUDIES IN 19TH-CENTURY GERMAN LITERATURE

This series of monographs is about post-Romantic literature during the nineteenth century in German-speaking lands. The series endeavors to embrace studies in criticism, literary history, the symbiosis with other national literatures, as well as the social and political dimensions of literature. Our aim is to offer contributions by American scholars, to renovate the reformation of the canon, the rediscovery of once significant authors, the reevaluation of texts and their contexts, and a renewed understanding and appreciation of a body of literature that was acknowledged as internationally important in the nineteenth century.

For additional information about this series or for the submission of manuscripts, please contact:

Peter Lang Publishing
P.O. Box 1246
Bel Air, MD  21014-1246

To order other books in this series, please contact our Customer Service Department:

(800) 770-LANG (within the U.S.)
(212) 647-7706 (outside the U.S.)
(212) 647-7707 FAX

Or browse online by series at:
www.peterlangusa.com